Taking it like a man

For Karen and Richard

and to the Memory of our Grandfathers

Pte William Young, 21st (Service) Battalion,
The Manchester Regiment 1914–1918

Pte Charles Caesar, RASC 1915–1918

Taking it like a man

Suffering, sexuality and the War Poets
Brooke, Sassoon, Owen, Graves

Adrian Caesar

Manchester University Press

Manchester and New York

Distributed exclusively in the USA and Canada by St. Martin's Press

Copyright © Adrian Caesar 1993

Published by Manchester University Press
Oxford Road, Manchester M13 9PL, UK

and Room 400, 175 Fifth Avenue, New York, NY 10010, USA
Distributed exclusively in the USA and Canada
by St. Martin's Press, Inc., 175 Fifth Avenue, New York, NY 10010, USA

British Library Cataloguing-in-Publication Data
A catalogue record for this book is available from the British Library

Library of Congress Cataloging-in-Publication Data
Caesar Adrian, 1955–
   Taking it like a man: suffering, sexuality and the war poets:
Brooke, Sassoon, Owen, Graves / Adrian Caesar.
      p. cm.
   ISBN 0-7190-3834-0
1. English poetry—20th century—History and criticism. 2. World War.
1914–1918—Literature and the war. 3. Soldiers' writings, English—History
and criticism. 4. English poetry—Men authors—History and criticism.
5. Sassoon, Sigfried, 1886–1967—Knowledge—Psychology. 6. Brooke, Rupert,
1887–1915—Knowledge—Psychology. 7. Owen, Wilfred, 1893–1918
—Knowledge—Psychology. 8. Graves, Robert, 1895- —Knowledge—
Psychology. 9. War poetry, English—History and criticism. 10. Masculinity
(Psychology) in literature. 11. Pyschoanalysis and literature. 12. Suffering in
literature. 13. Sex role in literature. 14. Men in literature
I. Title
PR605.W65C34 1993
821'.91209358—dc20   92–30538

ISBN 0 7190 3834 0 *hardback*

Printed in Great Britain
by Bookcraft (Bath) Limited

Contents

Acknowledgements

I would like to thank several people who have helped me in the preparation of this book. Victor Kelleher discussed the project with me in its early stages and, with Alison Kelleher, remained a constant source of support and encouragement whilst I was writing it. In the later stages, friends and colleagues at University College, Susan Lever and Peter Looker, gave me their critical opinion of parts of the manuscript. My wife and family have contributed by their forbearance through the inevitable moody moments! I should also like to thank Loes Baker for her cheerful and intelligent assistance with the proof-reading and preparation of the index. Margaret McNally, with great patience and good humour, contributed her expertise in word-processing.

It should be noted that an early and shorter version of Chapter 3 appeared in *Critical Quarterly* Vol. 29, No. 2 (Summer 1987), and some material from Chapters 2 and 3 appeared as an essay in H. Heseltine (ed.), *The Shock of Battle*, University College, ADFA, 1989, and I would like to thank the editors of those two publications.

All poems quoted are from the following sources: J. Stallworthy (ed.), *The Complete Poems* and *Fragments of Wilfred Owen* (2 vols.), Chatto & Windus, The Hogarth Press and Oxford University Press, 1983; G. Keynes (ed.), *The Poetical Works of Rupert Brooke*, Faber & Faber, 1946; Siegfried Sassoon, *The War Poems*, Faber & Faber, 1983; Robert Graves, *Over the Brazier*, St James Press, [1916] 1976, *Fairies and Fusiliers*, Heinemann, 1917, *Poems About War*, Cassell, 1988.

I would like to thank A. P. Watt Ltd, who, acting on behalf of the Robert Graves Copyright Trust, granted permission to quote from *Over the Brazier, Fairies and Fusiliers* and *Poems About War*. Thanks also to Faber & Faber Ltd for permission to quote from Siegfried Sassoon, *Diaries 1915–1918, Diaries 1920–1922* and *Siegfried's Journey*. All other quotations from Siegfried Sassoon are reproduced by kind permission of George Sassoon.

1

Introduction

The English writers of the First World War have achieved, I think, the status of cultural heroes. Rupert Brooke was the first of the poets to be so appropriated and mythologised. The 'young Apollo, golden–haired' of Frances Cornford's poem, who penned the now infamous 'War Sonnets', had only to die en route to Gallipoli, in order to be immortalised as a symbol of lost Edwardian youth and manhood. Winston Churchill's tribute in *The Times* (written by Edward Marsh) adopted a language which ensured Brooke's elevation into an English upper-middle-class pantheon: 'Joyous, fearless, versatile, deeply instructed, with classic symmetry of mind and body, he was all that one would wish England's noblest sons to be in days when no sacrifice but the most precious is acceptable, and the most precious is that which is most freely proffered.'[1] The god-like youth sacrificed in a noble cause, has obvious Christian as well as classical overtones to which we shall often return in the course of this study, but for now let it be noted that these are the terms in which Winston Churchill sought to justify and console the nation for its losses. If, in later times, Brooke's poems about the war were subject to an almost unanimous dismissal as the expression of a discredited, imperialist chauvinism, the idea of celebrating sacrificed youth was to have a longer and more powerful tenure. The work of the so-called 'trench-poets', and particularly that of Owen and Sassoon, is largely responsible for this. Their poems are credited with debunking traditional ideas of patriotism, heroism and glory, and of communicating to later generations the 'reality', 'horror' and 'futility' of war. Thousands, if not millions, of school children in the western world dutifully tell this story in their exam responses to the 'war poets'. Yet

1

Owen's 'visionary compassion' and Sassoon's righteous anger and indignation, have elevated the poets into archetypes of the suffering martyrs that their poems describe and celebrate. Just as Brooke was a symbol to many of his class and generation, Owen and Sassoon have taken on a similar mantle for later readers. The very depth of their sufferings commands our respect and homage; they are the heroes of their own poems, which, if read in humanistic ways may be said to represent a triumph of the human spirit in the face of appalling tribulation.

In a recent book, *The Neo-Pagans*,[2] Paul Delaney has offered an account of Brooke and his circle which goes well beyond the mythical, and restores something of the man and his psychological conflicts. Similarly Dominic Hibberd in *Owen the Poet*,[3] has done much to demonstrate the complexities of Owen's psyche, and the literary traditions his work develops from. I wish to build upon these fine studies in order to investigate the place of suffering in the life and work of Brooke, Owen, Sassoon and Graves. For it is my conviction that by an unfolding of their attitudes towards suffering we may come to a fuller and deeper understanding of their work and its appropriate place in our culture. It seems to me, that whilst we have been happy to teach our children that writers like Owen and Sassoon were noble in their expression of pity, grief, indignation, and anti-war sentiment, we have been less forthcoming about their positive responses to war, and our positive responses to their war writing. What I am suggesting here is that their work has been read and taught in particular ideological ways which elide a consideration of the psychological and cultural complexities involved in both the poetry and our responses to it. As well as communicating to the reader that war is wasteful, absurd, appalling, horrific, there is, I think, in this work a celebration of war as a vehicle of pain and suffering, which is shared by the voyeuristic reader who peeps at the horror through parted fingers and is consciously or subconsciously thrilled and excited by it.

Writing about her experience as a Voluntary Aid Detachment (VAD) nurse during the First World War, Vera Brittain concludes that, 'the war had made masochists of us all'.[4] Masochism rarely exists in isolation from its unlovely partner sadism. And in the same book Brittain hints at this when she also writes cogently about the 'excitement' of war and how this constitutes a barrier to pacifism. In this passage she is remembering her time of service in Malta:

I may see the rocks again, and smell the flowers, and watch the dawn sunshine chase the shadows from the old sulphur-coloured walls, but the light that sprang from the heightened consciousness of wartime, the glory seen by the enraptured ingenuous eyes of twenty-two, will be upon them no more. I am a girl no longer, and the world, for all its excitements of chosen work and individualistic play, has grown tame in comparison with Malta during those years of our anguish.

It is, I think, this glamour, this magic, this incomparable keying up of the spirit in a time of mortal conflict, which constitute the pacifist's real problem – a problem still incompletely imagined, and still quite un- solved. The causes of war are always falsely represented; its honour is dishonest and its glory meretricious, but the challenge to spiritual endurance, the intense sharpening of all the senses, the vitalising con- sciousness of common peril for a common end, remain to allure . . . The glamour may be the mere delirium of fever, which as soon as war is over dies out and shows itself for the will-o'-the-wisp that it is, but while it lasts no emotion known to man seems as yet to have quite the compelling power of this enlarged vitality.[5]

At the heart of this passage is 'anguish'. To suffer and watch other people suffering 'keys up' the 'spirit'; 'enlarged vitality' is bought at the ironic cost of other people's lives. It is something of this mystery, this real problem for pacifists, that I wish to illuminate in this study. It is a problem which in my view is intimately related to sado-masochistic responses to suffering which are enshrined in our culture.

It will be helpful then, to clarify what I mean by sadism and masochism. In using these terms singularly or conjoined as sado- masochism, I am interested in their usefulness to describe the gaining of pleasure or fulfilment through the suffering and inflic- tion of pain, whether conscious motivation is present or not. In using the words in this broad sense, it will be apparent that I am not primarily concerned with sado-masochism as a physical prac- tice in which orgasmic sexual fulfilment is gained from the admin- istration of suffering. Rather, I would see practices such as flagellation as relatively extreme and rare behavioural manifesta- tions of a much more widely experienced phenomenon, involving punishment and self-punishment of various kinds both mental and physical. This is not to deny that there may be an erotic compo-

3

nent in the aetiology of all sado-masochistic responses; but is to suggest that in the distinction between what Freud called 'moral' as opposed to 'erogenous' masochism (or sadism) the part played by sexuality becomes blurred. Indeed it should be admitted at once that there is no definitive answer to the causation of either 'erogenous' or 'moral' sado-masochism, and I do not wish to either reproduce or embrace here the manifold complexities of Freud's speculations on these matters. Nevertheless, Freud's idea that erogenous sado-masochism arises as a component of the death wish, and that the latter is brought into play when the erotic instincts are repressed seems to me a suggestive idea in the context of what follows. Similarly his notion that moral masochism arises from (often unconscious) guilt feelings and the resultant need for self-punishment, also seems to me helpful in looking at the lives and work of my four subjects. Where I wish to go further than Freud is in arguing that the dominant, traditional ideologies experienced by Brooke, Sassoon, Owen and Graves, which helped to constitute their subjective sense of self, were instrumental in the formulation of sexual repression with its attendant confusions and feelings of guilt, and that in my view this helped to produce in them ambivalent attitudes to their own and others' sufferings. Sado-masochism then, is not used in this study to describe a 'perversion' but a widespread, culturally inscribed phenomenon.

Although in the chapters that follow we will be discussing particular experiences of individual authors and the relationship between these and their writings, here we may usefully consider in broader, more general terms the traditions inherited by the young men and women who were to suffer in and write about the First World War. What attitudes had the 'generation of 1914' imbibed which led them to volunteer so willingly for self-sacrifice when the war broke out? And what was the relationship between these traditions and the creation of art? In suggesting answers to these questions, I begin with a discussion of Christianity which I take to be the central pillar supporting the dominant imperialist ideology of the Victorian and Edwardian era. Whether individual writers personally believed in Christianity or not is at this stage irrelevant to my purposes. What I wish to argue is that Christianity, and particularly the English middle-class Protestant variety, deeply influenced attitudes to pain and suffering in believers and non-believers alike, since the attitudes were institutionalised at every level of the society.

Christianity is a religion which takes as its central icon, the image of a young man nailed onto a cross. This is said to be an image which represents 'love'. God the father 'so loves' the world that he is prepared to have his son sacrificed, in the most painful, barbarous way, in order that 'we' may be 'saved'. To condone pain, to endure suffering are at the heart of Christian idealism. We, as followers of Christ, are called upon to 'take up' our 'cross' and 'follow him'. This path of faithful suffering will lead to treasures in heaven. Marx called this religion the 'opiate of the people' because he perceived how it was used to justify (and implicitly celebrate) the poverty, humility and suffering of the working classes. It was also used to justify their mass slaughter in order to preserve the very power structures which oppressed them. But in 1914 it was not only the working class who conceived their 'duty' to God, king and country to be synonymous. Self-sacrifice, the infliction and endurance of pain were necessary to the 'salvation' of the Empire. And the rulers of the British Empire were willing to sacrifice its sons, just as God was, and in just as brutal ways – the only difference being that the treasure at issue was not to be found in heaven, but on earth, and very unevenly distributed.

Important as these basic political ideas are, there are other subtle corollaries of the Christian inheritance which are more central to my concerns in this book. For Christianity not only provided a hierarchical model of service and sacrifice, but also underwrote the sexual mores which in turn perpetuated and supported nationalism and Empire. It need hardly be said that the Pauline theology which dominated the Victorian era was deeply sexist; women were the 'weaker vessel'– if they could not adhere to the ideal of chastity, then respectable motherhood within a nuclear family was their only possible way of avoiding the charge of uncleanliness. And one suspects that tragically, in the lives of many bourgeois women, the place of sexuality within marriage was abhorred rather than celebrated; the idea and ideal of the virgin mother thus being upheld and propagated. Males brought up in this tradition, tended to internalise this perspective in which all women were either virgin or whore, thus rendering all their relationships with women extremely ambivalent. Encouraging this ambivalence further was a notion of male power, which according to St Paul was also ideally chaste. That young men should be 'clean in thought word and deed' was an idea originating in Christianity which, as George L. Mosse has shown, had huge political ramifications for nationalism and imperialism.[6] Pure 'manliness', so the ideology implied, was necessary for the maintenance of the nation's imperial power, and to this end 'degeneracy' of any kind needed to be ruthlessly discouraged. Nowhere was such ideology so clearly expressed as in the English public schools. Here, where young men were actively segregated from women, and discouraged from associating with them, they were also, paradoxically taught religious and moral strictures against 'effeminacy' and homosexuality.

The consequent repression of sexual instincts and feelings within an individual constitutes a variety of pain, and the sufferer may vent aggression upon the person, male or female, who arouses 'forbidden' sexual feelings within him or her, precisely for 'causing' this pain. But such feelings are rarely pure, and, as I have already intimated, are more often mixed, so that the individual is also attracted to, and seeks out that which is forbidden thus tying, or at least helping to tie, the 'gordian knot of pain and pleasure', which constitutes the sado-masochistic response in either homo- or hetero-sexual love. And so we come back to the idea that love – true, real, chaste love – is centrally concerned with the endurance of pain, and we come back to that erotic figure of worship: the crucified Christ. Some might object to the circularity of my argument here: I have implied that the crucified figure of Christ is a revered image because it embodies sado-masochistic feelings and I have then proceeded to argue that these feelings are at least in part *caused* by Christianity and its icons. But this interdependence is, I think, the point, and tells us something about the survival of both Christianity and sado-masochism in our society: it is possible that indeed they are part of a very vicious circle.

However this may be, it is certain that evidence exists which demonstrates that the idealism inculcated by the English public schools, which had its basis in Christianity, gave rise to a code of 'manliness' immediately before the First World War which actively encouraged and rejoiced in pain. Writing about the 'rhetoric of cohesion, identity, patriotism and morality' to be found in public-school songs celebrating athleticism, J.A. Mangan remarks upon the co-existence of three motifs within Edward Thring's songs: 'masculinity, sensuality and pain'.[7] Thring was the headmaster responsible for transforming Uppingham Grammar School into 'an expensive national boarding school for the upper classes.'[8] Vera Brittain's brother, fiance and friends, killed in the war, were all educated at Uppingham. But it should not be thought that the phenomenon we are discussing was restricted to a particular school. It was, as Mangan has shown, widespread. Edward Lyttleton, headmaster of Eton between 1905 and 1916, 'bemoaned the removal of the element of pain from cricket, due to the development of smooth pitches'. This, he said, made the game 'comparatively worthless'. F.B. Malim, one-time assistant master at Marlborough and subsequently headmaster at a number of public schools 'considered golf and lawn tennis undesirable school games because they were insufficiently painful'.[9] The same man wrote in 1917: 'What virtues can we reasonably suppose to be developed by games? First I should put physical courage . . . for the security of the nation courage in her young men is indispensable. That it has been bred in the sons of England is attested by the fields of Flanders and the beaches of Gallipoli. We shall therefore give no heed to those who decry the danger of some schoolboy sport.'[10] Given such sentiments, it is not difficult to see how the songs which idealised suffering and dishing out pain on the games field, became a model for both moral exhortations and sentimental remembrances during the Great War. And, of course, the metaphors which proliferated during the war comparing fighting and killing to 'playing the game' had their source in the public schools' tradition.

Apart from this cult of athleticism, in which 'masculinity' was defined by the ability to endure and inflict pain, the public schools were also responsible for reinforcing the ideology of self-sacrifice, and the 'beauty' of pain and death via their teaching of the classics. The crucial point to be made about this is that the Victorian and Edwardian reading of classical literature was extremely Romantic and censored by a muscular Christianity. Peter Parker in his book, *The Old Lie,* admirably describes the process whereby 'dangerous' tendencies were expurgated from Greek and Roman literature, so that Anthony Powell at Eton in 1919 could experience, 'Homer metamorphosed into a Pre-Raphaelite poet, Plato seen as a great headmaster, Greek homosexuality merged into heroic comradeship'.[11] In both pre-war and immediately post-war public schools, *The Iliad* was apparently dealt with in such a way as to emphasise the heroic nature of death in battle whilst erasing ideas of 'the tragic futility of war'.[12] More important, however, to the classical curriculum, Parker suggests, was J.W. Mackail's *Greek Anthology*, which constituted a selection from the *Palatine Anthology* significantly bearing upon its title page a Pre-Raphaelite woodcut by Burne-Jones. The selection was suitably imbued with a late nineteenth-century taste for 'pessimism and despair, an over-ripe perfection', in which epigrams about 'love and death and the fate of youth and beauty' abounded.[13] Poems which overtly alluded to homosexuality or paederasty were omitted, but the death of youth in battle is fully treated. In his introduction to the anthology Mackail draws his readers' attention to epitaphs:

On the Athenians, slain under the skirts of the Euboean hills, who lavished their young and beautiful lives for Athens; on the soldiers who fell, in the full tide of Greek glory, at the great victory on the Eurymedon. In all the epitaphs of this class *the thought of the city swallows up individual feeling;* for the city's sake, that she may be free and great, men offer their death as freely as their life; and the noblest end for a life spent in her service is to die in the moment of victory.[14]

An ideal is made of beautiful male youth self-sacrificed in battle. It is no wonder that A.E. Housman's *A Shropshire Lad* was so popular with infantry subalterns on the Western Front: his 'lads that will die and never grow old' were clearly in the tradition.[15]

Brooke, Sassoon and Graves all attended public schools. Owen is the exception in this regard, as he came from a less elevated class background. Nevertheless the cultural traditions created and perpetuated by these schools were inevitably heavily influential in bourgeois society as a whole since it was from these schools that the ruling, preaching and teaching classes were drawn. As we shall see, if Owen missed the peculiar 'privileges' of a public-school education, other aspects of his biography conspire to bring his experience into close relationship with his more wealthy peers. Furthermore, like all writers of the Great War, my four subjects were writing into the Romantic tradition which is saturated with 'spilt religion'. The idea that 'beauty' is inextricably associated with pain, and that the artist must therefore suffer to create beauty is central to the Romantic tradition. Mario Praz extensively documents the darker corollaries of this equation in *The Romantic*

Agony, where the ubiquity of sado-masochistic sexuality in the writings of French, Italian and English Romanticism is demonstrated. Brooke, Owen and Sassoon had read their Shelley and Swinburne, wherein pain, violence, and flagellation are given awful expression and are inextricably entwined with the idea of love.[16] Graves, due to the influence of his father, was not quite so steeped in these authors, but certainly had an early familiarity with the Pre-Raphaelites in whose work we also find sensuality irrevocably bound with pain.[17] The poets I deal with here were also engaged, like those before them, in the Romantic quest to find an individual voice, and in doing so they were obliged not to be baulked by earlier writers, or by the pressing demands of Eros. As Frank Kermode has shown, it is in this way that the artist comes to see him or her self as a Christ-like figure, sacrificing themselves for art. Thus D.H. Lawrence, a non-combatant member of the generation that I am concerned with here, could speak of the artist's 'crucifixion into isolate individuality'.[18]

In the pages that follow, where I trace the place of physical and mental suffering and its relationship to sexuality in the lives and work of Rupert Brooke, Siegfried Sassoon, Wilfred Owen and Robert Graves, the bearing of Christianity, the public-school ethos, and Romanticism upon individuals will be discussed. This will inevitably lead into considerations of the formation of masculine identity in the late nineteenth and early twentieth centuries. It is important in this connection to observe that my attitude to 'masculinity' and 'femininity' is non-essentialist. That is to say that despite the obvious differences of male and female biological functioning, I do not believe that these confer different, specific human attributes upon their subjects. Masculinity and femininity are socially constructed, relative terms, and it is part of my project to suggest, along with others like Michael Adams in his book *The Great Adventure*,[19] that gentleness, emotional range and depth, the ability to nurture and to love unconstrainedly, need to be recognised as not only viable but also necessary qualities of masculinity as well as femininity. In the period I am dealing with here, however, it is quite clear that certain traits were considered to be specifically 'masculine' and others 'feminine', and we will have occasion to repeat such assumptions when they touch upon or are encountered in the lives and work of the poets with whom I am concerned. In such cases I have tried to ensure that the significations 'masculine' and 'feminine' are always rendered provisional by their appearance in inverted commas.

Male homosexuality will also be an issue here. As Jonathan Dollimore has recently stated there is no single satisfactory definition of homosexuality, and in theoretical terms it is preferable to think of a range of feelings and behaviours as 'homosexual*ities*'.[20] In my discussion I use the word 'homosexual' in its most basic sense of denoting sexual attraction between people of the same biological sex. The specific qualities of the 'homosexualities' dealt with, and their relationship to ideas of 'femininity' and 'masculinity', will, I hope, be clear from the contexts of each discussion. I occasionally use the word 'homoerotic' to describe eroticism with a specifically homosexual component, but not to suggest either overtly or covertly (as I think Fussell does) any clear distinction, moral or otherwise, between a chaste (and therefore acceptable) homoeroticism and a practising (unacceptable) homosexuality.

In discussing problems of sexual identity experienced by all four poets dealt with, I have not been primarily concerned with psychological speculations about the aetiology of homosexuality. In the following chapters I wish to suggest a different approach to this subject that moves away from inappropriate categorisations of 'homosexual' and 'heterosexual' which suggest that these two states are somehow 'fixed', opposite, and mutually exclusive to each other, and which concentrates rather upon the process of sexual choice in social interaction. I am indebted here to Hart and Richardson's book, *The Theory and Practice of Homosexuality*,[21] wherein the authors propose an 'interactive' model which attempts to explain how a man or woman might come to identify themselves with, and therefore live out a homosexual or heterosexual role. Hart and Richardson demonstrate how much thinking about homosexuality has been dominated by a concern with aetiology. They argue that biological, psychoanalytic, and social learning theories are all inconclusive, flawed, and seem unable to adequately explain how or why an individual might show homosexual behaviour at one time of their life, and heterosexual behaviour at another, and why some people choose bisexual identities. Rather, their emphasis is upon 'the complex question of how a person comes to identify as homosexual'. Hart and Richardson are anxious to distinguish between 'homosexual acts' and 'homosexual identities' arguing that 'many people engage in same sex acts without necessarily identifying as homosexual' or alternatively that 'a person may not have actually engaged in same sex acts, although they would define themselves as homosexual'. That most people view themselves as either homo- or hetero-sexual is because sexuality is a 'core construct' in the development of self-identity, and the idea that sexual identity is fixed and stable is one given much ideological and social support. But some people, because of the particular circumstances of their lives and the particular interactions of such circumstances, and because of their own dynamic reactions to these, choose different sexual identities at different stages of their lives.

We come back then to the 'lives', 'experiences' and work of Brooke, Sassoon, Owen and Graves. In making a distinction here and throughout the book between the 'life' and the 'work' of each poet, I am aware of using a convenient convention which is fraught with theoretical difficulties. What I mean by 'the life' or 'experience' of a poet is not, of course, some substantive 'reality' but rather those *texts* which reconstitute the biography, which tell the *stories* of the poet's life. There may be verifiable, historical 'facts' of biography, but as soon as these are formed into a narrative then we are in the realms of interpretive fiction. This does not, to my mind, invalidate the use of biographical conventions. After all, when we speak of our own lives, our own selves, we are constructing the fiction of our lives whether we are conscious of this or not. Previously published biographies of Brooke, Owen and Graves have then been used, sometimes for information, sometimes for points of agreement and disagreement. I have also utilised other texts that these biographies rely on, principally the poets' letters. From these materials I have fashioned a reading and a re-writing of the respective lives, and have related this to a re-reading of the poetry. I make no apology for this. Indeed it seems to me that in the mythologisation of the 'war poets' there is already an almost inseparable connection between their lives and work, perhaps even more so than is usual with other writers. Rupert Brooke's physical appearance, the way in which so many memoirs speak of his looks, is as important to the idea of the 'young Apollo' as are his poems. Similarly the idea that Owen's and Sassoon's poems are 'realistic' and full of 'pity', is encouraged by a selective 'reading' of their lives, wherein their 'experience' of suffering is used to authenticate the poems. In order to question such ideas it is, I think, essential to reconsider not only the poems, but the other texts which are intimately related to the poems in order to suggest new, and I hope useful, readings of both.

What will emerge in the course of these readings are patterns of suffering which crucially inform the way the war is written about, and which illuminate aspects of the writing that have not gained sufficient, if any, attention hitherto. In undertaking such a pursuit, and following Paul Delaney down the path of attempting to de-mythologise the writers and writings of the First World War, I am perhaps laying myself open to charges of disrespect for both the writers and their art. This is a particularly sensitive issue in the case of men who patently suffered so much. Yet it is my belief that to recover what we can of the complexity of both writers and their writings, and to mount a critique of ideologies formed by their work, is not a matter of disrespect, but on the contrary a recognition of the value and importance of their life and work.

One further matter requires clarification. I have chosen Brooke, Sassoon, Owen and Graves as the subjects for this study for several reasons. They are, I submit the most famous, most widely read of English First World War writers. Despite Owen's slightly less elevated class background, they share a specifically English, Protestant, middle-class inheritance. They also shared a web of social connections. Sassoon met Brooke before he was killed, through their mutual friend Edward Marsh. Graves also knew Marsh, and on meeting Sassoon because they were in the same regiment, realised that they shared this and other mutual aquaintances in literary London. Sassoon's meeting with Owen at Craiglockhart hospital was coincidental, but it was not long before Owen was introduced to Graves, and to Marsh and to the same London literary set. This then, together with constraints of space, provides the rationale for limiting my study to these four. To have introduced Rosenberg, Gurney, or Brittain to the argument would have added significant complications of class, religious and sexual difference. Nevertheless, it is my belief that much of what I say here about my chosen authors may be applied to one degree or another to these three. And in my conclusion this is remarked upon. But this is to anticipate far too much. We must proceed now to a discussion of that most mythologised of writers, Rupert Brooke.

Notes

1 Quoted by P. Delaney, *The Neo-Pagans: Friendship and Love in the Rupert Brooke Circle*, London, 1987, p. 212.
2 Delaney, *The Neo-Pagans*.
3 D. Hibberd, *Owen the Poet*, London, 1986.
4 V. Brittain, *Testament of Youth*, London (1933), 1978, p. 154.
5 Ibid., pp. 291–2.
6 G.L. Mosse, *Nationalism and Sexuality: Middle-Class Morality and Sexual Norms in Modern Europe*, Wisconsin, 1985, pp. 23–48.
7 J.A. Mangan, *Athleticism in the Victorian and Edwardian Public School: the Emergence and Consolidation of an Educational Ideology*, Cambridge, 1981, p. 187.
8 Ibid., p. 2.
9 Ibid., pp. 187–8.
10 Ibid., pp. 195–6.
11 P. Parker, *The Old Lie: the Great War and the Public-School Ethos*, London, 1987, p. 87.
12 Ibid., p. 95.
13 Ibid., pp. 88–9.
14 Ibid., p. 96.
15 Ibid., pp. 93–5. See also, P. Fussell, *The Great War and Modern Memory*, London (1975), 1977, pp. 270–309.
16 See M.Praz, *The Romantic Agony*, London, (1933), 1970.
17 Ibid., pp. 227–8 and *passim*.
18 Quoted by F. Kermode, *Romantic Image*, (1957), 1971, p. 18.
19 M.C.C. Adams, *The Great Adventure: Male Desire and the Coming of World War I*, Bloomington and Indianapolis, 1990, pp. 134–40.
20 J. Dollimore, *Sexual Dissidence*, Oxford, 1991, pp. 28–32.
21 J. Hart and D. Richardson, *The Theory and Practice of Homosexuality*, London, 1981.

2

Rupert Brooke

In recent years both John Lehmann and Paul Delaney have written biographical accounts of Rupert Brooke, which attempt to demonstrate that he was both more and less than either the upper-middle-class chauvinist of the war sonnets, or the Godlike youth of Frances Cornford's poem.[1] In what follows I am deeply indebted to both books, but wish to further our thinking about Brooke by re-examining the poems in the light of this new biographical material, and by suggesting some further clues to the mysteries of Brooke's psychological make-up. What I am interested in charting is the development of an attitude which finds the expression of physical love 'dirty' yet rejoices in the notion of killing and being killed on the battlefield as 'pure'; an attitude in which the creative principle is implicitly wicked, and the destructive aligned with virtue. What experiences were they that moved Brooke to write that love was 'a little emptiness' as against the implicit 'fullness' of death in battle? As we shall see he was not merely mouthing commonplace platitudes. His war sonnets are the corollary of his aesthetic, emotional, and psychological experiences up to the time of composition. And it is to a consideration of his biography and psychological development that we should now turn to gain what I hope will be further insight into those first and most famous of World War I poems.

Rupert Chawner Brooke was born in 1887. His father, William Parker Brooke, was a teacher at Rugby School who became the house master of School Field in 1891, a post he retained until his death in 1910. Parker was a rather mild mannered, and somewhat disappointed individual, known to the boys under his charge as 'Tooler', and rumoured to be dominated by his strong-willed and

Puritanical wife, Ruth. Certainly, as he grew up, it was Mrs Brooke who exerted the strongest active influence over Rupert, and she continued to be a very powerful figure for the rest of his short adult life. As a child, Rupert was rather sickly and this fostered a close and anxious relationship between mother and son. This circumstance may also have been exacerbated by Mrs Brooke's wish for a daughter. She later admitted to Rupert how disappointed she had been to give birth to a second son, and Rupert claimed that his own qualities of 'feminine intuition'[2] stemmed from this fact. Indeed it is quite clear that Brooke attributed his sexual confusions at least in part to the 'very female'[3] qualities which he believed he had inherited as a result of his mother's early wishes and feelings.

Whilst Rupert was young his mother fussed over him, and did not relish having him out of her sight. Consequently Rupert was sent to a 'prep' school, Hillbrow, that was only a hundred yards away from their home at Rugby school, and when he was old enough, Rupert became one of the pupils in his father's house. As Brooke's previous biographers point out, this put the boy into a very peculiar situation which might be described as the worst of both worlds: he had both the sexually sequestered and confusing experience of a public school education, and an intense family life. On one side of School Field he was one of the boys, indulging in the romantic intrigues of the dormitory, where his mother and father were referred to as 'Tooler' and 'Ma Tooler', but on the other side of the house he was the dutiful and conforming son.

It is not then entirely suprising that Brooke's career at Rugby was in some respects entirely conventional and in others less so. He did well at classics and games – the two primary desiderata of public school education. He played rugby football and cricket for both house and school, and by 1904 had attained the rank of colour-sergeant in the Officer Training Corps. Although never over-enthusiastic about classics, he seems to have done quite well in the subject, and Hassall remarks that the closest he ever came to his father was 'over a Latin or Greek grammar'.[4] At the same time, Brooke was developing his interest in poetry, and this was encouraged by an older friend, the twenty-five-year-old St John Lucas, a lawyer and poet who lived in London, but whose family were neighbours of the Brookes'. His published work was heavily influenced by the English Decadents, and Lucas himself was homosexual. Presumably Rupert's parents had not read Lucas's work and were ignorant of his sexual preferences. That he was the son of a neighbour, that he had attended the same school as Parker Brooke, and that he was pursuing a reputable career in the Middle Temple, were presumably enough to convince Mr and Mrs Brooke that here was a suitable mentor for their son. In fact Lucas's influence encouraged Rupert in an 'aesthetic' rebellion against the philistinism of school life. Dowson, Swinburne, and Wilde were recommended and avidly read, providing a creed of beauty, suffering and pain which the young poet found irresistible.

Between 1904 and 1906 Brooke was producing poems which were sent to Lucas for commentary and criticism. Because this work is so obviously derivative, critics and biographers have been quick to dismiss its importance, and to suggest that the subject matter is equally inauthentic. Hassall, for instance describes Brooke as 'extravagantly insincere' in his letters and remarks that he was making 'poetry out of a pose'.[5] Similarly Delaney notes the 'decorously homoerotic' poems of this period are those of a person who is a 'jester and poseur',[6] thereby implying that the poems themselves have little to tell us of the true state of Brooke's emotional and psychological life. John Lehmann also follows suit, speaking of 'affectations of sentiment' and of 'pose'[7] in these poems. In looking at some of this juvenilia again, I would want to acknowledge that the influence of Dowson, Swinburne and Wilde is often very plain, and in so far as the poems express hints of deep experience and world-weariness they are undoubtedly less than sincere. On the other hand, what seems to me important is the *kind* of pose adopted, and the expression of various attitudes and emotional states underlying the pretentiousness which do not seem to me necessarily 'fake', or necessarily unimportant in understanding Brooke's development.

We might begin by asking ourselves why it was that Brooke was so passionately attracted to the work of the Decadent writers? Doubtless Lucas was highly influential in promoting these writers to Brooke, and certainly their work represented a 'rebellion' against his parents' values and those of school. But it seems to me that there is more than this involved. That Brooke could so readily respond to and imitate the crepuscular, disembodied, world of Dowson and Swinburne, with their images of love, idealised yet sinful, their glorying in pain, despair, sorrow, their sado-masochistic images wherein eroticism is allied with bloodshed and sacrifice, seems to me to bespeak an emotional and psychological identification with this subject matter which goes beyond mere 'posing'. That Swinburne remained a particular favourite of Brooke's well after he had left school also attests to this.

The poems Brooke wrote in his last two years at school express thwarted desires, yearnings to escape from such desires, feelings of sinfulness and shame, notions of lost beauty, love, and purity, and a concern with sickness and disease. In 'It is Well' for instance, the speaker is a thwarted lover who addresses the beloved from a position of self-sacrifice. The poet is a Christ-like figure who forfeits 'joy unutterable' to save his beloved from sorrow. He bears 'the load of sin', sacrificing his own pleasure and even salvation for the sake of love. The only reward for this behaviour is to see from hell the beloved's face again in heaven.[8] 'Dedication' is a similar poem, but here the tone is more accusatory. The poet speculates that when he is dead, and has rest from all his 'sins and sorrows' his beloved will discover these 'broken rhymes, . . ./Fashioned and forged in the fierce hidden fire' of a love that the poet has died for, and will 'weep for great love given in vain'.[9]

A longing for death is expressed in poem after poem. In 'Evening', 'The Return', 'Afterwards' and 'The Lost Lilies', images of dissolution are juxtaposed with those of love. Death is habitually preferred to sexual love. In 'Evening' the poet and his beloved escape from the 'folly of youth's delight', and find 'Nothing of passion or pale sorrow' in the realm of death. Rather, oblivion provides healing:

> Rest for sick bodies and hearts aching!
>   We shall sleep very soundly, you and I,
> Sleep unbroken by passionate dreaming,
>   Silence unmarred by sob or sigh,
>   And – God guard us from waking![10]

Similarly in 'Afterwards' Brooke longs to escape from life in order to 'forget', and to relieve 'his festered soul' its 'dull hate/For this interminable hell of Life'. But in this poem, Brooke is cast as a youthful Hamlet who 'shrinks' from ending life for fear of what might 'wait/Behind the pitiless Silence of Eternity'.[11] 'The Lost Lilies' is a slightly more complicated effort wherein the 'heaven' of one love has 'been forfeited' by 'sin', and the poet attempts to persuade himself that other loves and passion remain to be explored. After 'desolate questing through the years' the poet achieves a 'dim languorous place' where he endeavours to forget the 'pale sorrow of . . .lost lilies' through the 'roses' purple kiss'. But passion, symbolised by the roses, is figured in the end as unsatisfactory, and at the close the poet pines for 'the perfect beauty' encapsulated by the 'immortal pallor' of 'lost lilies'. Thus a state of unfulfilled desire is idealised. Joy is merely lack of desire. The 'sick heart' longs for the 'purity' and perfection residing in the funereal lilies.[12] By implication passion is impure and imperfect. Only through pain and death can one commune with perfect love and perfect beauty.

Such mannered abstractions from the pen of a schoolboy may seem to be so far removed from the recognisable realities of experience as to be risible. I do not share this view. I think that the poems relate directly to the psycho-sexual dilemmas with which he was struggling at the time. What were these? It is quite clear from Brooke's letters that he was involved in the romance which characterised the relationship between so many older boys with their younger schoolfellows in English public schools.The most well-documented of these in Rupert's case is his 'affair' with Charles Lascelles which began in the spring of 1906. But it seems certain that there were other 'crushes' prior to this, as in a much later letter he recalls how his mother's mention of the 'boy of the moment in the House' over luncheon would turn him 'the level red of this blotting paper, and crying with silent wrath'.[13] That Brooke's mother could continue to have this effect on her son in later life, and that he spent much time and energy in subterfuge to prevent his mother discovering his love life, is indicative of the power she held within the relationship, and of at least one source of the guilt Brooke felt about his sexuality.

In his romantic dealings with other boys at school it seems likely that Brooke was chaste, and that matters did not proceed much further than a holding of hands and perhaps a furtive kiss. Writing to Geoffrey Keynes in February 1906 Brooke was firstly able to tell him of a 'romantic comedy' of the 'usual' kind which, 'the Schoolmaster delights to nip in the bud perhaps wisely, for most boys are beasts'. He goes on to furnish some information concerning his own personal life:

A purple and terrific scandal has arisen round me. It is tremendously intricate, and even I know only three-quarters of it. No one else knows more than a quarter . . . It began by Dean catching me one day & informing me that 'a gentleman' in another House, had been trying to buy a photo of me: Dean was willing, but my leave was necessary. My enormous conceit was swelled even more – and I gave leave. Dean unluckily mentioned the name of the House. And there were who overheard. Whence rose a scandal; which I yet nipped in the festering bud. (Forgive my archaic style it – is beautifully reasonless.) Sundry however heard of it, and theorized – to my much discomfort. H.F.R.[ussell] S[mith] for instance has an unfounded yet stubborn faith that it was the Anarchist!! But I secretly made inquiries and found it was one I knew of old – one with the form of a Greek God, the face of Hyacinthus, the mouth of Antinous, eyes like a sunset, a smile like dawn. . . It appears that the madman worships me at a pale distance: which is embarrassing but purple. . . So I wander around, taking a huge aesthetic delight in the whole mad situation.[14]

As we shall see, 'tremendous intricacy' was to attend all of Brooke's subsequent affairs, and although pain was more often the result than joy, this meant that his emotions could all the more readily be assimilated into the aesthetic realms of poetry.

In further correspondence with Keynes, Brooke continued to regale his friend with the progress of his 'affair'. He was enjoying himself immensely in a circumstance which had not gone beyond Brooke's giving of the photo, and their eyes meeting in chapel. It was this 'situation' that Brooke described as 'so exquisite, so delicately appealing' to his 'aesthetic heart', that he feared 'to move forward'. Nevertheless he recognised that though 'knowledge is so disillusioning' he must 'advance in the matter'. 'Real life', he says, cannot be 'left hanging as it might in a novel or a prose poem'. Furthermore, and in rather contradictory vein, he asserts that 'to retire would be inartistic'.[15] Keynes apparently was concerned that Brooke might do something ill advised, but he needn't have worried as Brooke contracted opthalmia and 'rose rash' which quarantined him for eight weeks, postponing the development of his relationship with 'Antinous' until the last term of Brooke's career at Rugby. That it was his last, tempted him, he declared, to 'rashness' ('except the rose variety') as he wished to 'make some actual material protest against the conventional hypocrisy of the public school', and because it was 'his obvious duty to live the aesthetic life' he 'preached'.[16] But apart from this, there is no evidence to suggest that his relationship with Lascelles went beyond the exchange of photographs, the writing of purple letters to each other, and a few walks in which the main subject of conversation seems to have been cricket![17] Delaney speculates that the relationship was ended by Lascelles during the Christmas vacation of 1906–7 after Brooke's first term at Cambridge.[18]

Keynes wondered, as have subsequent biographers, how much of Brooke's 'affair' was 'true'. Brooke's chastising answer has been taken as evidence that it was not, and that Brooke was merely playing at love. 'It does not do to inquire too closely', he wrote, and continued 'Even if it were only a romantic comedy, a fiction, who cares? Youth is stranger than fiction.'[19] One sympathises, I think, with Brooke's response. He is surely right in the sense that *all* romantic love *is* a fiction. The pertinent question concerns what *kind* of fiction we are dealing with. And this is why Brooke's relationship with Lascelles seems to me significant. It signals Brooke's response to the sexual difficulties so commonly engendered by the public schools. As Peter Parker has argued, the public school code was fraught with contradiction in its attitudes towards male relationships. Whilst promoting a situation which encouraged romantic friendship between boys, it simultaneously denounced the sexual expression of such feelings. 'The model for the Romantic Friendship was not that of Achilles and Patrolocus or Alexis and Corydon, but that love passing the love of women enjoyed by David and Jonathan. David's lament was frequently read as the lesson in chapel.'[20]

Brooke read this text at Rugby in 1904, and one cannot help wondering if two years later he sought out the eyes of 'Antinous' as this famous passage was read out again. However this may be, it is clear, I think, that Brooke was caught between romantic idealism and sexual fulfilment, between repression and expression. We recall his remark approving of the master's behaviour in the majority of cases on the grounds that most boys are 'beasts'. On the other hand, he speaks of the 'hypocrisy' of the public schools and of conventional attitudes. But it is clear that the latter were more prevalent in Brooke's behaviour, and he found an outlet for rebellion in the reading and writing of 'decadent' poems in which secret and 'sinful' desires are alluded to, and in which ideal love is fulfilled in death rather than erotic experience. The 'shadows', 'mists', 'dim languors' and 'weariness' of the poems figure the sexual confusion Brooke felt, as he yearned for the resolution of his ambivalences, and the fulfilment of his sexual drive.

This context helps explain another poem Brooke wrote in 1906 entitled 'The Song of the Beasts' wherein he equates sobriety and dullness with daytime, and the night with 'shame'. The reader is invited to join the poet's bacchanalia for, 'Have you not felt the quick fires that creep/Through the hungry flesh, and the lust of delight,/And hot secrets of dreams that day cannot say?' The progress of the 'beasts', 'By little black ways, and secret places,/In darkness and mire' is described, and although 'the touch and the smell of bare flesh sting', the followers are urged forward to find an ultimate consummation 'Beyond lust and fear' in a Swinburnian plunging into the sea, therein to drown.[21] It is surely short sighted to suggest that such a poem is divorced from Brooke's experience, just as it is with his other 'juvenilia' discussed above. The poem expresses the 'beastliness' yet the excitement of desire; it hints at sado-masochistic enjoyments of the flesh, and lastly shies away from the reality of sexual consummation to take comfort in an escape and a sublimated self-obliteration in the sea rather than in the arms of a lover. The poem is poised between the exciting 'shame' of sexuality, and the desire to escape from it.

The affair with 'Antinous' also demonstrates for us how inextricably love and art were entangled in Brooke's experience; how sexuality and the aesthetic were intimately related. And in both art and love, pain was of importance. In 1905 Brooke read Wilde's *De Profundis* and became highly enthused by Wilde's vision of Christ as the type of the Romantic artist. In the late summer of 1905, writing in response to a series of questions put to him by James Strachey, Brooke replied in the decided affirmative to the question, 'Are you in favour of war at any price?', asserting that war 'kills off the unnecessary'. He went on to give his view of the Saviour: 'For Christ – I am so obsessed by *De Profundis* that I have no other views on this subject than those expressed therein. The Perfect Artistic Temperament.'[22] Only a few months later, visiting Italy in April, Brooke recalled for St John Lucas an experience in 'the vaporous gloom of St Mark': '. . . gazing on the mosaics, [I] mused of all my religions, till everything became confused, the grand pulpit changed to an altar of Moloch, the figure of Mary grew like Isis, and the fair Byzantine Christ was lost in the delicate troubled form of Antinous'.[23] His beloved is likened to Christ who is also associated with the artist. There is more than a little narcissism here, as well as an association of love and art with pain.

Before going on to discuss Brooke's development after he left Rugby and took up his place at King's College Cambridge, we would do well to discuss the difficult issue of homosexuality. Delaney has suggested that Brooke at school and in his first year at Cambridge 'might be called homosexual, but that if he was it was more by chance than by choice'.[24] What I think Delaney means by this remark is that Brooke's attraction to boys was simply the product of being in their close proximity and separated from girls during his adolescence. It implies that Brooke was not 'really' homosexual. Brooke's other biographers, Christopher Hassall and John Lehmann agree on this subject. Hassall suggests that Brooke was 'not by nature' drawn to 'romance of this kind', that he was simply posing and playing with 'Antinous', and was therefore not seriously homosexual,[25] whilst Lehmann remarks that such relationships between a younger and older boy at a public school are 'too frequent a phenomenon to be considered other than normal'.[26]

It is at this point that the interactive model of sexual identity, outlined in my introduction, becomes helpful, as it avoids inappropriate, absolute distinctions between hetero- and homo-sexuality. It is also useful because Brooke's family circumstances might tempt a Freudian or neo-Freudian 'explanation' of his adolescent sexual difficulties since they provide a near-perfect example of the pattern of relationship posited as the 'cause' of homosexuality. That is to say that he had a domineering mother, a small, retiring father who 'hid behind his moustache', and Rupert was closer to his mother than his father. Added to this, Parker Brooke died when Rupert was only twenty-three and so distance became absence – both predisposing factors according to the Freudians of homosexuality. The interactive approach, on the other hand, whilst not seeking to deny the impact of parental relationships on the development of sexual choice, would see this familial pattern as only one of many factors which might influence the formation of sexual identity. In Brooke's case it may well be true that seeing his father so dominated by his mother did not induce in him, whilst he was at home and school, any particularly attractive reasons for choosing a heterosexual identity. Rather, the reverse may be true. But other interactive factors which might predispose him towards a homosexual identity include the lack of contact with girls, the general acceptance of homoerotic relationships amongst the boys, and last but not least, the identification by Brooke of art with homosexuality and homoeroticism, whereas games were traditionally 'hearty', implicitly 'manly' and therefore regarded as properly 'heterosexual'.

In his last years at school, Brooke encouraged by the examples of Wilde, Swinburne, and St John Lucas seems to have begun to construct a homosexual persona, if not a homosexual identity. It is apparent in several letters that his aesthetic rebellion against the Philistines involves a weariness with games and an infatuation with art.[27] As we have seen, the whole affair with 'Antinous' was intimately related to Brooke's aesthetic leanings. One might even speculate that Brooke saw a homosexual identity as a necessary condition of becoming the artist that he wished to be.

It was only gradually during his years at Cambridge that Brooke's direction began to change somewhat. On first going up he was miserable and lived the life of a 'hermit'.[28] He was pining for Lascelles, and finding the transition from school to university difficult. Things were not helped by the death of his elder brother, Dick, during the Christmas vacation; an event that crushed the remaining spirit out of his father and left Brooke as the 'single focus' of his mother's 'ambition and her powerful will'.[29]

Despite this troubled time for Brooke, it did not take him long after the first term to become involved in various Cambridge groups, notably Charles Sayle's salon in Trumpington Street, the exclusive discussion group known as the 'Apostles', the Fabian Society and the Marlowe Dramatic Society. These circles were not always mutually compatible as they constituted different and opposed sexual worlds. Sayle was a middle-aged librarian who was homosexual and, chastely paedophilic.[30] At his gatherings Brooke met other intellectuals who shared similar sexual and aesthetic orientations. Likewise the Apostles at this time were predominantly homosexual. Brooke's election to the group was engineered by a friend from 'prep' school days, James Strachey. Strachey was in love with Brooke and invited him to bed on several occasions without success. Nevertheless they remained friends for some years, and Brooke was often in his company.

If Sayle and the Apostles offered continuities with Rugby, the Marlowe Dramatic Society and the Fabians provided alternatives. These groups facilitated Brooke's introduction to the society of women, and to ideas and ideals derived from the thought of Edward Carpenter. Friends like Justin Brooke (no relation) and Jacques Raverat had been to the progressive Bedales School whose ethos and curriculum owed much to Carpenter's thought. The school was co-educational, and encouraged 'comradeship' between the sexes. Closeness to nature was a primary desideratum, such that hiking, camping, arts and crafts, manual labour and folk songs were all promoted. The politics implicit in all of this were a variety of socialism that had more in common with William Morris than Karl Marx. And although Fabian politics were sometimes slightly harder nosed, Brooke's 'revolutionary' and atheistical enthusiasms were always more sentimentally liberal than bluntly materialist. The sexual politics deriving from Bedales, though mildly progressive, were nevertheless extremely Puritanical. Despite Carpenter's championing of homosexual love, he subordinated sexuality to the rather chilling concept of 'rational comradeship', and as Delaney has intimated, this idea was to have a profound and unfortunate effect on Brooke's subsequent heterosexual relationships.

Before arriving at Cambridge Brooke's only contact with women of his own generation seems to have been his correspondence with his cousin Erica Cotterill. But by November, 1907 Brooke is clearly excited by the prospect of serving on the committee of the Fabian society because many of the members are women: 'Most of the Committee are Newnhamites, strange wild people, whom I shall infuriate by being utterly incompetent. I am greatly looking forward to it.' The same letter continues to speak of his forthcoming trip to Switzerland during the Christmas holidays. It was to be a large party of twenty-eight young people mostly, according to Brooke, 'young, heady, strange, Females'. He is, he says, 'terrified' and wonders if he has the 'courage to go'. But, reassuringly, he remarks that Mrs L, the chaperone for the party, is 'a good woman'.[31] Writing to Erica Cotterill whilst actually in Switzerland, Brooke is moved to exclaim, 'Even the Newnhamites and others of their age and sex are less terrible than they might be. Several are no duller to talk to than males. There is One! . . . oh there is One . . .aged twenty, *very* beautiful & nice

24

& everything . . .'[32] This 'one' was Brynhild Olivier, the first of the four Olivier sisters that he met.

Brooke's defensive, but nevertheless insulting remarks about women in the letter quoted above, are symptomatic of the sexual 'terror' they induce in him. Hence the remark about the chaperone. Mrs Leon is evidently to be trusted as someone who will 'protect' Rupert from any sexual advances from the Newnhamites. The other side of this coin, of course, is the Romantic, idealised response to Brynhild's beauty. But it was not Brynhild, who was to cause Brooke overmuch pain or anxiety, but her sister Noel whom he met in May 1908. She was only fifteen, and had just been enrolled at Bedales. There followed over the next several years a tortuous courtship of Noel which found no satisfactory resolution. But it was an unlikely affair to produce such an issue. Brooke chose to fall 'in love' with someone whom he could necessarily have only very limited opportunities to meet, get to know, or be with. For her part, Noel was reserved, aloof, self-contained, aristocratic and rather cold.[33] It was not a promising scenario. But this was surely the point. On the one hand Noel represented for Brooke someone much younger than himself, so that he presumably felt less threatened by her than by his contemporaries. Her youth in those days would also have ensured for Brooke her 'virginity' and her 'purity'. On the other hand it was a situation which would necessarily hurt Brooke; a situation guaranteed to make him endure the pain of sexual frustration, the pain of separation, and the pain of dealing with someone much less passionately involved than he was himself. It thereby guaranteed him material for his poetry.

1909 found Brooke trying to steer a delicate course between his conflicting interests. In a manoeuvre which might suggest that Brooke was increasingly forging a heterosexual identity, his association with Sayle seems to have lapsed somewhat in his third year at Cambridge, and, encouraged by Jacques Raverat, Justin Brooke, Gwen and Francis Darwin, and the Olivier sisters, Rupert became 'a wild, rough elementalist'. This back-to-nature programme, which Virginia Woolf (then Virginia Stephen) christened 'Neo-Paganism', had long walks, camping, nude bathing, sandals and sometimes vegetarianism as the attractive tenets of its creed. But the simplicity of this scheme of life was ironically at odds with the complications in Brooke's affairs, as his plans for his Easter holidays of 1909 admirably demonstrate. Even recording these is difficult, since Brooke told different groups of people three different itineraries so as to placate his parents, keep the Apostles in the dark, and enable him to orchestrate a 'chance' encounter with Noel.

He began his vacation staying near Manaton in Devon with James Strachey where he reported a strict regime of physical exercise, cold baths etc. in keeping with his new found beliefs. From there he progressed to a meeting of several Apostles at the Lizard in Cornwall. Here there was nude bathing and Strachey perhaps inspired by the beauty of Rupert's nakedness invited that recalcitrant friend to his bed, only to be refused again. Brooke had other developments in mind. Unbeknown to the Cornwall contingent Brooke had been plotting with Dudley Ward to 'escape' to the New Forest for four days, there to encounter the Olivier sisters who had hired a cottage in the forest. Ward's diplomacy, and Brooke's subterfuge worked, and the result was, for Brooke at least, an outstanding success:

I was, for the first time in my life, a free man, and my own master! Oh! the joy of it! . . . And all in England, at Eastertide! And so I walked and laughed and met a many people and made a thousand songs – all very good – and, in the end of the days, came to a Woman who was more glorious than the Sun and stronger than the sea, and kinder than the earth, who is a flower made out of fire, a star that laughs all day, whose brain is clean and clear like a man's and her heart is full of courage and kindness; and whom I love.[34]

In his letters of 1908 and 1909, Brooke's family are variously alluded to as 'abominable', 'sad', 'accursed'.[35] It was clearly the sense of having escaped their watchfulness which leant this particular escapade its special piquancy. And then it was springtime, and here was another meeting with Noel. One suspects that it was precisely the difficulty of seeing her that Brooke enjoyed – it added excitement, romance, secrecy – heady ingredients which manifestly off-set the difficult practicalities of being 'in love' with a sixteen-year-old school girl. Of her attractions listed above, the most intriguing, and the most significant is the remark about Noel's 'manly' brain which is 'clean' and 'clear'. The implication that women's minds are dirty and unclear, demonstrates the depth of Brooke's psychological ambivalence which kept him allied to a

Victorian sexism quite out of tune with Fabianism. The Fabians were feminists: Brooke never was, and as we shall see, in all his dealings with women, habitually referred to those he professed to love in superior, condescending, tones.

But for now he was captivated by Noel, and continued further plotting to see her again in the summer. Brooke took his classical tripos exams in May and gained an indifferent Second. There followed a 'Neo-Pagan' camp at Penshurst in July when Rupert and Noel were again together. In August Rupert persuaded his parents to rent a house in Clevedon in which to entertain his friends. This did not work well, and his mother particularly mistrusted and disliked the Olivier sisters, though Noel was kept from attending this party by her elder sister Marjory. The Olivier girls who did visit had been brought up in free-thinking circles. Their unconventional attitudes were construed by the 'Ranee' (as Brooke referred to his mother) as a lack of morals and manners. After the Clevedon episode, Rupert was regaled by 'nightly anti-Olivier lectures'[36] from his mother. To make matters worse, Marjory Olivier made life difficult for Rupert. She acted as chaperone and guardian to her younger sister, and decided to put every obstacle in his path to seeing Noel. In a letter of September 1909, Marjory chastised Brooke for his 'wild writing' to Noel, and pointed out that 'love' at such an early age was apt to destroy a woman's intellectual development.[37] Therefore, Brooke was to be shut out of Noel's existence as much as possible.

Rupert was distraught, and there followed in October, a drastic reaction to his frustrations and confusions. If his own account is to be believed, Brooke, rather coldbloodedly, decided to seduce Denham Russell-Smith, brother of Hugh, both of whom he had known from Rugby School. Brooke's vivid account of this episode is quoted at length by Delaney.[38] Here Brooke makes mention of a schoolboy 'affair' with Denham, and how on a week-end visit he decided to lose his virginity with the same person, to whom he was at this time hardly close at all. Brooke's account of his first sexual consummation was written in 1912 whilst Brooke was 'recovering' from a nervous breakdown, and he had just heard of Denham's death. Perhaps due to these circumstances Brooke's rendition is so detailed as to have a rather self-obsessed prurience which need hardly detain us here. Only one salient particular is of interest. In the throes of making love Brooke speaks of treating

Denham with 'the utmost violence'. Although he speaks of feeling 'tenderness' for Russell-Smith after he has left the room (they did not spend the rest of the night together) still one cannot, I think, ignore the sadistic overtones of this description. Love and pain were inextricably related for Brooke, although the pain both given and received was more often mental than physical. Despite losing his virginity in a homosexual act, this did not propel Brooke down the path of forging a coherent homosexual identity. Rather he continued to pine for the unattainable Noel, thereby inflicting more pain upon himself.

The poems Brooke wrote between 1906 and 1909 as we might expect are replete with sufferings of various kinds. But in these years he steadily refined his style away from the lush, sensuous ornamentation of his 'Decadent' phase, and under the influence of various Renaissance writers, worked towards a plainer, more conversational mode, which nevertheless retained some poetic diction and always relied upon strict metrical and rhyming patterns. The influence of his reading and involvement in the drama at Cambridge had a salutary effect on his writing. Donne became the chief influence on his later work, but Cowley, Milton, Webster and Marlowe, were also important. It should also be said that some of these poets must also have suggested to Brooke that to be an 'aesthete' or an artist did not necessitate a homosexual orientation.

Of course, the broad development outlined here was a matter of gradual process, and in 'The Beginning', a poem dated variously by different people as belonging to either July 1906 or January 1907, one can still hear echoes of Swinburne. This poem, almost certainly written about Charles Lascelles, is important as it introduces us to concerns which are central to much of Brooke's oeuvre; it is indeed the 'beginning' of various obsessions which were to dog Brooke to the end. But the title of the poem refers to the beginning of his affair with Lascelles, and the poem contrasts this with an imagined and very bitter close. The poet suggests that though they are parted now, in later life he will seek out his beloved who will be recognised, 'Though the sullen years and the mark of pain/Have changed you wholly'. In that meeting, however, lies not joy or fulfilment, but only a sense of loss and betrayal:

So then at the ends of the earth I'll stand
And hold you fiercely by either hand,
And seeing your age and ashen hair
I'll curse the thing that once you were,
Because it is changed and pale and old
(Lips that were scarlet, hair that was gold!),
And I loved you before you were old and wise,
When the flame of youth was strong in your eyes,
– And my heart is sick with memories.[39]

The paraphernalia of 'Decadent' poetry has here given way to a clarity of utterance which strikes one immediately as more deeply felt than some of his earlier work. Nevertheless, the influence of Swinburne is still manifest in the very musical, predominantly anapaestic rhythm, which at moments precisely emulates the measure employed by Swinburne in his great elegy to his lost beloved, 'The Triumph of Time'.

Brooke's poem is not merely about the worship of youth and the fear of old age. It is also about his equation of love with youthful innocence, and with certain bodily characteristics. What he remembers most passionately are 'Touch of your hands and smell of your hair' and 'Lips that were scarlet, hair that was gold'. It is physical decay, as well as 'wisdom', or experience, which leads Brooke to an aggressive denunciation of the past. This hankering for an 'innocent', ultimately childish romance lies at the heart of many of Brooke's poems. As a corollary, there is a distrust of the body, not only because it declines with age, but also it partakes in sexual experience thereby, according to Brooke, destroying innocent, young beauty.

In poems like 'The Call', 'The Wayfarers', and 'Choriambics I', written between February 1907 and December 1908, the focus is upon a beloved lost in the past, who will later be reclaimed in a place 'beyond' the confines of earth. In 'The Call', a difficult and confusing poem to unravel entirely, all of the action seems to proceed in the realms of the metaphysical. The poet is woken out of 'slow dreams of Eternity' by the voice of the beloved. But this does not result in any earthly experience. Rather the poet goes on to celebrate the 'immortality' of their love and of the poet's celebratory song in which the beloved's 'mouth' is said to 'mock the old and wise'. Their love will withstand the destruction of heaven and hell, and Death will fear their 'glory'. The poem concludes with the immortals 'clothed about with perfect love,/Alone above the Night, above/The dust of the dead gods, alone'.[40] Love, communion, consummation are not experienced physically, they belong to the spiritual. Youthful beauty is celebrated, but not sensuously enjoyed.The same pattern is apparent in 'The Wayfarers' and 'Choriambics I'. In both poems the poet yearns for a consummation in death or in some spiritual after life.

If this kind of chaste communion in the realms of the metaphysical represents one side of the coin which preserves youthful love, the other side is represented by a deep revulsion from old or even middle age and particularly physical aspects of that condition. Anything physical that was less than beautiful seems to have caused Brooke great discomfort. Testament to this is 'Dawn', a poem written whilst travelling in Europe in 1907. The poet is in a compartment where opposite him 'two Germans snore and sweat'. The poem, in which the sonnet form is used to heighten ironic effect, describes the fetid claustrophobia of the compartment in horrified tones. One of Brooke's unwitting fellow-travellers 'wakes, and spits, and sleeps again'. As dawn breaks the 'foul air' becomes 'fouler than before' and the final line repeats for the third time the implicit cause of the poet's discomfort, 'Opposite me two Germans sweat and snore'.[41] There is an unpleasant xenophobia at work here, as well as an equally unpleasant Puritanical disgust with ordinary bodily functions. The poem is an inverted love poem; here is everything that Brooke believes to be opposed to love and romance.

In three other poems of this period there are virulent portraits of old age. 'Wagner' (1908) describes an older man attending a concert of that composer's music. Brooke dwells upon the details that revolt him. The man is described as having a 'fat wide hairless face', of liking 'love-music that is cheap', but worst of all he is accused of liking women, and of 'thinking himself the lover'. That somebody whom Brooke finds physically repelling should have such feelings is too much for the young poet, who betrays his own psychological problems in the last lines:

> The music swells. His gross legs quiver.
> His little lips are bright with slime.
> The music swells. The women shiver.
> And all the while, in perfect time,
> His pendulous stomach hangs a-shaking.[42]

There is a kind of horrified fascination in all of this, as if Brooke finds it monstrous that older, corpulent people should have sexual feelings at all. If he could write with this depth of feeling about a chance observation in the Queen's Hall, it is not surprising that in other poems about situations closer to him, an even greater passion underwrites the utterances.

This is the case in both 'Jealousy' and 'Menelaus and Helen'. The latter poem distances the poet's emotions through the use of the Trojan story, but in these twin sonnets it is not only sex in old age that horrifies Brooke, but also the whole notion of matrimony and domesticity. The first sonnet describes the Romantic passion of 'The perfect Knight before the perfect Queen', whilst the second provides an ironic commentary which describes the 'long connubial years' that follow, wherein Helen 'grows a scold' and Menelaus 'waxes garrulous'. At the close we hear of Helen 'gummy-eyed and impotent', and of her 'dry shanks' which 'twitch' at Paris's name. In the concluding couplet marital disharmony in old age is compared disadvantageously with death.[43] The poem adds another dimension to Brooke's puritanical fear and distaste for sexuality and things of the body. Surely his 'abominable' parents have not only imbued him with this Puritanism, but also given him an appalling example of marriage. Brooke was much enamoured with *Peter Pan*. People who do not wish to grow up usually have introjected very negative messages from their parents about what it is to be an adult. It seems that this was Brooke's unhappy position.

In 'Jealousy' the fate of matrimony is wielded like a curse. There is some evidence to suggest that this poem relates to the camp at Penshurst held in the summer of 1909, and is about Godwin Baynes and Bryn Olivier. We recall Brooke's early infatuation with Bryn, and now he sees her flirting with a man whose physique offends the poet with, 'the empty grace /Of those strong legs and arms, that rosy face...'. Brooke goes on to offer a vision of the couple in later life, which is remarkable only in the depth of its rancour. The poet imagines them to have been married for years:

When all that's fine in man is at an end,
And you, that loved young life and clean, must tend
A foul sick fumbling dribbling body and old,
When his rare lips hang flabby and can't hold
Slobber, and you're enduring that worst thing,

Senility's queasy furtive love-making,
And searching those dear eyes for human meaning,
Propping the bald and helpless head, and cleaning
A scrap that life's flung by, and love's forgotten, –
Then you'll be tired; and passion dead and rotten;
And he'll be dirty, dirty!
                    O lithe and free
And lightfoot, that the poor heart cries to see,
That's how I'll see your man and you! –
                              But you
Oh! when *that* time comes, you'll be dirty too! –

The things of the body are 'dirty'; by implication, cleanliness is about youth, beauty and innocence. We remember Brooke's praise of Noel Olivier's 'clean' mind.

These lines also, I think, help to explain Brooke's enthusiasm for Renaissance and Jacobean drama. The macabre fascination with the difficulties of this 'too, too solid flesh' is clearly part of Brooke's own psychological experience, and like so many of the Elizabethans and Jacobeans, Brooke's response to this problem is to look to the mystical, platonic and disembodied, to find 'real' love. Hence in poems like 'Choriambics II' or 'Finding', the beloved appears 'in vision white', or as a 'white dream' which comforts the lover and brings him rest. Significantly too, in the former poem the 'vision' is also a child. As we might expect from the discussion so far, 'children' in Brooke's poems are always romanticised, and always equated with beauty, love and innocence. It is surely no coincidence that he habitually addressed every woman he was ever in love with, as 'dear child'.

Other poems in praise of Noel Olivier, have the beloved safely located in realms beyond the earthly. In the sonnet 'Oh! Death will find me, long before I tire/Of watching you', the poet awaits his beloved's arrival beyond the grave, and when she obliges, a 'Most individual and bewildering ghost', she treats the ancient dead with proud, amused disdain.[45] Or in 'Victory' the couple take part in a peculiar pageant of the Gods, 'Alone, serene beyond all love or hate'.[46] It is only when Brooke confronts the physical presence of the beloved, or the reality of physical desire, that love turns away from comforting white visions to the experience of pain. In poems like 'The Voice', 'Blue Evening' and the infamous 'A Channel Passage' for instance, love and pain are strangely mixed.

'A Channel Passage' is a cruel poem. One senses Brooke relishing not only the shocking of an older generation's sensibilities, but also his delight at inflicting hurt upon a loved one. The poem describes a rough sea crossing, during which the poet thinks of the beloved in order not to be sick. But memories of her only give rise to 'sharp pain and dole' – he is faced with a choice between a 'sea-sick body, or a you-sick soul!' This proves no choice at all, and the sestet of this ironic sonnet brings together Brooke's fascinated horror with things physical and his difficulties with heterosexual love:

> Do I forget you? Retchings twist and tie me,
>   Old meat, good meals, brown gobbets, up I throw.
> Do I remember? Acrid return and slimy,
>   The sobs and slobber of a last year's woe.
> And still the sick ship rolls. 'Tis hard, I tell ye,
> To choose 'twixt love and nausea, heart and belly.[47]

Love is sickness, love is pain, and the poet's response to this is to cause some himself by writing this less than pretty 'love' poem. What Noel Olivier made of it can only be guessed. It appeared in Brooke's volume, *Poems* (1911), which he offered to dedicate to Noel. It is hardly any wonder that she refused this magnanimous gesture.

'A Channel Passage' was written in December 1909, when Brooke was struggling with his frustrated and frustrating passion for Noel. He had hardly seen her since the Penshurst camp in June, and she was not to attend the Christmas skiing party to which he was en route when he experienced the 'sea-sickness' of the Channel crossing. Things did not improve over the next few months, for in January 1910 Brooke's father died and Rupert was obliged to remain at Rugby for the first term of the New Year in order to take his father's place. Apart from disrupting his immediate plans of returning to Cambridge to do work on the Elizabethan dramatists, his father's death also further ensnared Brooke with his mother, and re-introduced him, however briefly, to the world of the public school where, as we have seen, so much was emotionally invested. In March, writing to Dudley Ward, Brooke included some lines of verse he had written about the boys under his charge. They are, he says, 'young, direct and animal', yet he perceives in them a 'certain dim nobility', and so loves,

>   each line
> Of the fine limbs and faces; love, in fine,
> (O unisexualist!) with half a heart,
> Some fifty boys, together, and apart,
> Half-serious and half-sentimentally . . .[48]

The word 'unisexual' is usually applied to flowers or plants which have pistils or stamens but not both. In its syntactical context here, Brooke suggests that he feels the bisexual position to be impossible. Since he can only have one physical gender he implies that he can never love wholeheartedly; his full self-hood can never be realised. This highlights a particular difficulty Brooke faced. As we have seen, he was deeply uncertain as to his sexual identity, but seems to have wished to choose either homosexuality or heterosexuality. The bisexual option seems either not to have been available to him, or if it was, it does not seem to have impinged upon Brooke's consciousness. The circles in which Brooke moved were either homo- or hetero-sexual. None of his close friends seems to have shared his sexual confusion to the same degree. There was no example to follow, or social context to allow Brooke to be at ease with a bisexual identity, and so he was faced with the difficulties of an either/or choice.

That he loved schoolboys half-heartedly has an obvious corollary with respect to Noel. Despite all his apparent protestations of love for her, it seems certain that this 'love' depended for its existence upon non-consummation or non-reciprocation. We have already seen what Brooke thought of the prospect of marriage, and there is little to suggest that he considered his own case with Noel to be an exception. In January 1910 Brooke wrote two poems which confirm this view. His sonnet, 'I said I splendidly loved you; it's not true' makes a nice companion piece to the lines about schoolboys quoted above. For here he figures a province of indetermination where: 'there are wanderers in the middle-mist/Who cry for shadows, clutch, and cannot tell/Whether they love at all, or, loving, whom . . .'.[49] Brooke counts himself as one such 'wanderer'. He is still psychologically lost in the crepuscular mists that he wrote of as a schoolboy. And it is the 'innocence' of his love for Charles Lascelles that seems to be the template for all his other relationships. His poem 'Success' makes clear that as soon as the affair with Noel threatens to become physical Brooke sheers off, frightened and repelled.[50]

It was the chase that Brooke enjoyed, and the inevitable pain inflicted on himself by choosing to pursue the unobtainable. Brooke spent the spring and summer of 1910 in pursuit of Noel in various locations. In July at a Neo-Pagan camp on the Beaulieu River in Hampshire, Brooke actually went so far as to propose to Noel. She replied in the affirmative, but insisted that this 'engagement' remain a secret. Noel was seventeen, Brooke twenty-three. It may be guessed that this arrangement was precisely to Brooke's liking. He had manoeuvred and persuaded Noel into a position where she had declared her love, but nothing too formal, nothing irretrievable had occurred. It was simultaneously a commitment and not a commitment. And it soon became obvious that the state of affairs between the parties was clear to neither of them. In August Brooke and his friends (including Noel and Bryn Olivier) were involved in re-enacting a production of *Faustus* which had been produced originally by the Marlowe Society at Cambridge in 1907. This presumably afforded Brooke the opportunity for daily contact with Noel, but this increased intimacy does not seem to have helped the couple to resolve their difficulties, rather the reverse. Brooke's ambivalent ardour was too much for Noel, and in letters of September and November she sought to distance herself from Brooke and from their pact of July. She describes herself as in 'unresponsive mood' and elsewhere questions the validity of marriage as an institution. Meanwhile she immured herself at Bedales, and remained aloof from Brooke for about eight months. Their correspondence, however, continued sporadically through this period.

It was in this hiatus in his dealings with Noel that Brooke's relationship with Katharine Cox began to develop. He had been friendly with Ka (as she was habitually referred to) since joining the Fabians, and she was often included in Neo-Pagan camps and walking expeditions. She was also close to Brooke's friend Jaques Raverat, and through 1910 into 1911 Jacques and Ka seemed to be on the verge of matrimony. Brooke saw Ka at a Fabian summer school of late 1910, before he began term in Cambridge where he was working on his essay about 'Puritanism and the Drama' which would eventually win the Harness prize. A more apposite field of research could not be imagined. Although Brooke mounts a critique of Puritans in this piece, his understanding of the subject is, as we might expect, very acute. 'Puritanism' is defined as, 'a democratic desire for more popular control of religion, a strong fear and dislike of Rome, a patriotism which went hand in hand with it, very individualistic religious feeling, and the "puritanical" instinct for restraining worldly pleasures. All amusement was considered as interfering with the individual's communion with God; for by the insidious dualism which lay, psychologically as theologically, behind Puritanism – that which was not of the soul was material and dangerous'.[51] This was the inheritance Brooke was emotionally and psychologically grappling with. In the essay he sounds confidently superior to the problems of Puritanism, but his life and his poetry betray the reality that he could not escape from them. And it was his relationship with Ka Cox which brought this conflict to a head.

During the Christmas holidays of 1910–11, Brooke joined a group of friends at Lulworth. He had attempted to lure Noel to this gathering, but she refused. If Brooke embarked on this holiday in a state of irresolution, so did Ka. Jaques proposed to her for a second time at Lulworth, and was refused again. It was in this atmosphere, with both parties on the rebound, that the first emotionally intense exchange between Rupert and Ka took place. What precisely occurred is not entirely certain, but that more than Platonic friendship was at stake is clear. An incident in a book shop provoked an outburst from Brooke written immediately after the Lulworth party had broken-up. Hassall speculates that Ka had offered to purchase Rupert a present, and that he had been ungracious in acceptance. This seems a fair inference, but whatever the precipitating cause, the significance of the following letter is that it expresses the pattern of their future relationship:

I'm red and sick with anger at myself for my devilry and degradation and stupidity. I hate myself because I wickedly and unnecessarily hurt you several times. (I don't mean that I'm sorry – for my own sake – for all that happened; or that I'm an atom changed from what I said and suggested. That stands.) But I hurt you, I hurt you, Ka, for a bit, unforgiveably and filthily and infamously; and I can't bear it; I was wild to do anything everything in the world to *undo* the hurt, or blot it out (but what could I do? I waved my arm in the bookshop at thirty books – but that'd have meant nothing. And I couldn't, as I wanted, take hold of you and put mouth hard to mouth, for you had somehow put that aside, and it would have confused other issues, – and I daredn't.) – Oh, tell me that you're unhurt, for I hurt you in *such* a way, and I was mean and selfish, and you're, I think, one of the most clear and most splendid people in the world.[52]

Ka may have been 'splendid', but she certainly was not 'clear' in the sense of being decided or decisive. This exacerbated Brooke's own ambivalent emotions towards her. The hurting of Ka, followed by mental self-flagellation and self-abasement before her, were to become a seemingly inescapable aspect of their relationship. Ka, as we shall see, responded in kind by imposing mental cruelty upon Brooke, and offering the same kind of apologies. They were caught in a circle of mental sado-masochism. The problematic place of physical love in their relationship is also prefigured in this letter. Brooke simultaneously wants and does not want to kiss her, and first she is blamed, and then he blames himself for this situation. One cannot help but feel that an unfettered, guilt-free expression of their sexual desires, would have broken the increasingly embroiled cycle of accusation, recrimination and reconciliation that constituted their relationship.

In the twelve months from January 1911 to his breakdown early the following year, Brooke's affairs moved from chaos to crisis. Apart from the ongoing irresolution of his relationships with Ka and Noel, Brooke added a third complication. He spent the first months of 1911 in Europe, ostensibly studying philology. There he became enmeshed with a Belgian sculptress, Elisabeth van Rysselberghe. It will come as no surprise that this relationship followed the familiar pattern of simultaneous attraction and repulsion that characterised his other close relationships with women. Delaney suggests that this particular liaison turned sour because Brooke wanted to plan a rather cold-blooded affair (in the manner of his relations with Denham Russell-Smith perhaps) whereas Elisabeth was in love with Brooke and wanted more commitment from him before she engaged in sexual relations.[53] But it seems to me that whatever Brooke was writing to others about his 'determination' to have an affair, he was in fact and as usual, extremely ambivalent about the sexual act itself, and was busy creating circumstances which would make sexual fulfilment impossible. His sonnet 'Lust' is about this, and describes his passion which proceeds until his physical desire is threatened with consummation at which point Brooke apparently experiences a loss of libido. Predictably Brooke's parting from Elisabeth in Munich was less than happy. He described it in a letter as 'most painful', with Elisabeth in tears and threatening to kill herself, and Brooke full of self-recrimination. He felt, he says, 'an awful snake' and speaks of being 'very bitter with himself'.[54]

But matters did not rest there. Brooke returned to England and Cambridge in May, and during the following summer continued to lead a very confused emotional life. He was now working on his dissertation about Webster and the Elizabethan drama whilst Ka was living variously in Manchester and London, and Noel, to whom he had made several protestations of love in correspondence between March and May,[55] was still proving evasive and difficult to meet. Elisabeth van Rysselberghe turned up in London in July, and Rupert entered into further, necessarily secret negotiations with her. It seems that he met her several times in London, and then attempted to arrange a meeting (possibly of a sexual kind!) outside London. But predictably he then admitted to being 'tired and confused' and the affair did not proceed. He saw her occasionally during the autumn, but she returned to Paris without Rupert and without consummating their relationship.

Meanwhile there was an eighteen-day camp in August which was fraught with tensions. It involved people from various groups – the Apostles, Bloomsbury and the Neo-Pagans – whom Rupert had assiduously tried to keep separate. Both Noel and Ka were there, as well as James Strachey who was still passionately enamoured of Rupert. This is to mention only four participants at an occasion attended by at least thirteen people all of whom knew each other to one degree or another, and none of whom were married or settled partners. The living may have been 'simple', the bathing nude and chaste, but the social dynamics, the hot-house emotions, the clash of intellects was anything but wholesome and healthy. On one occasion, it all got too much for Rupert who went off on his own to spend the night weeping under the stars. One can hardly blame him.

Through the autumn, turmoil in his private life continued, as his emotional life wove a delicate counterpoint between Noel and Ka. Furthermore, there are rumours that he added to his troubles at this time by embarking upon another homosexual liaison.[56] At the same time Brooke was also working extremely hard since he had to have his dissertation finished by December. He completed it on time, and it demonstrates that psychologically he was still fascinated with the macabre, the grotesque, the difficulties of the flesh. His commentary upon several dramatists indicates Brooke's attraction to violence and pain. In Marlowe's work he detects, 'bloody and vital violence', not to mention the 'superb insolence and lovely brutality of youth'.[57] But it is in his remarks about Marston that Brooke waxes most passionate: 'It was because he loved truth in that queer, violent way that some men do love, desirous to hurt. It fits in with his whole temperament – vivid, snarling, itching, dirty. He loved dirt for truth's sake; also for its own. Filth, horror, and wit were his legacy; it was a splendid one.'[58] We detect here (as elsewhere in his thesis) Brooke's own fixation with 'cleanliness' and 'dirt'. His passionate attraction to Marston and Webster is the obverse side of his own Puritanism.

After spending some time at home with his mother, recovering from the labours of academic work, Brooke proceeded to Lulworth, where a reading party was convened which rather than being dominated by Brooke's Neo-Pagan circle was so by Apostles and members of the Bloomsbury group. As Delaney puts it, 'Rupert had expected a soothing week in the company of Ka and a few trusted friends. Instead, he had a house full of Stracheys.'[59] But worse was to come. Earlier in December Ka had met the painter, Henry Lamb, and conceived a passion for him. True to the 'clean' idealism of Brooke and friends, she immediately confessed her feelings to Rupert. He was not pleased. He was even less so when at Lulworth Lytton Strachey met Lamb from the train and introduced him to the party. Lytton was apparently in love with the flamboyantly heterosexual Lamb, just as his brother was in love with Rupert. Lytton seems, somewhat mischievously, to have engineered a situation where he could, as it were, be of service to his beloved by procuring Ka for him. It nearly worked. Ka disappeared for a long walk with Henry, and according to Rupert was nearly seduced by him. Whatever happened, it is certain that Ka returned to announce that she was in love with Henry. This was enough to precipitate a crisis for Rupert, and he immediately abandoned his vacillations and proposed to Ka. She refused and told Rupert that she wanted to marry Lamb. But that gentleman was already married, and was something of an opportunist and philanderer; when things threatened to become serious he decamped back to London. But as far as Rupert was concerned, the damage was already done, and he fell into a state of nervous collapse.

The precise symptoms of Brooke's illness are by no means clear. He later recalled 'a week or so in the most horrible kind of Hell; without sleeping or eating – doing nothing but suffering the most violent mental tortures'.[60] Delaney further refers to 'an acute manic-depresssive condition that lasted for six months or more'.[61] Whatever label one cares to apply to the condition (and I am not sure that 'manic-depressive' is terribly accurate or helpful)[62] it is clear that the neurotic tensions in his position had become unbearable and were causing fairly acute symptoms of distress. Not only was Brooke torn between Noel and Ka, and between heterosexuality and homosexuality, he was now also confronted by the 'dirtiness' of Lytton Strachey, Lamb, and Ka. Furthermore, he was manoeuvred into a position where he had to make a commitment which implicitly involved not only sex, but also marriage – and he was terrified of both. He found himself in a situation where it must have been very difficult, if not impossible to envisage a positive solution.

Brooke had already planned to spend some time abroad early in the New Year with Ka. Now he was shuffled off to Europe with his mother to recuperate from his breakdown, having first consulted an eminent Harley Street Physician who specialised in mental disorder. Dr Maurice Craig was a leading psychiatrist who also treated Virginia Woolf. Like most physicians of his generation he had no idea how to treat neurosis, and proceeded by means of 'common sense' laced with strict, not to say Puritanical morality and very conservative politics. Craig's textbook, *Psychological Medicine* has been described as 'more a political treatise than anything else'.[63] Insanity is diagnosed as behaviour inappropriate to the sex and class of the individual concerned. Characteristics of the insane, according to Craig, include an imperfect aesthetic sense, (finding beautiful things ugly and vice versa), uncleanliness, gaudy, bizarre or inappropriate dress, solitariness, and hatred. Tears in a man are considered to be a very serious symptom, whilst for women adopting the 'divided skirt' is taken to be a step towards wearing mens' clothes which the 'arm of the law', he says, needs to control. Furthermore, a woman when healthy may be 'reserved and maidenly' but when insane 'frequently becomes forward and immodest'. And so the book goes on. Craig implies that any attitude or behaviour which is not thoroughly conservative,

Puritanical, and in harmony with the majority, is aberrant and a sign of mental illness.[64]

Craig's treatment consisted of an initial consultation or two in Harley Street after which the patient was packed off somewhere quiet to eat and sleep their way back to health. This 'cure' has been given the soubriquet 'stuffing', since so much importance was placed upon the patient's weight. No record remains of what went on between Craig and Brooke in Harley Street. Certainly Rupert was diagnosed as having suffered a 'nervous breakdown', and was said to be still struggling with a 'seriously introspective condition'![65] He was advised to join his mother in Cannes, and to eat and sleep his way to health. He was forbidden to do any literary work, or take any exercise, and was ordered to breakfast in bed, not rising before ten, and that he must keep no late nights. He was also prescribed drugs to suppress his libido. One suspects also that Rupert, in his meetings with Craig, imbibed the idea that sanity meant conformity, for it is from this time onwards that Brooke's social and political beliefs began to turn rapidly to the right. The anti-semitism that he and Raverat had entertained beforehand, now surfaces in more virulent outpourings in the letters, together with viciously sexist tirades about women and homosexuals.[66]

Needless to say, Craig's advice did little to help Rupert. Through the early weeks of 1912, Brooke wrote constantly to Ka, using her to unburden his very troubled mind, and to assure her of his love. He was not, however, at this stage completely won over to conformity. He decided that his breakdown and introspection were 'mixed up with this chastity',[67] and that if he consummated his relationship with Ka, all would be well. To this end he bombarded her with letters insisting that they meet soon for this purpose. But the tortured nature of the relationship is clearly signalled in rather chilling assertions like this: 'We'll both be so strong and wonderful at Munich, that we'll be able to burn or tear or hurt each other; and laugh.'[68] In the event, there was to be plenty of pain and very little laughter.

The letters demonstrate Brooke's confusion, and continues the pattern of all his correspondence with her. He hurts her and then follows with self-recrimination. He is 'feeble, silly and mean',[69] he is 'worthy of treading to death in dung',[70] he has a 'tight and dirty self',[71] he has a 'horrible nature' and is a 'dirty abyss'.[72] His ambition is to be 'strong and clean and sane'; an ambition, he says,

that Ka will help him to achieve.[73] Ka, on the other hand, is
alternately praised and insulted. She is 'divinely the nicest person
in Europe',[74] she has 'splendid strength and beauty',[75] she is 'fine'
in a 'slow way',[76] she is the possessor of 'funny blue infantile eyes
that almost shame one'.[77] But being in love with her is likened to
'having black beetles in the house'.[78] She is both 'Devil and
God'.[79] Mention is made of the 'furry atmosphere of her inconse-
cutive ideas',[80] and she is a 'fool'.[81] Furthermore, when he hears
that she is to attend a ball in Munich before they meet, his
suspicion and jealousy are aroused. She will, he says, be surrounded by 'naked men', and is concerned since, 'Virgins like you,
you know, give in immediately if they see a naked man'.[82] Ka is
exhorted not to be so 'wicked and unfeeling and unimaginative as
to be soft'. She has, he says, 'done enough harm with her toler-
ance.'[83] This hardly veiled imprecation clearly refers to her behaviour with Lamb at Lulworth. Brooke is nervous, and considers
Ka to be 'weak' and in need of protection.

But when they did meet in Verona, it was Brooke who was in
a state of near collapse. He had practised an elaborate subterfuge
to keep his mother in ignorance of his arrangements, and there
had been a terrible row when Brooke announced to the Ranee that
he was leaving Cannes. This apparently exhausted him and Brooke
looks forward to Ka's 'lap' and the 'peace' and 'comfort' she will
afford him.[84] Ka is clearly cast in the role of surrogate mother. Ka
duly obliged and took him back to Munich the next day, where
they stayed for some time and she looked after him. On February
17 they left for a week-end together at the Starnbergesee. On the
way Ka told Brooke how she had been seeing Lamb since their
meeting in London. Ka it seems could be cruel as well as Rupert.
Her 'confession' caused a violently jealous reaction on Rupert's
part, but it also, perhaps, moved him to action, and on that
week-end he at last made love with Ka. As Delaney remarks the
circumstances were hardly propitious for a carefree night of love.[85]
Not only the tortured emotional life of the couple, but also his
ignorance of women's physiology, and their struggles with contra-
ceptive devices all must have played their part. Despite the note of
triumph in one of Brooke's letters that records this event,[86] it was
not enough to induce in either a desire for elopement or marriage.
Four days after the event they returned to England, he to Rugby
and she to London.

Their correspondence continues in the by now familiar pattern. Brooke upbraids Ka continually for her 'filthy behaviour' with Lamb, whilst she apparently showed no mercy in revealing all her meetings with that individual. Just as Brooke had promised, they were busy hurting and tearing each other. Ka was then invited to Bilton Road, but was warned to behave not like a lover, but only as a friend. The visit was a disaster, with Rupert alternating between rows with the Ranee, and treating Ka badly. With Ka back in London their immensely painful correspondence continued. But Rupert's thoughts also kept returning to Noel. By now she had attracted other admirers, and to Brooke's dismay they were from amongst those he had associated with his 'other' life: the Apostles. Both James Strachey and a Hungarian named Ferenc Békássy were both taking an interest in Noel now that she was living in London as a first year medical student.

This situation was not one to aid Rupert's peace of mind. He considered Lytton Strachey to be vile and loathsome, blaming him in part for Ka's indiscretions with Henry Lamb. Now James was in danger of meddling with Noel. Things staggered on until April when Brooke is talking of suicide, and further confuses the situation by re-igniting his passion for Bryn Olivier. But he had plans to meet Ka again in Europe in order to try to consolidate their relationship. Before he left on this expedition he went to the Olivier household at Limpsfield in order to try to explain himself to Noel. His letters to Ka at this stage are full of aggressive intensity, and in one he admits to feeling 'mentally better for being beastly to you'.[87] Elsewhere he accuses her of sacrificing himself as well as 'love honour good fineness cleanness truth' on her 'lust'.[88] That his sexual confusions had not been entirely resolved in favour of heterosexuality is signalled by this effusion: 'Oh my God, I *want* you so tonight. Your nakedness and beauty – your mouth and breasts and cunt. – Shall I turn in a frenzy and rape James in the night? I'd burn you like a fire if I could get hold of you.'[89] That Brooke's love–hate relationship with James Strachey was not dissimilar to his relationship with Ka is signalled in another letter to Virginia Stephen, who had also suffered a nervous breakdown. Rupert exclaims: 'What tormented and crucified figures we literary people are! God! how I hate the healthy unimaginative hard shelled dilettanti, like James and Ka.'[90] It might be legitimately added that if artists see themselves as 'crucified' they will also take their turn as the Roman soldier with the nails.

As the time for departure came near, Ka tried to withdraw from her promise to meet Rupert in Germany. But he insisted. They met in Berlin in May, Ka having first settled things with Lamb. She had wished to live with Lamb as his mistress, but he only wanted a casual affair. So Ka came to Rupert prepared to love him entirely, and there is some evidence to suggest that their previous attempts at contraception had failed and that she was pregnant with Brooke's child. It is thought that the pregnancy was either aborted or Ka miscarried sometime between April and June.[91] However this might be, when it became clear to Brooke that she was prepared to give herself entirely to him, he could not cope. The couple left Berlin for Neu Strelitz and a fortnight's holiday when they were to present themselves as man and wife. Things went from bad to worse, and finally Ka had news from England that her sister's engagement had been broken, and so she returned home whilst Brooke remained in Berlin. He wrote many letters over the next few months which allude to the failure with Ka. Brooke seems to have felt that Ka had sullied herself in her dealings with Lamb. But it is also surely transparent that he could not deal with her sexuality. His mind reverts to the 'purity' of Noel:

I was afraid, beforehand, I might – when I saw her – be dragged down into that helpless tortured sort of love for her I had all the first part of the year, and had just crept out of. The opposite. I remain dead. I care practically nothing for any person in the world. I've anxiety, and a sort of affection, for Ka – But I don't really care. I've no feeling for anybody at all – except the uneasy ghosts of the immense reverence and rather steadfast love for Noel, and a knowledge that Noel is the finest thing I've ever seen in the world, and Ka – isn't.[92]

To say that he had no feelings was disinguous. He had feelings of a very aggressive kind, as the following extracts from letters to and about Ka written over the next few months indicate:

Love her? – bless you, no: but I don't love anybody. The bother is I don't really *like* her, at all. There is a feeling of staleness, ugliness, trustlessness about her. I don't know. Dirt. – hu – . . . I've a sort of hunger for cleanness.[93]

...it's hard to get up love for anyone whom one associates only with the evil things of one's life: and whom one always catches oneself thinking degraded, slightly noisome or at least contemptible; and for whom one has – all unwillingly – continual feelings of unforgiveness.

And then – I'm terrified of leaving her.[94]

Ka's done the most evil things in the world. She has – or she's on the way to have – dirtied good & honour & all high things, & betrayed & degraded love. Think of the filthiest image you can for the fouling of the best things by the worst. Ka is doing that. For the sake of all those things, & for the sake of the Ka I used to know, & for the sake of the good love there was between us, I'd not care if I saw Ka *dying* of some torture I could inflict on her, slowly.[95]

It's no good. I *can't* marry you. You must see. If I married you, I should kill myself in three months. I may, I daresay I shall, anyway . . .You had two ways before you, a dirty one and a clean one; coming to Germany was not even deciding; it was only giving the clean one a chance. You refused to marry me. You refused to forswear filth . . .

I felt ashamed because you were better and honester than I (ashamed – and yet superior, because you are a woman).[96]

Brooke vacillates between self-denigration, praise, and a violent hatred for Ka. But it was obvious to him that the affair could not prosper. He spent the summer in the company of various Apostles, and he went on another trip to Germany in November-December. It was not until the following June that Brooke wrote to Ka, formally suggesting that they should cease communication with each other, but by the end of 1912, the most tempestuous year of his life, his relationship with her was all but over.

Predictably, as his relationship with Ka disintegrated, Brooke increasingly turned to Noel for solace. Between March and August 1912, he wrote her desperate letters articulating his love and his fears lest she be contaminated by the 'poisonous lot' with whom she was mixing in London.[97] He went so far as to insist that they should get married. Noel remained cool and 'fond' throughout this barrage, but insisted that on no account would she marry Brooke.[98] From thence forward communications about her to other friends reveal a 'compulsive viciousness'.[99] This was not only to do with her rejecting him, but also concerned with James Strachey's courtship of her. Brooke was still attempting to maintain his relationship with James, but the latter's attraction to Noel finished it. By the end of the year any hope of a romantic relationship with Noel had fallen apart completely, and he refers to her in January of 1913 as 'that swine Noel'.[100] Finally, Brooke cut himself off from everything to do with Bloomsbury, and began to mix in a new circle to which he was introduced by Eddie Marsh. His social life from now to his death would be centred on London and on the people entertained by the Prime Minister and Violet Asquith at 10 Downing Street. His flirtation with Fabianism, with Neo-Paganism, with unconventional relations between the sexes in England was over.

The poems Brooke wrote between 1910 and 1912 elaborate on the themes we have already encountered in his work. There is, however, further technical development, and a penchant for rhymed octosyllabics becomes evident. This is exemplified in 'Dining Room Tea', a poem about Noel in which we are re-introduced to Brooke's obsessions with disembodied love. The poem begins with the poet in happy laughter with friends over tea. The description is of youthful vitality wherein companionship is Romanticised and gaiety prevails. But in the midst of this, a further abstraction takes place. The poet gazes upon the beloved's 'innocence', and experiences a 'timeless' moment wherein he perceives the eternal, Platonic forms of everything and everybody around him including the beloved:

> And you, august, immortal, white,
> Holy and strange; and every glint
> Posture and jest and thought and tint
> Freed from the mask of transiency,
> Triumphant in eternity,
> Immote, immortal.[101]

The rest of the poem describes a return to time-bound perception, in which Brooke asks the rhetorical question: 'How could I cloud, or how distress/The heaven of your unconsciousness?' This is how Brooke liked to love. The beloved is removed to a higher plain where she is pure, white, eternally innocent, and where he cannot intrude upon her 'unconsciousness'. It was no wonder that Noel was something of a disappointment to him when she opened her mouth; she was in the impossible position of being regarded as an 'eternal holiness'.

In other poems of 1910–11 Brooke returns us to the world after death; the world of so many of his schoolboy poems. Inspired by the Elizabethan and Jacobean dramatists, however, these later poems often include elements of the macabre, and predictably dwell upon the contrasts between spirit and flesh which obsessed his progenitors as much as himself. That Brooke himself was very aware of this is attested to in 'Mummia', a poem which is about the intertextuality of love. Here Brooke says that rather than take Mummia to inflame his passion, he takes 'love's infinity' from 'paint, stone, tale and rhyme'. Art of the past informs his love, and in every action he makes he is taught and accompanied by the 'invisible, lovely, dead':

> For the uttermost years have cried and clung
>> To kiss your mouth to mine;
> And hair long dust was caught, was flung,
>> Hand shaken to hand divine,
>
> And Life has fired, and Death not shaded,
>> All Time's uncounted bliss,
> And the height o' the world has flamed and faded, –
> Love, that our love be this![102]

Despite the abstraction of the last stanza, this nevertheless remains one of Brooke's most ingenious and impressive poems. That he and his partner's love should be as it is, involves the life and art of past lovers and artists whose love has transcended death and time through art. And so Brooke wishes to join their company. The poem is not only about his ambitions for his relationship with Noel, but also and perhaps more strikingly it is about his ambitions for his pen. 'This' surely refers to the poem itself, as much as to the lovers. And so Brooke demonstrates the way in which flesh is transcended and transmuted into art.

'The Life Beyond' and 'Dead Men's Love' are less confident, and much more grim. Both poems are about mental states of living death, though the circumstances of each are quite different. Brooke describes a state of being in 'The Life Beyond' where the protagonist is surprised to find himself still alive in a dead land. He does not survive as himself but as, 'An unmeaning point upon the mud' or 'a fly/Fast-stuck in grey sweat on a corpse's neck.' This is what life constitutes after the death of his feelings for the beloved. The poet thought that if his love died so would he, but 'most strangely' he lives on.[103] The poem is an extreme expression of self-denigration, and appears to prefigure the 'dead' feelings he experienced with Ka on their second meeting in Germany, and which he recorded in more than one letter.

'The Life Beyond', however, dates from 1910 and is therefore more likely to be another complaint about Noel. But 'Dead men's Love' was written in Munich in the February of 1911, after Brooke's first exchange of deep feelings with Ka. That this poem focuses on the 'deathly' nature of sexual relationships also suggests that Ka is the subject of the poem. For from the first, physical attraction seems to have played a bigger part in his relations with Ka, than with the younger Noel. 'Dead Men's Love' posits a couple who are dead, but have not yet realised their condition:

> There was a damned successful Poet;
>   There was a Woman like the Sun.
> And they were dead. They did not know it.
>   They did not know their time was done.
>   They did not know his hymns
>   Were silence; and her limbs,
>   That had served Love so well,
>   Dust, and a filthy smell.[104]

The poem goes on to recount their physical pleasure in touch, until in the final lines they realise that they are dead and in hell. They experience 'Chill air on lip and breast,/And, with a sick surprise,/The emptiness of eyes'. The implication is that physical love results in a spiritual death. Brooke's revulsion from the body is signalled throughout the poem, but nowhere more so than in his image of the 'beloved's' limbs disintegrating to 'Dust, and a filthy smell'.

The most explicit poem in Brooke's oeuvre which articulates his attitude to the human anatomy was also written in 1911 and is rather unimaginatively entitled, 'Thoughts on the Shape of the Human Body'. It is a stark expression of Brooke's difficulties in which he projects these onto the whole of the human condition. We are, he argues, 'gaunt zanies of a witless Fate/Who love the unloving, and the lover hate', and who are consigned to desire, but do not know what or whom we want or how to find fulfilment. The reason given for all of this is the body, which unlike the mind cannot achieve perfection:

> Love's for completeness! No perfection grows
> 'Twixt leg, and arm, elbow, and ear, and nose,
> And joint, and socket; but unsatisfied
> Sprawling desires, shapeless, perverse, denied.
> Finger with finger wreathes; we love, and gape,

Fantastic shape to mazed fantastic shape,
Straggling, irregular, perplexed, embossed,
Grotesquely twined, extravagantly lost
By crescive paths and strange protuberant ways
From sanity and from wholeness and from grace.[105]

If only, the poem goes on to say, we could be as perfectible as
thought, then we could rise 'disentangled from humanity' and
experience passion perfected in eternity. Brooke dismembers the
body thereby denying *its* wholeness, beauty and integrity. He turns
away from the physical in Puritanical loathing in order not only
to exalt a fictional 'higher' reality, but also to produce an implicit
definition of 'sanity' which is very close to Dr Craig's, and presumably to his mother's.

By 1913 Brooke was in full retreat from the Apostles and
Neo-Pagans. Both groups were now considered to be 'dirty' and
to have sacrificed their idealism to sexual philanderings which he
could not tolerate. Particularly abhorrent to Brooke was the mixing of the two groups. The implication is that Brooke felt that one
ought to be either homosexual or heterosexual but certainly not
both. He projects his own self-disgust with his bi-sexuality onto
other people, and strives from now on to live a committedly
heterosexual life in a considerably more conservative milieu. He
was introduced into the elevated social circles of the Prime Minister and friends by Eddie Marsh. It was through his agency that
Brooke also met Cathleen Nesbitt, with whom he fell in love,
chastely. She became the new Noel in his life. In late 1912 and
early 1913, his passion for Elizabeth van Rysselberghe was also
inflamed again. This was never going to be a happy relationship.
Some time earlier Brooke recorded feeling an uneasy mixture of
'lust and dislike' for this unfortunate woman, and his renewed
dealings with her promised no advance upon this. As Delaney has
noted, Brooke had merely replaced Noel and Ka with Cathleen
and Elizabeth without resolving the ambivalence which led to the
bifurcation of his intellectual and physical life.[106]

Neither woman could deter Rupert from leaving England in
May 1913 on a trip which he hoped would clear himself of Ka
forever, and return his mental balance. He travelled to Canada and
the United States and from there toured the South Seas. He was
away for over a year, during which time the most significant
psycho-sexual event in his life was his relationship with a Tahitian

woman named Taatamata. In Tahiti Brooke found a kind of Neo-Pagan paradise which was without the Puritanical restraints of England. He wrote of enjoying the 'most ideal place in the world, to live and work in',[107] and for company he had 'the lovely and gentle brown people'.[108] In such an environment Brooke could indulge his sexual desires apparently without difficulty or remorse. But it did not finally change his attitude to women of his own class and nationality. One reluctantly concludes that his easy relations with Taatamata were predicated precisely on Brooke's racism and sexism. She hardly spoke English, and so he could wield power over her without being threatened, and without having to cope with any intellectual relationship with her. It would be unfair to suggest that no tenderness existed between the two. It certainly did. The point that needs to be made is that this event, which might be interpreted as one in which Brooke came to terms with his own sexual nature, in fact did not serve that function. He returned to England with all his sexual difficulties unsolved; he had merely found some temporary physical relief.

Back in England in June 1914 Brooke took up again with Cathleen Nesbitt, though the relationship remained strictly Platonic. His sexual interest was aroused by Lady Eileen Wellesley, but the outbreak of war prevented Brooke from repeating the destructive cycle in which he had engaged with Ka and Noel. The story of Brooke's last months is well known. Through the offices of Eddie Marsh via Winston Churchill, Brooke was accepted into the Royal Naval Division and gained his commission. He was briefly in Belgium at the siege of Antwerp, but saw no action. Nevertheless the sight of Belgian refugees moved him to pity and to anger, serving to convince him of the justice of England's cause. And so he wrote the famous war sonnets, before embarking for Gallipoli with his comrades. He died not the hero's death, but rather ignominiously from malaria contracted from a mosquito bite, and was buried on the island of Skyros.

The poems of 1913 exhibit a distance and control, a cooler tone than much of his earlier writing. This is in keeping with Brooke's circumstances. Physically removed from the source of his disquiet, he is able to write poems which recall his relationship with Ka in various moods. In some he is jauntily resigned, in others wistful, and in a few bitter. What is constant is the alliance of love and pain. In 'The Chilterns' we hear of the 'splendour and the pain' of his lost love,[109] whilst in 'One day' he recounts the pleasure to be gleaned 'from that old dust of misery'.[110] 'Waikiki' has the poet listening to a ukelele which suggestively 'thrills and cries/And stabs with pain the night's bright savagery'. This provides an apt prelude to the 'empty tale, of idleness and pain' which constitutes his failed love affair.[111] And in the opening lines of 'The Great Lover', which will significantly celebrate Brooke's 'love' for things both man-made and natural, or moods, rather than for people, he refers to the 'pain, the calm, and the astonishment' of love.[112]

Although it could be argued that there is some technical advance in these poems – there is for instance a willingness to use a wider variety of metrical and stanzaic pattern, and there is a welcome absence of the derivative macabre – there is little thematic advance. The same ambivalences that by now we are familiar with inform the poems. The mutability of love, the passing of youth, the yearning for abstract perfection, discontent with bodily love, and sometimes a quite overt aggression towards the beloved run through the poems. The only possible exception is 'Tiare Tahiti', which is about Taatamata. The first fifty-six lines of the poem represent Brooke at his Platonic best. Here he describes heaven to his beloved, where exist only the great eternal forms. But in the last few lines of the poem, there is a tentative celebration of the temporal and sensory. Delaney has argued that here Brooke 'suddenly embraces what his poetry had always evaded, the sexual here and now'.[113] This is, I think, to attribute a conviction to the poem which it does not possess. Certainly Brooke invites the beloved to walk along the sand and bathe at night washing 'the mind of foolishness'. But what constitutes the foolish, what the wise is cast into doubt by the final lines:

> Spend the glittering moonlight there
> Pursuing down the soundless deep
> Limbs that gleam and shadowy hair,
> Or floating lazy, half asleep.
> Dive and double and follow after,
> Snare in flowers, and kiss, and call,
> With lips that fade, and human laughter
> And faces individual,
> Well this side of Paradise! . . .
> There's little comfort in the wise.[114]

The 'foolishness' alluded to earlier seems to be of the mind and to refer to the Platonic ideas which have preceded. This gives way to sensual pleasure, yet this implicit 'wisdom' is said to give forth 'little comfort'. It might also be noted that although these lines are sensuous, they are not specifically sexual. The 'gleam' of limbs and 'shadowy hair' sound somewhat ethereal, and floating half asleep does not sound terribly passionate. And the subterranean play only leaves the poet with a recognition that he is *not* in Paradise. It is perfectly possible to read the final lines in concert with the rest of Brooke's oeuvre, as expressing finally a dissatisfaction with earthly pleasures.

It is significant too that water, the element of cleanliness, is where this sensuous play proceeds. We recall those early poems, written at school, wherein the 'beasts' driven by lust, find a final consummation by plunging into the sea. And we are thus given a nice introduction to the first of the war sonnets:

> Now, God be thanked Who has matched us with His hour,
>   And caught our youth, and wakened us from sleeping,
> With hand made sure, clear eye, and sharpened power,
>   To turn, as swimmers into cleanness leaping,
> Glad from a world grown old and cold and weary,
>   Leave the sick hearts that honour could not move,
> And half-men, and their dirty songs and dreary,
>   And all the little emptiness of love![115]

Brooke had, since being at school, consistently denied Christianity. Yet his poems are full of references to 'God' and 'gods'. As late as December 1913 Brooke was jesting in a letter about the Victorian poets' propensity to 'refer suddenly to God in the last line'.[116] Brooke's sudden mention in his opening line, constitutes a reversion to the Victorian inheritance of his mother and father, against which he had fought so hard, for so long. But the outbreak of war enabled Brooke to revert to the Puritanism and chauvinism at the bedrock of his psyche.

'God' had only just 'caught' Brooke's 'youth'. We have seen as a constant expression in his poems an obsession with youth, and a deep fear of old age. Nobody, he once said, over thirty is worth talking to. In December 1913 Brooke spoke in a letter to Jacques Raverat of being 'middle-aged',[117] and in August of the following year he turned twenty-seven. The war enabled Brooke to resurrect his Romantic worship of youth, and in particular the idea of sacrificed youth as 'beautiful' and 'clean'. He turns away from his

own coldness and weariness, his sexual failures, his bisexual tribulation. No longer 'a half-man' the implication is quite clear that
the war will make 'real men' of the nation's youth. The sestet
speaks of those who have known 'shame' who will now find
'peace' through sacrifice of the body, and through 'agony'. The
'cleanness' being leapt into is death. This is the final answer to
Eros, just as it was in his schoolboy poems. Here it is expressed
without the linguistic trappings of decadence, and converted into
a patriotic rhetoric. But the ideas expressed sublimate sexuality
into death wish.

Sonnets II and IV merely expand upon the 'safety' and peace to
be found in death. More interesting are the third and fifth. 'The
Dead', makes even larger claims for the 'immortality' of sacrificed
youth. The celebration is enthusiastic and wholehearted. Again we
have the joyful idea that 'age' will not be reached. The 'red/Sweet
wine of youth' is going to be 'poured' in battle. The 'bugles' have
rescued Brooke and his generation from 'dearth' and conferred
'Holiness, lacked so long, and Love, and Pain.'[118] The equation of
love and pain here is entirely symptomatic of Brooke's sado-masochistic impulses. And it is worth pausing to consider what or
which 'Love' is alluded to in the line quoted. Is it simply patriotic
'Love' or is there an implication that the 'Pain' of sacrifice will be
suffered for the 'Love' of one's comrades? After all, joining the
Royal Naval Division allowed Brooke to re-enter an all-male
society populated by ex-public schoolboys like himself. It was a
world wherein physical expression of homoerotic feeling would be
discouraged, but homoerotic solidarity encouraged. It was the
world which represented in its clearest form the idealism of public
school life. We are back to David and Jonathan. The last line of
sonnet III, 'And we have come into our heritage', is apt to ring
somewhat ironically in our ears. Their heritage was death, destruction and pain; an ideology which equated 'nobleness' with killing
and being killed, whilst Eros was considered to be 'shameful' and
'dirty'.

The last of the war sonnets is the most famous and most
vilified. 'The Soldier' expresses a passionate patriotism of place.
As in his earlier poem 'Grantchester', here Brooke romanticises
and sentimentalises rural England. More interestingly, for my
purposes, it equates the 'body' of a dead soldier with the beauty
of England. If he dies, a 'corner of a foreign field' will be 'forever

England':

> There shall be
> In that rich earth a richer dust concealed;
> A dust whom England bore, shaped, made aware,
> Gave, once, her flowers to love, her ways to roam,
> A body of England's, breathing English air,
> Washed by the rivers, blest by suns of home.[119]

The racial, and implicitly racist arrogance of these lines hardly requires comment. What I find most interesting is the way in which the body is, as it were, purified in death as it becomes one with the 'dust' of England. In the sestet we hear of 'evil' being shed away, and in the lines quoted we find that cleansing water again. The 'body', which for Brooke is the source of 'dirtiness' due to its sexuality, is rescued from that state by death in battle.

That Brooke's less than heroic demise did not hinder his elevation into a National hero cannot come as a surprise. These war sonnets succeeded in expressing cultural values that were (and still are) exceedingly strong. Much I have said might lead the reader to conclude that Brooke himself was less than a pleasant individual. This may or may not be the case. The point, however, lies elsewhere. From adolescence onwards Brooke fought strenuously against his parental inheritance. The poets of the decadence, Fabianism, Neo-Paganism, were all means of attempting to break the shackles of dominant Victorian ideologies. But in the end he could not escape. The traditions of art which he wrote into, both the Decadent poets of the 1890s and the Renaissance and Jacobean poets and dramatists, did not lead Brooke away from his dilemmas, but merely reinforced them. The Puritanical dichotomy of mind and body, the elevation of the former at the expense of the latter, the fascination with the grotesque and macabre, the equation of love and pain, images of sado-masochism were all there for his mind to respond to and react with. The absence of a sense of pleasure in the physical act of love was as absent in this literature, as it was in Brooke's life and art.

Delaney has argued that Brooke was 'nothing so simple as a sexually repressed puritan. Rather, his desires were so various and contradictory that they had to be rigidly segregated'.[120] This, I think, needs to be put in a slightly different way. It surely was Brooke's inability to come to terms with his sexuality that lies at the heart of his neurosis. He subordinates bodily pleasure from a very early age, and in both homo- and hetero-sexual encounters found little pleasure. Sexuality was viewed as 'dirty' and 'beastly'. And it was, I think, his bisexuality that exacerbated this view. The lack of a viable bisexual lifestyle and identity, forced Brooke into the situation where he had to choose either homosexuality or heterosexuality. In choosing either one or the other he was denying himself, but the pressure was clearly very great to make this choice. His hatred of both women and homosexuals was surely a projection of the loathing he felt towards aspects of his own make-up. The escape from this confusion into 'cleanliness' and clarity, was offered by death rather than life, by *Thanatos* rather than *Eros*.

The frustration of sexual desire in Brooke's life inevitably caused him great pain. No wonder then that he in turn caused pain to others in all his close relationships. And in the end, as in the beginning, it is suffering which becomes the only source of pleasure. We recall how the youthful Brooke confused his beloved 'Antinous' with Christ, and as he went to war he implicitly celebrated again, through his war sonnets, the act of sacrificial love. As we shall see in later chapters, the idea of the soldier as a Christ-like figure was to become a leading icon of the First World War. Looking back it is difficult not to see Brooke's life and death in terms of tragedy. He wrestled with his demons but was defeated by himself certainly, but also by a combination of social, political, and cultural pressures well beyond his control. There is every excuse for him, but none for us in perpetuating such ideologies. The response since the First War, has been to reject Brooke for his politics, and to elevate poets like Owen and Sassoon for their 'anger' and 'pity', which implicitly at least hint at a more palatable politics. What has not been sufficiently recognised and criticised is the elevation of pain and suffering in all of their work. Ironically, as we shall see, the poets who came after Brooke had much in common with him, and were grappling with similar problems. The difference is that they saw action, and experienced kinds of suffering that Brooke did not.

Notes

1   J. Lehmann, *Rupert Brooke: His Life and His Legend*, London, 1980, P. Delaney, *The Neo-Pagans: Friendship and Love in the Rupert Brooke Circle*, London, 1987. I am also indebted for biographical material to C. Hassall, *Rupert Brooke: a Biography*, London, 1964.
2   Hassall, *Rupert Brooke: a Biography*, p. 26.
3   Geoffrey Keynes (ed.), *The Letters of Rupert Brooke*, London, 1968, p. 375. This text will hereafter be referred to as *LRB*.
4   Hassall, *Rupert Brooke: a Biography*, p. 38.
5   Ibid., p. 44.
6   Delaney, *The Neo-Pagans*, pp. 8–9.
7   Lehmann, *Rupert Brooke*, pp. 22–3.
8   G. Keynes (ed.), *The Poetical Works of Rupert Brooke*, London, 1946, p. 199.
9   Ibid., p. 196.
10 Ibid., p. 184.
11 Ibid., p. 195.
12 Ibid., pp. 172–3.
13 Quoted by Delaney, *The Neo-Pagans*, p. 8.
14 *LRB*, p. 41.
15 Ibid., pp. 41–2.
16 Ibid., p. 43.
17 Ibid., p. 54.
18 Delaney, *The Neo-Pagans*, p. 22.
19 *LRB*, p. 49.
20 P. Parker, *The Old Lie: the Great War and the Public-School Ethos*, London, 1987, p. 107.
21 *The Poetical Works*, p. 168.
22 Quoted by Hassall, *Rupert Brooke*, pp. 68–9.
23 *LRB*, p. 50.
24 Delaney, *The Neo-Pagans*, p. 8.
25 Hassall, *Rupert Brooke*, p. 83.
26 Lehmann, *Rupert Brooke*, p. 23.
27 See *LRB*, pp. 7–59.
28 *LRB*, p. 66.
29 Delaney, *The Neo-Pagans*, p. 22.
30 Ibid., pp. 17–18.
31 *LRB*, pp. 115–16.
32 Ibid., pp. 117–18.
33 That these characteristics are not merely unsympathetic inventions from the pen of Brooke's biographers, see the recently published, *Song of Love: the Letters of Rupert Brooke and Noel Olivier*, P. Harris, (ed.), London, 1991.

34 *LRB*, p. 164.
35 See for example *LRB*, pp. 136, 147, 155, 161, 166, 167, 174, 175.
36 *LRB*, p.180.
37 Ibid., pp. 180–1.
38 Delaney, *The Neo-Pagans*, pp. 78–80.
39 *The Poetical Works*, p.166.
40 Ibid., p. 164.
41 Ibid., p. 162.
42 Ibid., p. 153.
43 Ibid., p. 125.
44 Ibid., p. 128.
45 Ibid., p. 134.
46 Ibid., p. 114.
47 Ibid., p. 113.
48 *LRB*, p. 232.
49 *The Poetical Works*, p. 105.
50 Ibid., p. 104.
51 C. Hassall (ed.), *The Prose of Rupert Brooke*, London, 1956, pp. 161–2.
52 *LRB*, p. 269.
53 Delaney, *The Neo-Pagans*, pp. 116–18.
54 Quoted by Delaney, *The Neo-Pagans*, p. 118.
55 *Song of Love*, pp. 77–93.
56 Delaney, *The Neo-Pagans*, pp. 139–40.
57 *The Prose of Rupert Brooke*, pp. 128–9.
58 Ibid., p. 131.
59 Delaney, *The Neo-Pagans*, p. 150.
60 Quoted by Delaney, *The Neo-Pagans*, p. 153.
61 Delaney, *The Neo-Pagans*, p. 154.
62 It would seem to me more accurate to describe Brooke's condition in terms of anxiety neurosis, since manic depression proper is a psychosis, and as such has perceptual distortions of reality as one of its primary symptoms. It is true that the vicious tirades against women, Jews and homosexuals which are scattered through his letters at this time (see Delaney, p. 153) are indicative of paranoid delusion, but we should remember that these were intensified expressions of feelings that he had had earlier and which, moreover, were to some extent at least endorsed by society at that time. In short I do not think they represent evidence of psychotic illness.
63 S. Trombley, *All That Summer She Was Mad, Virginia Woolf: Female Victim of Male Medicine*, New York, 1982, p. 196.

64 Ibid., pp. 189–208.
65 Delaney, *The Neo-Pagans*, p. 156. See also *LRB*, p. 343.
66 Delaney, *The Neo-Pagans*, p. 153.
67 *LRB*, p. 335.
68 Ibid., p. 333.
69 Ibid., p. 336.
70 Ibid., p. 349.
71 Ibid., p. 334.
72 Ibid., p. 341.
73 Ibid.
74 Ibid., p. 349.
75 Ibid., p. 335.
76 Ibid., p. 336.
77 Ibid., p. 333.
78 Ibid., p. 337.
79 Ibid., p. 339.
80 Ibid.
81 Ibid., pp. 341 and 352.
82 Ibid., p. 345.
83 Ibid., p. 349.
84 Ibid., p. 354.
85 Delaney, *The Neo-Pagans*, p. 160.
86 Quoted by Delaney, *The Neo-Pagans*, p. 160.
87 *LRB*, p. 366.
88 Quoted by Delaney, *The Neo-Pagans*, p. 171.
89 Ibid., p. 170.
90 *LRB*, p. 364.
91 Delaney, *The Neo-Pagans*, pp. 172 and 179–80.
92 *LRB*, p. 378
93 Ibid., p. 379.
94 Ibid., p. 382.
95 *Song of Love*, p. 168.
96 Quoted by Delaney, *The Neo-Pagans*, p. 192.
97 *Song of Love*, pp. 171, 185–9, 195–214.
98 Ibid., p. 216.
99 Delaney, *The Neo-Pagans*, p. 181.
100 Ibid., p. 195.
101 *The Poetical Works*, p. 110.
102 Ibid., p. 81.
103 Ibid., p. 95.
104 Ibid., p. 83.
105 Ibid., p. 85.
106 Delaney, *The Neo-Pagans*, p. 205.

107   *LRB*, p. 562.
108   Ibid., p. 566.
109   *The Poetical Works*, p. 53.
110   Ibid., p. 38.
111   Ibid., p. 37.
112   Ibid., p. 30.
113   Delaney, *The Neo-Pagans*, p. 206.
114   *The Poetical Works*, p. 25.
115   Ibid., p. 19.
116   *LRB*, p. 541.
117   Ibid., p. 539.
118   *The Poetical Works*, p. 21.
119   Ibid., p. 23.
120   Delaney, *The Neo-Pagans*, p. 181.

3

Siegfried Sassoon

If the name of Rupert Brooke has become synonymous with the idealistic patriotism and enthusiasm with which the outbreak of World War I was greeted by so many, then the name of Siegfried Sassoon has become equally identified with protest against war in general, and the carnage on the Western Front during World War I in particular. His poems, like those of Wilfred Owen, appear in anthologies and on school syllabuses all over the English-speaking world, where they excite high school children into essays which dutifully speak of the 'futility of war', and of the anger and compassion expressed in the work of these poet-heroes. Academic criticism has done little to discourage such responses. As I have already mentioned, there has been some attempt recently to move away from cliches, and to deal with the complexities of Owen's response to the war, notably in Dominic Hibberd's fine study, *Owen the Poet.*[1] But there has been little advance with regard to Sassoon. The account of his poetry in Bernard Bergonzi's *Heroes' Twilight,* and Jon Silkin's *Out of Battle,* provide a model of response which has been widely accepted and shared. Bergonzi speaks of the 'strictly realistic' impulse 'behind the more mature war poems', and asserts that Sassoon was a poet of 'narrow but direct effects'. Sassoon's gifts are said to be 'pre-eminently those of a satirist', and mention is made of the 'complexities of actual experience' being 'reduced to a single satisfying gesture'. In summary, the poems according to Bergonzi, express 'a mood of anti-heroic revolt with . . . fervour and harsh wit', and constitute a 'new and incisive note in the literature of war'.[2] Silkin, in an account which is perhaps more thorough, is no less commendatory, and the grounds for that commendation are little different.

Sassoon's message is said to be 'burningly direct'. His attitude to the war is summarised as a change from 'a Brooke-like idealism to angry satire'. We hear again of 'realism', and there is speculation that 'the prolongation of the war through 1916–17 may have convinced him [Sassoon] that he should produce direct, simple work as the best way of marshalling opinion against the war's continuation'.[3]

Here we have the lineaments of what has come to be a stock response to Sassoon's poetry: it is considered to be realistic, anti-war, anti-heroic, satirical, direct, angry, and by implication full of the sorrows of war. Paul Fussell's otherwise brilliantly insightful book, *The Great War and Modern Memory*, does little to further this picture. Essentially, Fussell sees Sassoon's poems as exemplary of what he calls 'binary vision'; the way in which First War writers habitually view the world and the war in terms of simple polarities. These polarities, Fussell suggests, are exploited in the service of irony and satirical attack thereby providing a poetry of public protest against the war and its conduct.[4]

In my view, this is to ignore the complexities of Sassoon's poetry, and to read it in a way which expunges or denies what may be considered the more interesting if less palatable aspects of his response to war. And so I am moved to look again at Sassoon's work, concentrating particularly upon a re-reading of his war-time writing, his attitudes to the war, and more specifically to the place of suffering in his world view. In doing so, there are some manifest difficulties which it is best to rehearse at once. These largely concern Sassoon's six volumes of autobiography published between 1929 and 1945, all of which deal with Sassoon's pre-war life and his war-time experiences. They provide a wealth of material, but are written with the benefit of hindsight and quite clearly attempt to re-write his contemporaneous reactions to the war as we find them expressed in his war diaries and poems. In this chapter I am primarily concerned with the latter, but in the absence of any reliable biography of Sassoon, I have on occasion used the later autobiographies as a means to establish the sequence of events in Sassoon's life. And, where it is clear that the subsequent autobiographies are using the diaries and poems as source material, or when the autobiographies seem to be illuminating the same 'version' of Sassoon as that found in the earlier writing, I have felt able to use the autobiographies to illustrate and expand my arguments. I have then gone on to suggest briefly the pattern of re-writing that Sassoon embarked upon in the post-war years. I begin with an account of Sassoon's life before the outbreak of war, as this is crucial, I think, in understanding the ambivalence of his response to his army experience.

Siegfried Lorraine Sassoon was born into the wealthy merchant-banking family of that name in 1886. The great good fortune of thus entering life as a member of the upper classes who would never have to worry unduly about financial or material comforts, was only off-set in childhood by the difficult disintegration of his parents' marriage. In the volume of his autobiography dealing with this, Sassoon admits a desire 'not to remember unpleasant things very clearly',[5] and so the tone of the narration is affable, urbane, benign and yet the events recounted are not, on the whole, very cheerful. After he was five years old Sassoon saw little of his father who had left the family home in Kent to live in London. His father's periodic visits to see his sons (Siegfried had two brothers) were marred by tensions between the parents. Sassoon admits to realising that his mother was often unhappy and that he was 'living in a family situation which did not promise to have a happy ending'.[6] This intimation proved correct as his father contracted consumption and from 1893 until his death in 1895 was an invalid. Sassoon recalls praying desperately that his father would be spared, and describes himself as too distraught to attend the funeral.

Like Rupert Brooke then, Sassoon's early life was dominated by his mother and other female influences in the shape of successive governesses, and for a time his maternal grandmother also lived with the family. Perhaps because of the father's departure and then death, it seems that Mrs Sassoon was very protective of her sons, and they were not sent away to school until they were well into their teens. They were educated firstly by governesses, Mrs Mitchell and Miss Batty, and subsequently by two tutors, Mr Moon and Mr Hamilton who taught Greek, Latin and Maths in a typically public school manner. At the age of fourteen, Siegfried was sent to a nearby 'prep' school which he describes as 'jolly decent',[7] and from there he went to Marlborough until he was eighteen. Apart from being somewhat coddled early on, it was a very conventional education, and if Sassoon's memories are accurate it imbued him with the dominant Christian and imperialist ideologies of the time. He recalls, for instance, Mrs Mitchell instigating in her young charge a terrible fear of God's retributions against the wicked such that Siegfried suffered 'horrible dreams' in which he was being pushed into the furnaces of hell.[8] Miss Batty had a version of Christianity which was somewhat gentler but no less staunch. The young Sassoon was taught notions of Christian good and evil which were mixed with imperialist notions of heroism. God, he was taught, 'wanted little boys . . . to grow up into splendid soldiers who won the Victoria Cross, or gallant sailors who got the Albert Medal for saving someone from drowning . . . or else missionaries who taught black men – and even cannibals – to believe in Jesus and read the scriptures'. This less than progressive teaching was bolstered by readings from *Deeds that Won the Empire* and the elevation of General Gordon of Khartoum into the epitome of Christian manhood. Being a 'hero', Sassoon observes, 'nearly always meant getting killed'.[9]

Through all this time the only mildly unconventional aspect of Sassoon's development was his interest in poetry which began he says, at about the age of ten, and was enthusiastically encouraged by his mother. His early reading was of Longfellow, Shelley and Tennyson. To these Romantic writers he later added an admiration for the Pre-Raphaelite poets and painters, and was, like Rupert Brooke, enamoured of Swinburne. From the first, Sassoon testifies, poetry and music were for him associated with 'an undefined heartache'.[10] That this had something to do with his father's death seems highly likely, and in the Romantic writers he first discovered a longing for death which he found fascinating: 'Eternity and the Tomb were among my favourite themes, and from the accessories of Death I drew my liveliest inspirations.'[11] The Romantic celebration of suffering and of death provided an appropriate inheritance for one who would become famous as a poet of war.

At 'prep' school and Marlborough Sassoon found that poetry was 'an occupation to be almost ashamed of'.[12] The 'hearty' (as opposed to the aesthetic) atmosphere prevailed and began a bifurcation in Sassoon's interests which was to have lasting and profound consequences. Marlborough, like Brooke's Rugby, emphasised the importance of classics and games. The desperately shy Sassoon was anxious to be accepted at school, and games were the easiest way to accomplish this. Due to his unconventional early education Sassoon never shone academically, and he was only in the lower fifth – approximately half-way through the school – when he left at the age of eighteen. So Sassoon developed cricket as his ruling passion for most of his school career, although he recalls the re-awakening of his poetic impulses in his final terms at Marlborough. Sport represented for Sassoon a medium through which he could socialise and project a persona of acceptable 'normality', whereas poetry was an activity that had to be pursued secretly and alone. The conflict between Sassoon the conventional sportsman and Sassoon the unconventional aesthete was one which shaped his life. That he felt this difference to be of crucial importance is signalled by the way in which he approached his autobiographical writings. The three volumes of fictionalised auto-biography in which Sassoon adopts the persona of George Sherston are, according to Sassoon, the story of his 'outdoor', sporting self. He then wrote another trilogy which purports to trace his intellectual and aesthetic development.[13]

It is my contention that the opposition between athlete and aesthete also involved a conflict of sexual identity. Performing as a sportsman was the mark of a 'real man', whereas writing poetry was identified with homosexuality. Further, I think that the un-happiness consequent upon this sense of self-division explains Sassoon's haste to join the army. He joined up two days before war was declared upon Germany. This occurrence has gone largely unremarked by commentators, the assumption presumably being that Sassoon was caught up in the idealistic war fever and fervour which led so many young men to voluntarily rush towards their brutal demise. There may be some little truth in this, but in looking again at this decision and Sassoon's situation when he made it, I wish to suggest that the war provided the central event in Sassoon's life when what he considered to be the two opposed aspects of himself were in closest harmony.

Sassoon was twenty-eight years old in 1914. Having left Marl-borough, he had proceeded via a 'cramming' institution, to Cambridge to study for a law degree. But this didn't last long as Sassoon found the intellectual labours involved uncongenial. So he went down without a degree and spent the following years living upon a private income, dividing his time between fox-hunting, cricket, golf, and the penning of mellifluous verse which, as Bergonzi has nicely remarked, is the product of a 'poetic talent minor to the point of debility'.[14] In *The Weald of Youth*, his autobiographical volume which deals with the years 1909–14, Sassoon records a sense of moving between two worlds which were mutually exclusive. On the one hand there were the active, unintellectual, country pursuits of the hunt and cricket, whilst on the other was Sassoon's involvement with a circle of intellectuals and aesthetes in London. He describes himself as 'a hybrid product' of his 'double life': 'One half of me was hunting-field and the other was gentleman writer.'[15] He goes on to speak of the impossibility of amalgamating his 'contrasted worlds of Literature and Sport'.[16] What is not admitted in this account is that sexuality was at least partly responsible for this impossibility. The most obvious omission from all the autobiographical volumes, with the exception of his diaries, is of any discussion of sexuality. This no doubt proceeds from the difficulties attendant upon admitting to homosexual preferences in a society which outlawed the physical expression of such desire, and from Sassoon's own Victorian attitudes to such matters. Nevertheless what may be asserted is that by 1911 Sassoon was corresponding with Edward Carpenter on the subject of homosexuality, and his war diaries make clear that he was very aware of his sexual attraction towards men during his army career. And in his pre-war life Sassoon mixed freely with other homosexual friends and patrons of the arts in London, but could not share this side of himself with his more conventional sporting cronies like Norman Loder.

Sassoon's correspondence with Carpenter is particularly important in understanding the young poet's pre-war attitude towards his own sexuality. In *The Intermediate Sex* Carpenter had articulated an explanation and defence of homosexual love, which despite its progressive intentions was deeply permeated by Puritanism. Inherited stereotypes concerning 'male' and 'female' qualities are used by Carpenter to argue that homosexuals, or 'Urnings' as he preferred to call them, constitute a 'female soul' in a 'male' body.[17] He is anxious to speak of the 'cleanliness' and 'dignity' of male comradeship and Platonic love, and leaves the place of physical affection between men very blurred indeed.[18] Carpenter argues that 'Urnings' are less given to 'lust' than 'normal' men, and that their love is 'gentler, more sympathetic, more considerate, more a matter of the heart and less of mere physical satisfaction than that of ordinary men'.[19] He also argues that at the basis of the male

Urning's 'nature' is 'the artist's sensibility and perception'.[20] How attractive and enlightening all this was to Sassoon can be measured by the opening letter of their correspondence. Here Sassoon says that Carpenter has 'opened up a new life for him, after a time of great perplexity and unhappiness'. He goes on:

Until I read *The Intermediate Sex*, I knew absolutely nothing of that subject (and was entirely *unspotted*, as I *am now*), but life to me was an empty thing, what ideas I had about homosexuality were absolutely prejudicial, and I was in such a groove that I couldn't allow myself to be what I wished to be, and the intense attraction I felt for my own sex was almost a subconscious thing, and my antipathy for women a mystery to me . . .. I cannot say what you have done for me. I am a different being, though of course the misunderstanding and injustice is a bitter agony sometimes. But having found out all about it, I am old enough to realise the better and nobler way, and to avoid the mire . . . I take as my watchword those words of yours, – 'strength to perform, and pride to suffer without sign'[21]

Here, starkly expressed, is the pathos engendered by naivety and prejudice. Sassoon is evidently much reassured to gain some understanding of himself, and to be able to admit his attraction towards men. Nevertheless, we cannot help but be aware of the Puritanical shunning of physical love ('the mire') and the self-conscious pride in suffering which Sassoon embraces as Carpenter's acolyte.

To return to the months immediately preceding the outbreak of the war then, we find Sassoon moving unsatisfactorily between two worlds. He spent the winter of 1913–14 hunting with Loder, who was the Master of the Atherstone hunt, and then went to London to complain to Edward Marsh of mental stagnation. Marsh, that friend and mentor of Georgian poets and poetry, suggested that Sassoon move to London. One of the main motivations for Sassoon complying was to find subject-matter for poetry: 'I was going to counteract cricket and hunting by leading an enterprising existence which would give me something real to write about.'[22] But the routine of lunch at the club followed by theatre, concert, and dinner parties at night could not provide the required stimulus, and the muse remained stonily unforthcoming. If we are to believe his autobiography, and I can see no reason for not doing so, in the July of 1914 Sassoon was adrift, and discontent. The sporting life could not appease his intellectual and artistic ambitions, and the smart life of upper-middle-class London could not move him into creativity. In neither world did he find love. And so it does not seem too much to suggest that the threat of war provided Sassoon with a convenient avenue of escape from these difficulties. In *The Weald of Youth* Sassoon pretends to be mystified at being so 'unwontedly quick off the mark'[23] in joining up. But this is disingenuous. The war surely promised Sassoon a way of integrating the man of action with the creative artist. In war he would find his subject matter, and enough to last him a lifetime. It also promised to remove him into an all-male environment wherein notions of suffering and sacrifice could ennoble relationships between men in ways similar to those outlined by Carpenter in *The Intermediate Sex*. Mars and Eros would combine to lift Sassoon from boredom to passion.

And so we find Sassoon writing his first 'war poem' in 1915 whilst undergoing training. The poem is entitled 'Absolution' and begins like this:

> The anguish of the earth absolves our eyes
> Till beauty shines in all that we can see.
> War is our scourge; yet war has made us wise,
> And, fighting for our freedom, we are free.[24]

In the remaining stanzas Sassoon asserts that 'Horror of wounds and anger at the foe,/And loss of things desired' all must pass, and that by joining the 'happy legion' the poet has claimed a 'heritage of heart' which implicitly immortalises himself with his 'comrades' and 'brothers'.

This poem has been dismissed by critics as an exercise in patriotic enthusiasm, and Sassoon himself encouraged this view when he subsequently wrote a note to the poem saying that this is how people 'used to feel when they joined up in 1914 and 1915'. 'No-one', he asserts, 'feels it when they "go out again"'. But this is part of that larger re-writing of his war experience that was carried forward in his autobiographies. 'Absolution' remains a more interesting and seminal poem than has been recognised thus far. For it expresses ideas and attitudes which are not entirely destroyed by Sassoon's subsequent experience, and which continue to surface in later poems which are very different in tone and method. The first stanza introduces us to the notion of an unspecified guilt which interestingly is equated with the sense of sight.

Lust is the obvious 'sin' for which sight may be blamed, and so, like Brooke in 'Peace', Sassoon expresses the idea that the war will be the harbinger of a 'beauty' that will absolve sexual guilt. We notice too that this beauty is explicitly related to 'anguish'. The contemplation of suffering is seen as a positive. If this introduces sadism into the poem we do not need to wait long for the introduction of its unlovely partner, masochism. 'War' we are informed, is 'our scourge' which is going to make us 'free'. Of course fighting for 'freedom' was (and is) a political cliché, but the language in the first stanza allows us to read its final line as the expression of a wish for freedom from guilt. The sufferings of war will absolve the soldier. The rest of the poem is less suggestive, more banal. Yet even here we may detect the impulse to find consolation for 'horror' and 'anger' in an idealisation of male relationships; an impulse which, as we shall see, informs a great deal of Sassoon's war poems.

'Absolution' was written between April and September 1915, most of which time Sassoon spent training with the Royal Welch Fusiliers. He had been commissioned into that regiment in May, and on 24 November he joined their First Battalion in France. Sassoon's first few months in France were relatively quiet, although sometimes uncomfortable. In his early days there were working parties to be led, but then the battalion was moved back into a rest area and afterwards, in January 1916, Sassoon was made transport officer which meant that he remained behind with company headquarters when his colleagues went into the line. Thus, it is only his subsequent reputation as an anti-war writer, which makes it surprising that his diary entries at this time are exceedingly cheerful, and there is no hint of protest against the war. On the contrary, we hear repeatedly and paradoxically that in France Sassoon has found 'peace'. Part of the diary entry for 3 December, for instance, reads like this:

My inner life is far more real than the hideous realism of this land of the war-zone. I never thought to find such peace. If it were not for Mother and friends I would pray for a speedy death. I want a genuine taste of the horrors, and then – peace. I don't want to go back to the old inane life which always seemed like a prison. I want freedom, not comfort. I have seen beauty in life, in men and in things; but I can never be a great poet or a great lover. The last fifteen months have unsealed my eyes. I have lived well and truly since the war began, and have made my sacrifices; now I ask that the price be required of me.[25]

We are immediately reminded here of 'Absolution'. The war affords peace and 'freedom' from the boredom and the tribulations of civilian life. His implicit failures in both love and art will be made good by the war; by making sacrifices and being sacrificed. The will to suffer is quite clear. And, it is surely not too much to suggest that in perceiving the horrors and then sacrificing himself, Sassoon saw the possibility of achieving great art and great love?

The themes of 'peace', 'freedom' and 'sacrifice' are constant in the diary over the following two months. On 7 December we hear that a few soldiers, implicitly including himself, will find in battle the 'splendours of the spirit' made manifest, and will earn the 'peace after sacrifice'.[26] Three days later there is the reiteration that peace has been found in France, and that 'the old inane life of 1913–14 seems lopped right off, never to return'.[27] The following week Sassoon expresses his happiness at having 'escaped and found peace' in this 'extraordinary situation' which he thought he would 'loathe'. He also strikes the heroic note again here, asserting that a 'cushy' wound would be an 'awful disaster' and that he 'must endure or else die'.[28] Early January finds him looking forward to action and to falling 'as best befits a man, a sacrifice to the spring'.[29] Soon afterwards he remarks upon the strangeness of coming to the war prepared to 'suffer torments and to see horrible sights' and finding instead 'hours in heaven', 'noble counties' at his feet, and 'love inhabiting the hearts of men'.[30] On being made a transport officer, Sassoon asks the unanswered question, 'why does this safe job come my way when I wanted danger and hardship?'[31]

Apparently Sassoon was relishing his time in France and positively wanted to be in action, to perceive horrors, to suffer, and as a corollary we might add, to inflict some suffering upon the enemy. Notwithstanding the extreme privilege of his social position, he expresses an enthusiasm to escape the confines of peacetime England thereby finding 'freedom'. In this he shared something with the thousands of working-class men who volunteered for the war, thereby trading the suffering of their menial jobs and meagre livelihoods at home, their hefty responsibilities and their social obligations, for the paradoxical 'freedom' of army life in which they were guaranteed food, clothes, a little money and were absolved from responsibility. The Tommies also experienced some freedom from the constraints of civilian life. Brothels provided them with opportunities for fornication, estaminets for drink, and in battle, however appalling it was, they were allowed a licence for unlimited aggression. That many volunteers seriously underestimated the suffering entailed in all of this may have at least something to do with the depth of suffering that the working class were inured to anyway, as well as being a result of heroic, imperialist propaganda. Given the conditions of life and work for most of the working class in 1914, it can hardly be wondered that so many felt that they had so little to lose.

But Sassoon's position was not that of the working class. And yet he felt society to constitute a prison. That this had much to do with Sassoon's sexuality cannot I think be doubted. Despite the predominantly homosexual circles of literary and artistic London, centring upon Eddie Marsh and Robbie Ross to which Sassoon was admitted before his service in France, society at large was brutally intolerant towards homosexuals and to the expression of physical love between men. Part of Sassoon's escape was surely from the demands of his libido and the guilt arising from its direction, into an arena where close relationships between men were the norm, and were 'ennobled' by the idea of sacrifice for each other. In the few poems that Sassoon wrote between November 1915 and the beginning of March 1916, the idea of male sacrifice is ever-present. And, not surprisingly given the ideological baggage of his upbringing, in more than one poem Sassoon compares and contrasts the soldier with Christ.

'The Redeemer', Sassoon's first trench poem, constitutes a narrative in which the poet attempts to convey the physical realities of the trenches. He describes a working party lugging 'clay-sucked boots' along the trenches on a wet and miserable night, illuminated only by the explosion of shells and rockets. The persona turns and sees 'Christ' in the form of a soldier floundering through the mud:

> No thorny crown, only a woollen cap
> He wore – an English soldier, white and strong,
> Who loved his time like any simple chap,
> Good days of work and sport and homely song;
> Now he has learned that nights are very long,
> And dawn a watching of the windowed sky.

But to the end, unjudging, he'll endure
Horror and pain, not uncontent to die
That Lancaster on Lune may stand secure.
He faced me, reeling in his weariness,
Shouldering his load of planks, so hard to bear.
I say that He was Christ . . .[32]

This constitutes an idealisation of a working-class soldier which is both condescending and sentimental. Sassoon presumes that his hero is 'simple', 'unjudging' and 'content to die'. He also presumes that the soldier's life prior to the war was some kind of idyll. Sassoon is seeing his experience through an upper-class lens, and through the pre-war Georgian poetry of such people as Masefield, who wished to write into the Wordsworthian tradition and glorify the life of 'simple folk'. That the industrial revolution had all but wiped out the class of people Wordsworth wrote about does not seem to have impinged on the Georgian poets' consciousness. And it should not be countered in Sassoon's defence that his regiment was made up of Welsh farm workers. A good proportion of the regiment were men from the industrial Midlands, and of course many of the Welsh would have been miners and steel workers from the industrial centres of that country.[33] It is also worth making the point that many of the soldiers in the Royal Welch Fusiliers were regulars, and all of them at this stage were volunteers. We should be aware too, that in talking of the soldier as Christ, Sassoon at once celebrates the idea of suffering and of victimhood. The soldier is seen as passive rather than active; a vision which is as morally questionable as it is politically damaging, suggesting as it does that the working class do not have volition. All this is not to suggest that the working-class soldiers were not 'good' men or to denigrate their undoubted endurance of suffering. What I am anxious to illuminate is the way in which Sassoon simplifies such men since he sees them as different in *kind* to himself because of their class, when in fact they were not. Some of them may have been duped by propaganda into a situation they imperfectly understood. But the same can be said of the officers, including Sassoon. This does not, I think, constitute an argument for perceiving them all as victims. It is surely the case that volunteers must take some moral responsibility upon themselves, particularly since they are not merely enduring suffering, but also likely to be causing it as well.

For an author who is so constantly praised for his 'realism' then, it is salutary to ponder just what these notions of 'realism' constitute, and whose 'reality' is being alluded to. And as we do so two further points should be raised about 'The Redeemer'. It is, I think, important to recognise the element of homoeroticism in the poem. The 'English soldier' is 'strong and white' and implicitly 'redeems' the persona through a sacrificial love. Apart from the chauvinism and the racist overtones of the word 'white' here, it is also possible to detect the influence of Edward Carpenter via Whitman with their idealisation of working-class manhood. Sasson's experience is redeemed by the sacrificial love of the young man. This is not a religious point. The poem ends with a soldier blaspheming: 'O Christ Almighty now I'm stuck', a line which points up the ironic contrast between the official religion and the soldier's experience. What Sassoon is celebrating is a sacrificial love between men.

In other poems written at this time, like 'Golgotha' and 'The Prince of Wounds', Sassoon at once wishes to question the conventional metaphysics of Christianity, whilst simultaneously suggesting that the troops' experience is equivalent to that of Christ. Other poems, such as 'To My Brother' and 'Victory' are less complex and rely upon a naive and abstract enthusiasm to forge consolation. The former poem indirectly alludes to Sassoon's younger brother who was killed at Gallipoli in 1915. In the opening quatrain, Sassoon exhorts his brother: 'Look in these eyes lest I should think of shame;/For we have made an end of all things base.' The example of his brother's death, we learn from the second and concluding stanza, is going to inspire Sassoon away from what is shameful and base towards a laurelled 'victory'.[34] The equation of 'eyes' with 'shame' here reminds us again of 'Absolution', as does the notion that death will absolve the protagonist. The underlying idea is that war will be 'cleansing'.

Sitting perhaps a little oddly with the poems we have discussed so far is 'In the Pink', which Sassoon describes as 'the first of my "outspoken" war poems'.[35] It was written in February 1916, and in some respects develops the method employed in 'The Redeemer', but this time without any of the religious imagery, and less overt homoeroticism. The poem describes 'Davies' writing to his 'sweetheart' after a drink of rum and tea in the shelter of a barn. He is, he says, 'In the pink'. But that night he is portrayed sleepless, thinking of 'Sundays at the farm' when he would go walking 'cheerful as a lark' with 'brown-eyed Gwen'. He thinks forward to the hardships to come, and the narrator finishes the poem with the following couplet: 'Tonight he's in the pink; but soon he'll die./And still the war goes on – *he* don't know why.'[36] This is the prototype of Sassoon's later satirical poems aimed at raising public awareness in England of what the 'reality' of the situation in France was like. This particular poem, Sassoon tells us, was refused by the *Westminster Gazette* on the grounds that it 'might prejudice recruiting'. But how are we to read the poem today? As in 'The Redeemer', it is difficult not to find the cameo of 'Willie' and 'Gwen' both idealised and sentimentalised. Sassoon calls his character 'typical', and yet, as I have already noted, it is very questionable whether the 'innocent' countryman portrayed *was* typical of working-class Tommies in the trenches. We might also note that Davies is portrayed as an 'innocent' victim; the audience is implicitly asked to feel 'sorry' for Davies just as the poet does. Davies is made into a hero precisely because of his suffering and his innocence. We are also left with the unanswered question as to *who did* know why the war was going on. There is certainly no evidence to suggest that Sassoon did, and yet there is an implication that Davies' class prevents him from such understanding.

That Sassoon perceived 'love inhabiting the hearts of men' in France is central to his response. And it was not only in the working class that Sassoon observed this. In 1915 at the base depot of the Royal Welch Fusiliers in Litherland, Sassoon first met David Thomas, and when Sassoon went out to France so too did his fellow subaltern. In *Memoirs of a Fox-Hunting Man* Sassoon describes the first meeting between his persona, George Sherston, and 'Dick Tiltwood'[37] (David Thomas) like this:

He looked up at me. Twilight was falling and there was only one small window, but even in the half-light his face surprised me by its candour and freshness. He had the obvious good looks which go with fair hair and firm features, but it was the radiant integrity of his expression which astonished me. While I was getting ready for dinner we exchanged a few remarks. His tone of voice was simple and reassuring, like his appearance. How does he manage to look like that? I thought; and for the moment I felt all my age, though the world had taught me little enough, as I knew then, and know even better now. His was the bright countenance of truth; ignorant and undoubting; incapable of concealment but strong in reticence and modesty. In fact he was good as gold, and everyone knew it as soon as they knew him.

Such was Dick Tiltwood, who had left school six months before and had since passed through Sandhurst.[38]

There is more of the same in the following paragraph, but I have quoted enough of Sassoon's rapturous prose, I think, to demonstrate that Sassoon was in love with David Thomas (whom he nicknamed 'Tommy') in the manner of an older boy to a younger at an English public school. It is an idealised love which the protagonists see as 'pure', and the place of sexuality in the relationship is hardly admitted even though implicitly it is the source of the emotional bond.

David Thomas served in the same company as Sassoon in France, and so for the first few months they were often together. But when Sassoon was made transport officer it meant that Thomas went into the line whilst Sassoon remained behind. On one such occasion in March, Thomas, the 'young Galahad'[39] of Sassoon's memory, was killed, shot through the throat. The impact of this upon Sassoon should not be under-estimated. Much has been said about the way in which the Somme battle of July 1916 changed attitudes towards the war, and this case has been mounted with respect to the poetry of Owen and Sassoon. There may be some truth in this, but there is substantial evidence to suggest that in Sassoon's case, the first, most crucial factor in intensifying his response to the war, was the death of Thomas. In his diary entry for 19 March, he movingly, if somewhat self-consciously, records his immediate reaction:

they came afterwards and told that my little Tommy had been hit by a stray bullet and died last night. When last I saw him, two nights ago, he had his notebook in his hand, reading my last poem. And I said good night to him, in the moonlit trenches. Had I but known! – the old, human-weak cry. Now he comes back to me in memories, like an angel, with the light in his yellow hair, and I think of him at Cambridge last August when we lived together four weeks in Pembroke College in rooms where the previous occupant's name, Paradise, was written above the door.

So, after lunch, I escaped to the woods above Sailly-Laurette, and grief had its way with me . . .

Grief can be beautiful,when we find something worthy to be mourned.

To-day I knew what it means to find the soul washed pure with tears, and the load of death was lifted from my heart. So I wrote his name in chalk on the beech-tree stem, and left a rough garland of ivy there, and a yellow primrose for his yellow hair and kind grey eyes, my dear, my dear.

Sassoon goes on to describe the burial of his friend, and before concluding remarks that Tommy was 'a gentle soldier, perfect and without stain'. The diary entry for that day ends with the following quatrain:

> For you were glad, and kind and brave;
> With hands that clasped me, young and warm;
> But I have seen a soldier's grave,
> And I have seen your shrouded form.[40]

I have quoted Sassoon's response at length because it is important to try to understand as nearly as we can, what kind of a relationship we are dealing with. Despite the references to 'living together' for four weeks, and the 'young, warm hands' of the quatrain above, it seems to me highly unlikely that the relationship was consummated physically. The tone of Sassoon's utterance, and its concentration upon moral 'purity' suggests to me the idealisation of male love encouraged by the public schools, wherein physical expression of that affection is regarded as 'beastly'. On the other hand, there is no mistaking Sassoon's passion, and this now gained expression in a different way. Sassoon's 'soul' may have been 'washed pure' on that particular evening, but the masochism implicit in talking of the 'beauty' of grief gave way to fierce sadistic impulses: he wanted to get into action and kill people. He was helped in this pursuit by the army who relieved him of his duties as transport officer and attached him to a rifle company. Between late March and late April 1916 Sassoon saw his first 'tours' of the front-line trenches near Morlancourt. For a thirty-day period the battalion spent six days in the trenches followed by a four-day rest period. During this time there were patrols in no man's land, and raids on German trenches. For his part in these Sassoon earned a reputation for 'deeds of reckless daring' such that he gained the nickname 'Mad Jack'. Following these escapades Sassoon had some respite as he was sent on a four-week course at the 4th Army School in Flixecourt. On returning to the battalion he again briefly experienced the front-line trenches, and for an action on 24 May, in which he rescued dead and wounded colleagues from no man's land whilst under enemy fire, Sassoon was awarded the MC.

The first full-scale battle in which Sassoon was involved was the dreadful Somme offensive which began on 1 July. Sassoon's part in this, however, was very limited. He spent the first few days in reserve, and when the battalion were engaged at Mametz Wood on 4 July, Sassoon became involved only by defying his orders. Nevertheless he again fought with distinction, and was recommended for another decoration, which was only refused on the grounds that the action as a whole was a failure. There followed a few days rest before the battalion again moved up to the line near Mametz. But Sassoon once more found himself in reserve at 'Transport Lines close to Meault', and there he stayed until 22 July. On the following day Sassoon felt unwell and was admitted to the New Zealand Hospital at Amiens with 'Trench fever'. He was subsequently evacuated to England where he remained until February 1917.

His diary entries and poems covering this period bear witness to the psychological trauma induced by David Thomas's death. The 'deeds of reckless daring' seem to have been motivated by a desperate carelessness about himself which was tantamount to a death wish. On 31 March he records his fascination with no man's land, and continues, 'I know I ought to be careful of myself, but something drives me on to look for trouble.' He also recalls the laughter of 'sheer delight'[41] which concluded their patrolling activities the night before. On 1 April the 'something' that drives him becomes clearer:

I used to say I couldn't kill anyone in this war; but since they shot Tommy I would gladly stick a bayonet into a German by daylight. Someone told me a year ago that love, sorrow, and hate were things I had never known (things which every poet *should* know!) Now I've known love for Bobbie and Tommy, and grief for Hamo and Tommy, and hate has come also, and the lust to kill. Rupert Brooke was miraculously right when he said 'Safe shall be my going, Secretly armed against all death's endeavour; Safe though all safety's lost'. He described the true soldier–spirit–saint and hero like Norman Donaldson and thousands of others who have been killed and died happier than they lived.[42]

Sassoon articulates the desire to kill and be killed, to be hero and saint; he is living out the Christian–Romantic heritage in all its violence.

And, there is a further dimension to this. Not only does he want to kill Germans and 'smash someone's skull' in order to avenge Tommy, but also Sassoon articulates on more than one occasion the determination to fight well 'for the sake of poetry and poets, whom I represent'.[43] He wishes to 'let people see that poets can fight as well as anybody else'.[44] This, I think, is very significant. We perceive how the Romantic idea of the 'poet' as someone who sacrifices everything for art and who must suffer to create, conveniently meshes with Sassoon's situation and self-image. The man of action and the contemplative aesthete instead of being at odds with each other are brought together in a common pursuit of enduring and inflicting suffering, the product of which is poetry. We may speculate further that Sassoon's ambition to 'fight well' had something to do with 'proving himself' not only to others but also to himself. As George Mosse has shown, the late-nineteenth-century 'Decadents' had fostered the idea that aesthetic experience was allied to a 'feminine' sensitivity and sensuality, as opposed to bourgeois ideals of 'manliness' which constituted the dominant ideologies and bolstered the Empire. Thus art and homosexuality became related to each other. 'Homosexuality is the noble disease of the artist' writes Gautier, whilst Krafft Ebing in 1898 remarked upon the 'medically proven' connection between 'homosexual decadence' and 'artistic feeling'.[45] As we have already seen from the writings of Carpenter, such astonishing ideas were still current in pre-war England, and as I have pointed out the literary circles in which writers like Rupert Brooke and Sassoon moved were predominantly homosexual. But it is crucial to understand that, as George Mosse has also indicated, many homosexuals reacted very ambivalently to this inheritance, demonstrating a self-hating desire to be 'virile' and 'manly' despite their sexual orientation or their aesthetic sensitivities. This seems to me to illuminate Sassoon's (and Rupert Brooke's) situation. Sassoon is politically conservative and wishes to 'prove' his 'manhood' in defence of the Empire, whilst simultaneously writing poetry and sublimating his homosexuality into a chivalrous, idealistic and chaste homoeroticism.

However this may be, it is certain that much of his writing is increasingly angry, violent and sado-masochistic. His poem 'Peace' written on 2 April 1916 provides an equivalent in verse to his other diary entries:

> In my heart there's cruel war that must be waged
> In darkness vile with moans and bleeding bodies maimed;
> A gnawing hunger drives me, wild to be assuaged,
> And bitter lust chuckles within me unashamed.[46]

Having thus expressed his 'lust' to kill and to participate actively in war, he then in the following and concluding stanza wishes Death to 'Stoop' like 'a lover' and afford him 'peace'.

Even more sinister than this poem, however, is 'The Kiss' which Sassoon wrote whilst at the army school in Flixecourt after hearing a 'brawny Highland Major' lecture on the bayonet. Sassoon records that all who heard this oration 'caught fire from his enthusiasm'.[47] The poem, which Sassoon later tried to pass off as satire, is nothing if not enthusiastic. Emulating the dubious literary skills of the major, Sassoon begins the poem by referring to bullet and bayonet as 'Brother lead and Sister steel'. The 'blind power' of both is celebrated, but it is the 'beauty' of the bayonet which gains emphatic attention. 'Her beauty' is guarded by the soldier, and 'she' is said to glitter 'naked, cold and fair' through 'nobly marching days.' This is the prelude to a final stanza which articulates a sadistic wish, in overtly sexual language:

> Sweet Sister, grant your soldier this:
> That in good fury he may feel
> The body where he sets his heel
> Quail from your downward darting kiss.[48]

This is vicious stuff in more ways than one. As well as the obvious celebration of violence here, we have evidence of a tortured psychological attitude towards sexuality. That the phallic bayonet is metaphorically transformed into a woman who demonstrates a powerful, destructive sexuality, suggests both a self-hating fear of male sexuality and a fear and hatred of women. The creativity of Eros is transformed into a celebration of destructive potential.

Sassoon records being 'happy and peaceful – and free'[49] during his time at Flixecourt, and it was there that as well as writing 'The Kiss', he also penned his elegy for David Thomas and wrote a cheerful verse letter to Robert Graves. The elegy, as we might expect, is highly Romantic and pursues the same argument as Shelley's 'Adonais'. David Thomas is said to have become one with nature; he is 'lost among the stars' and returns to us in their light, and in the whispering of trees, and in the leap and tumble of brooks.[50] The tone of this consolatory celebration is maintained in the letter to Graves, wherein again Sassoon proposes a Romantic solution to the ardours of war. The 'spark' of imagination provides 'dreams' which 'will triumph though the dark/scowls'. Thus war, Sassoon asserts, is turned into 'a joke'.[51] Until his evacuation with trench fever in July, Sassoon's diary remains resolutely consolatory. We hear of there being 'more delight than dread in the prospect of the dangers',[52] of 'having fun' with his men in no man's land, of the 'undying sense of valour and sacrifice'[53] in the hearts of the dead, of a determination to find 'beauty' at the front, and a desire to retain the 'freedom' he has found there.[54] But once evacuated to England, the poems that flood from his pen[55] articulate an increasingly complex response in which the anger and sado-masochism of 'The Kiss' is elaborated, together with other, somewhat gentler, more compassionate utterances.

Some of these poems are of the satirical, epigrammatic kind which previous critical opinion has deemed 'typical' of Sassoon's output. But there are many other poems which do not conform to this description. There are several longer dramatic–narrative poems which tend towards the documentary, and there are poems which articulate personal thoughts and feelings in a lyrical mode. For the most part the satirical poems deploy fairly unsubtle ironies with the ostensible purpose of alerting the civilian population of England, who are assumed to be blind, ignorant and complacent, to the grimmer aspects of war. 'The One-legged Man' and 'Died of Wounds' for instance play brutally upon the 'happiness' to be gained from incurring a 'safe' wound, whilst 'They' and 'The March Past' direct an attack upon the Church and the military command respectively. In other poems the focus of attack is the 'complacent' civilian population themselves; 'Decorated' satirises the enthusiasm of the crowd who give a hero's welcome to a VC. winner, and 'Blighters' wishes death and destruction upon a chorus line and its audience in a London theatre. The former exploits the moral ambiguity whereby a multiple murderer in peace time would be reviled by the crowd, whereas 'Corporal Stubbs, the Birmingham VC.' is revered for killing 'five of 'em'. 'Blighters' is less subtle. The poet wishes for a tank to 'come down the stalls/Lurching to ragtime tunes, or "Home, sweet Home"'.

Then, he says, there would be 'no more jokes in Music-halls/To mock the riddled corpses round Bapaume'.[56]

These poems are full of Sassoon's anger. It is as if being removed from the front and therefore from venting his emotional frustration in action, he now turns his attention to others who do not share the front-line soldiers' predicament. This is very understandable. But it is, in my view imperative, that we perceive the problematic position in which these poems place their audience. Implicitly the front-line soldier is assumed to be in a morally superior position to any civilians. Unless we share the soldiers' experience, it is implied, we can have no proper response. Far from being pacifist in their implications, they seem to me bellicose in so far as they imply that participation in battle is a prerequisite to forming a moral attitude to that activity. And, in the case of 'Blighters', Sassoon's aggression towards civilians is overt in defence of the 'victims' of Beaumont Hamel.

That Sassoon was not entirely unaware of such problems is attested to by another satirical poem 'The Hero', which articulates a more complex situation with its attendant moral dilemma. The poem describes an officer visiting the mother of a deceased comrade. She is in receipt of a letter from the colonel which moves her to tears, and to articulate the sentiment that, 'We mothers are so proud/Of our dead soldiers'. The poem continues:

> Quietly the Brother Officer went out.
> He'd told the poor old dear some gallant lies
> That she would nourish all her days no doubt.
> For while he coughed and mumbled, her weak eyes
> Had shone with gentle triumph, brimmed with joy,
> Because he'd been so brave, her glorious boy.
>
> He thought how "Jack", cold-footed, useless swine,
> Had panicked down the trench that night the mine
> Went up at Wicked Corner; how he'd tried
> To get sent home, and how, at last, he died,
> Blown to small bits. And no one seemed to care
> Except that lonely woman with white hair.[57]

The narrative voice seems to delight in the cruel ironies it discovers. Nevertheless, the poem illuminates a problem central to all writing about war. The 'Brother Officer' is in the position of having to choose between 'gallant lies' and a brutal 'reality'. He chooses the former on compassionate grounds, so as to leave the bereaved with some measure of consolation. Sassoon is attempting to tell the 'truth' by contrasting the callous indifference of the 'Brother Officer' towards 'Jack' with his attitude to the bereaved mother. But the poem implicitly demonstrates that the bereaved *need* consolation, and this militates against the truths of war being told. And, as we have already seen in the case of his elegy for David Thomas, some of Sassoon's poetry has a strong consolatory element itself which is as 'fictional' as the 'lies' suggested in the poem above. When David Thomas was shot through the throat, he did not become 'lost among the stars' as Sassoon states in his poem, but buried in the ground in close proximity to further, ongoing carnage.

Sassoon's 'documentary–narrative' style poems from this period are an interesting attempt to render the actualities of trench and hospital experience, again presumably motivated by a wish to 'educate' the public. 'A Night Attack' is perhaps the most success-ful of these as it turns upon the narrator's memory of a dead German, and the dramatic recreation of how this 'Young, fresh and pleasant' youth was killed. The poem is unusual in its concen-tration upon compassion for the enemy, a compassion which nevertheless avoids sentimentality by virtue of its uncompromising language, and one suspects, by Sassoon's greater emotional dis-tance from the subject of his utterance. In other poems Sassoon seems to have difficulty maintaining such perspective. In poems like 'A Working Party' and 'Conscripts' for instance, the respective descriptions of action are rendered less powerful by Sassoon's sentimentalisation of working class soldiers. 'Conscripts' suffers particularly in this way. The persona here describes training the unwilling soldiers and then shipping them to France where 'most of those [he'd] loved too well got killed'. Furthermore, 'many a sickly, slender lord' who had, in the past, filled the speaker's soul with 'lutanies of sin' together with the personified 'Rapture', 'pale Enchantment' and 'Romance' are said to have been sent home because 'they couldn't stand the din'. This clears the way for the concluding paean to the 'common man':

> But the kind, common ones that I despised
> (Hardly a man of them I'd count as friend),
> What stubborn-hearted virtues they disguised!
> They stood and played the hero to the end,

Won gold and silver medals bright with bars,
And marched resplendent home with crowns and stars.[58]

It is easy to sympathise with Sassoon's critique of his own snobbish class preconceptions here. And, again, one would not wish to
deny or denigrate the fortitude of the working class during the
war. But there are more disturbing notions than this in the poem
that concern Sassoon's sexual identity. The juxtaposition of the
'common ones' who are 'virtuous' with 'lords' who are 'sickly' and
implicitly 'sinful', serves to celebrate an idea of 'manliness' which
is inextricably bound up with military values. Far from providing
a critique of conscription or the war, the poem extols the heroism
of the staunch who are appropriately rewarded with military
medals and promotions (it is impossible to ignore this implication
of 'crowns and stars' representing the insignia of officers). Meanwhile the gentler propensities of men are implicitly equated with
'weakness' and cowardice. The conflict within Sassoon between
the false oppositions of aesthete and soldier, a homosexual identity
and 'manliness', are resolved by denigrating the former to the
enhancement of the latter. It is also important to notice how
Sassoon equates survival on the battlefield with 'virtue', when in
fact it was largely a matter of luck. And, of course, the last but
not least of the criticisms to be made of this poem (albeit with the
benefit of *post facto* knowledge) is that far too few 'working-class
heroes' returned at all, and many more returned maimed rather
than 'resplendent' with medals or promotions.

The consolatory tenor of 'Conscripts' is also evident in overtly
personal lyrics like 'A Mystic as Soldier', 'Secret Music', and 'The
Poet as Hero'. The first two of these may be read as companion
pieces. In 'A Mystic as Soldier' the persona recalls a time when he
lived 'Dreaming fair songs for God', with 'glory' in his heart.
Now, he asserts, 'God is in the strife' and must be sought there
amidst 'death' and 'fury'. The poem concludes rather limply:

I walk the secret way
With anger in my brain.
O music through my clay,
When will you sound again?[59]

The only intriguing aspect of this is the 'secret way' of the first
line. The poem ensures the secrecy by refusing to divulge any
further precisely what is meant, but speculation is invited. And it

is surely not too fanciful to suggest that what is 'secretive' in the life of Sassoon the heroic soldier, is the life of Sassoon the homosexual artist who finds in war the subject of his poetry.

This interpretation is bolstered if we turn to 'The Secret Music', which answers the question with which 'A Mystic as Soldier' concludes. In this poem the potential conflict between the roles of poet and soldier is triumphantly resolved. The poet here unashamedly celebrates that in war he finds the stuff of poetry. 'Music' is found in 'Glory exulting over pain,/And beauty, garlanded in hell.' The poet's 'dreaming spirit' can ignore the threat of death because 'Proud-surging melodies of joy' may be discerned amidst the 'gloom'. The poem concludes in an assertion that suffering has been transmuted into art: 'But in my torment I was crowned,/And music dawned above despair.'[60] Interestingly, this is the kind of sentiment that later critics have endorsed with reference to the war poets, and it is one that is by no means pacifist in its implications. On the contrary it validates the war through its generation of suffering which in turn enables the poetry which heroically records that suffering.

This provides a neat introduction to Sassoon's poem, 'The Poet as Hero'. The self-congratulation of the title is rather breath-taking, and it is possible that some irony was intended, or at least some implicit re-definition of the term 'hero'. But again what is striking is that Sassoon prefigures the response of his later admirers. The poem constitutes an imaginary dialogue with an interlocutor who has questioned why the poet has given up his 'old silly sweetness', and changed ecstasies into an 'ugly cry'. The poet responds by admitting that in the past he dreamed of chivalric values and glory, but now he has said 'goodbye to Galahad.' The poem concludes:

> For lust and senseless hatred make me glad,
>   And my killed friends are with me where I go.
> Wound for red wound I burn to smite their wrongs;
> And there is absolution in my songs.[61]

We will recall that Sassoon refers to David Thomas as a 'young Galahad', a circumstance which makes the farewell of the poem even more pointed. Not only has the poet said goodbye to chivalry, he has also said goodbye to idealised love. It is replaced by lust and hatred. Sadism, masochistic guilt, and the need for absolution are given economical expression. The poem is the means whereby the violence is to be forgiven; the new hero is not the chivalric knight, but the soldier-poet.

Sassoon went out to France again in February 1917. In the preceding month his diary entries continue to express an enthusiastic will to suffer and sacrifice. On more than one occasion Sassoon congratulates himself upon his willingness to die in comparison with the 'gross majority' of both soldiers and civilians who belong to a 'decayed' society and who have no purpose, no courage, and 'little souls'. He also celebrates his 'luck' in surviving thus far, and that this has enabled him to write 'all those decent poems'. In marked contrast to his mood in 1913, he now finds that there is 'such a lot to say' about 'Love and beauty and death and bitterness and anger'.[62] On one occasion the soldier-artist explicitly compares himself with Christ.[63] So it is no wonder that when he arrived in France again, Sassoon speaks of how he loathes 'the very idea of returning to England without having been scarred and tortured once more',[64] and remarks upon how 'absolutely happy and contented' he is to choose battle over a return to England.[65]

Battle was joined in the spring offensive of April 1917. Up to that point Sassoon's battalion had been in reserve, and was then marched up to the Somme front in stages until they entered the front line on 14 April. Sassoon records ghastly sights in and around his position. He did not have to endure them for long, however, as on 16 April he was sniped in the shoulder whilst engaged in an attack upon Fontaine la Croiselles. He was evacuated to England and there began the process which was to see him bundled off to Craiglockhart Hospital having been labelled 'neurasthenic' following a public protest against the continuation of the war. Since it is as 'bitter pacifist' rather than 'happy warrior' that Sassoon has been remembered, and since this period in 1917 was his most poetically productive, it is worth considering in some detail Sassoon's state of mind at this time and the complex motivations which governed his behaviour and his writing.

On 17 April Sassoon records 'still feeling warlike', and expresses a wish to return to the line within a few weeks, rather than go back to England. He also exults in his 'luck', which makes it 'inevitable' for him to 'be cast for the part of "leading hero!"'[66] A week later, however, safely back at Denmark Hill hospital in

London, Sassoon records that his 'brain is screwed up like a tight wire', and describes terrible nightmares:

All day I have to talk to people about the war, and answer the questions of friends, getting excited and over-strained and saying things I never meant to. And when the lights are out, and the ward is half-shadow and half glowing firelight, and the white beds are quiet with drowsy figures, huddled outstretched, then the horrors come creeping across the floor: the floor is littered with parcels of dead flesh and bones, faces glaring at the ceiling, faces turned to the floor, hands clutching neck or belly; a livid grinning face with bristly moustache peers at me over the edge of my bed, the hands clutching my sheets. Yet I found no bloodstains there this morning. These corpses are silent; they do not moan and bleat in the war-zone manner approved by the War Office . . . I don't think they mean any harm to me. They are not here to scare me; they look at me reproachfully, because I am so lucky, with my safe wound, and the warm kindly immunity of the hospital is what they longed for when they shivered and waited for the attack to begin, or the brutal bombardment to cease.[67]

Ironically, England rather than France had become the place of suffering for Sassoon. And it seems clear from the above that guilt was the primary source of this mental anguish; but guilt which had more than one source as is made clear from his lines 'To the Warmongers', also penned at Denmark Hill.

This poem, like many others written in the following months, displays Sassoon's anxiety to rub the noses of civilians into the mud and blood and slaughter of the western front. In the case of real warmongers this may be justified, but reading Sassoon's poems of this kind can lead to the very mistaken impression that every civilian was a heartless coward. Sassoon's fury is very evident in these poems, and nowhere more so than in 'Warmongers'. The poem begins with a series of images closely related to the nightmares quoted above, and concludes like this:

For you our battles shine
With triumph half-divine;
And the glory of the dead
Kindles in each proud eye.
But a curse is on my head,
That shall not be unsaid,
And the wounds in my heart are red,
For I have watched them die.[68]

Part of the cost of war is guilt. Sassoon's lines are couched in such a way as to suggest both guilt for engaging in the killing and guilt for surviving the fighting whilst others, implicitly in his care, have died. These feelings I suggest, led him to the conclusion drawn in his diary entry on 21 May: 'I still think I'd better go back to the First Battalion as soon as possible, unless I can make some protest against the War.'[69]

If Sassoon experienced mental and emotional 'peace' whilst in battle, once he was experiencing physical peace in England he engaged in mental and emotional warfare. The anger he could no longer express in combat was directed against civilians, and the reckless daring, the will to sacrifice, was turned into a moral rather than a physical proposition. Encouraged by meetings with H.W. Massingham, the editor of the left-wing journal *The Nation,* with Bertrand Russell and with other pacifists, Sassoon decided to make a public protest against the continuance of the war on behalf of the troops at the front. He was following what he called the 'way of martyrdom',[70] for he was inviting court martial and severe punishment. He was also risking losing various close friendships. But just as he wished to be 'tortured' at the front, so now he wished to suffer at home. And just as he was motivated by sexual guilt, by love, and by anger on the battlefield, so now guilt and love and anger were the emotions which drove Sassoon on. But this time his efforts were directed towards peace, not war. His statement was sent to several eminent politicians and writers, and by arrangement became the subject of a question in the House of Commons and was subsequently published in *The Times*. It reads in part:

I believe that this War, upon which I entered as a war of defence and liberation, has now become a war of aggression and conquest . . . I have seen and endured the sufferings of the troops, and I can no longer be a party to prolonging those sufferings for ends which I believe to be evil and unjust. I am not protesting against the military conduct of the War, but against the political errors and insincerities for which the fighting men are being sacrificed. On behalf of those who are suffering now, I make this protest against the deception which is being practised upon them.[71]

Sassoon began to think of making his protest in May, wrote it in June and sent it to his commanding officer at the beginning of

July. It appeared in *The Times* later that month. Many of Sassoon's friends, including Robert Ross, Eddie Marsh, and Robert Graves were appalled at what he had done. They sought reassurances from the War Office that Sassoon would not be too severely punished, whilst Graves wrote to Sassoon's CO suggesting that his friend was suffering from neurasthenia. This suited the army admirably, as the last thing they wanted to do was to make a martyr out of Sassoon. Graves accordingly went to work to persuade Sassoon to attend a medical board. After some obstinacy Sassoon gave in, having realised that nothing was to be gained from further self-sacrifices. At the board Graves testified that Sassoon had suffered hallucinations of 'corpses strewn along Piccadilly',[72] and after a brief interview they found that Sassoon was indeed suffering from neurasthenia, and he was duly posted to Craiglockhart War Hospital in Edinburgh to undergo some gentle 're-education'.[73] He arrived there on 23 July.

Sassoon's doctor at Craiglockhart was W.H.R. Rivers, an anthropologist and psychologist, who was a fellow of St John's college Cambridge, temporarily acting as a Captain in the Medical Corps. He belonged to the enlightened vanguard with respect to the treatment of shell shock, avoiding the physical brutalities practised by some of the medical profession,[74] and relying instead upon therapeutic conversations and suggestions in order to help patients face their fears and anxieties. Rivers was clearly influenced in his approach by Freud, but disagreed with the great Austrian physician about the sexual aetiology of all neuroses. Shell shock, Rivers argued, was the result of a conflict between fear and duty. Martin Stone summarising Rivers' position writes: 'Rivers claimed that "fear" was the affective aspect of an instinct of self-preservation – a mental function which in Freudian terms was not associated with the libidinous drives of the unconscious.'[75] The aim of Rivers' therapy was to decrease fear and reinforce a sense of duty. It is not difficult to perceive how such an ambition might involve moral and political interventions in the name of medicine. As Stone remarks, Rivers' position 'incorporated a notion of discipline on the one hand and therapy on the other.'[76] He was unable to perceive shell shock as anything other than a 'failure' which had to be made good.[77] This was the approach he took with Sassoon.

We come now to the vexed question of whether or not Sassoon

was 'ill'. As we have already noticed, in April Sassoon had been suffering nightmares and hallucinations both common symptoms of shell shock. In the same month he speaks in a letter of being very near 'the snapping point'.[78] By May the nightmares seem to have subsided, but there is still evidence of considerable mental anguish in his diary entries. In June and July it is clear that some of Sassoon's friends thought that he was mentally unstable. Graves was certainly of this opinion, as was Robbie Ross who described Sassoon's condition as 'very abnormal'.[79] That Sassoon himself came to think of his behaviour as aberrant is signalled in a diary entry of 9 May 1918, when he was back in France: 'I must never forget Rivers. He is the only man who can save me if I break down again. If I am able to keep going it will be through him.'[80] Rivers has taken on the mantle of saviour and protector, whilst Sassoon implies that he has already 'broken down' once and may do so again.

This diary entry takes on particular significance when one considers other conflicting evidence. Sassoon, writing to Ottoline Morell shortly after arriving at Craiglockhart, has this to say:

My fellow patients are 160 more or less dotty officers. A great many of them are degenerate-looking. A few are genuine cases of shell-shock etc. One committed suicide three weeks ago. The bad ones are sent to another place.

My doctor is a sensible man who doesn't say anything silly. His name is Rivers, a notable Cambridge psychologist. But his arguments don't make any impression on me. He doesn't *pretend* that my nerves are wrong, but regards my attitude as abnormal. I do not know for how long he will go on trying to persuade me to modify my views.[81]

Very much later in *Siegfried's Journey* Sassoon quotes from Rivers' written diagnosis at Craiglockhart, wherein the 'patient' is described as 'a healthy-looking man of good physique' who shows 'no physical signs of any disorder of the nervous system', who 'discusses his recent actions and their motives in a perfectly intelligent and rational way,' and who exhibits 'no evidence of any excitement or depression'.[82] What was 'wrong' with Sassoon was an attitude that Rivers on another occasion called his 'anti-war-complex'.[83] It was this that Rivers set out to modify, and did not give up until he had done so. The only thing that was considered to be 'mad' in Sassoon's behaviour was in fact the most sane: his suing for peace.

Rivers 'treated' Sassoon in the same way that he treated his other neurasthenic patients with a one-hour consultation every other day. Sassoon's sessions took place in the evening, and he was otherwise encouraged by Rivers to play golf, and to get out and about in the surrounding countryside. For the first few weeks Sassoon seems to have been relatively contented, but as time went on he began to become increasingly miserable.[84] That this had something to do with Rivers' efforts to modify his opinions seems certain; tensions in the doctor–patient relationship are manifest in Sassoon's October letters. He writes for instance of Rivers becoming very 'war like' recently, arguing that the Germans 'will admit defeat suddenly in the face of superior American power'. Sassoon continues that he still likes Rivers although he (Rivers) has implied that Sassoon is a 'pernicious person'.[85] In *Sherston's Progress,* which is a far more cheerful account of Craiglockhart than is to be found in the diary and letters, we also hear of Rivers pointing out that 'Sherston's' argument about the war is 'emotional and inconsistent', and we learn that Rivers was of the opinion that peace at that time would constitute a victory for pan-Germanism and nullify all the sacrifices that the English had made.[86] Meanwhile Sassoon maintained that he would not retract his statement and would not change his opinion.[87] But Rivers' pressure was beginning to tell. Sassoon began to think more and more of his comrades in France. It seems likely that Rivers encouraged this train of thought. For in his published writings on the treatment of war neurosis, he makes much of his technique of suggesting to patients that they should dwell upon the positive aspects of their appalling experiences in France. That Sassoon felt sacrificial love between comrades to be the principal positive of the war cannot, I think, be doubted. And since Sassoon had made his protest on behalf of the troops, he would be particularly vulnerable to the argument that an officer could best serve his men by being with them at the front. Several October letters show this idea taking shape in Sassoon's mind.[88]

At the same time, Sassoon was becoming increasingly depressed about Craiglockhart and its inmates. In a letter of October 4 he speaks of the 'truly awful atmosphere of this place of wash-outs and shattered heroes'.[89] And thirteen days later he is writing to Ottoline Morell, one of his pacifist friends, that she 'must' see 'how futile' it would be for him to remain in 'these intolerable surroundings'.[90] We remember that in his initial responses to the hospital he had remarked that many of his fellow sufferers looked 'degenerate' and the thought that he might share something with these men, that he too might be considered a 'wash-out' or 'shattered' or 'degenerate' played upon his mind. In *Sherston's Progress* where he recalls his time at Craiglockhart, he speaks of the 'tacit understanding' amongst the inmates that they 'were all failures', and that this made him wish to reassure himself that he wasn't the same as the others.[91] Doubtless this was another chink in Sassoon's armour that Rivers, could exploit. Undoubtedly Sassoon had wished to aquit himself well on the battlefield for the sake of 'poets' as he put it; in other words he had been anxious to prove his 'manliness' to himself and to others. As I have suggested it was in the army in France that the aesthete and the sportsman could happily co-exist; where anxieties about his homosexuality could be allayed by 'manly' heroism. Once back in England, however, the old self-divided Sassoon emerges again, and the conflict between his aesthetic, pacifist gesture and his soldierly duty becomes extraordinarily intense. Once he allowed himself to think that he might be behaving like a 'coward' or a 'degenerate', the only solution was to go back to France.

In his letters and memoirs there is ample evidence of the terrible mental struggle that ensued. On the one hand he remained adamant in his views about the war, on the other he felt increasingly guilty about 'abandoning' his men, and uncomfortable with his position at Craiglockhart. So intense were his feelings that by November he was experiencing war nightmares again.[92] Far from dealing with Sassoon's anxieties, Rivers had generated some more. Sassoon pursued his only option. He told Rivers that he was prepared to go back to the war, if it could be guaranteed that he would be posted to active service. He did not want a 'cushy' job at home. One road of martyrdom having failed, he pursued the other with the full approval of Rivers, who agreed to make representations to the War Office to guarantee that Sassoon would be posted overseas. By this time, what the Freudians call a 'transference' had taken place between Rivers and his 'patient', such that Sassoon was viewing his doctor as a 'father-confessor'.[93] Having been deprived of his father early in life, Sassoon had now found a surrogate.

But there was further drama before Sassoon's inner conflicts were resolved. A medical board was arranged to review Sassoon's case. Very interestingly and significantly Sassoon, in a fit of impatience, took a walk around Edinburgh instead of attending. This, I think, signals his ambivalence towards the decision he was taking. But this was overcome by Rivers who reacted vehemently to Sassoon's insubordination. In a letter of 29 October Sassoon remarks that 'they are very fed up' with him at Craiglockhart for missing the board, and that Rivers views one of his recent poems as 'very dangerous'.[94] In *Sherston's Progress* the incident is dealt with like this:

Rivers, as I have already attempted to indicate, was a wonderful man. He certainly made me aware of it after I'd offered him my wretched explanation. [For missing the medical board] It was, thank heaven, the only time I ever saw him seriously annoyed with me. As might be expected, he looked not only annoyed, but stern. The worst part was that he looked thoroughly miserable. With averted eyes I mumbled out my story; how I'd lost my temper because I was kept waiting; how I really didn't know why I'd done it; and how it was nothing to do with backing out of my decision to give up being a pacifist. When he heard this his face changed. He looked relieved . . . he threw his head back and laughed in that delightful way of his. For me it was the best laugh he had ever indulged in.[95]

As in all three volumes of the *Memoirs,* the tone here is considerably lighter than in the contemporaneous writings. Nevertheless, we are able to perceive in this passage that Sassoon is playing naughty boy to Rivers' stern, but loving father. It also demonstrates the kind of emotional pressure that was brought to bear upon Sassoon, and that an element of counter-transference had taken place. This is an idea substantiated in the only book about Rivers that I have been able to find. Therein Richard Slobodin attests that Rivers, who remained a bachelor all his life, was a changed man after he had met Sassoon; he became happier, more invigorated and more fulfilled.[96] The two men remained close friends until Rivers' death in 1922.

Another medical board was convened, and Sassoon was passed fit for active service. And so his second prolific period of writing war poems drew to a close. Between arriving back in England in April 1917 and returning to his regiment in December, Sassoon had written thirty poems. These may be roughly categorised in the same way as his previous year's output into dramatic-narratives, satires, and personal lyrics. The dramatic narratives are few and far between. There may be good reason for this since poems like 'The Rear-Guard' and 'Counter-Attack' recreate, in so far as this is linguistically possible, both the atmosphere and the physical detail of trench warfare. Such rememberings must have been extremely painful, and it is interesting to note that the former poem was written in April when at least one of Sassoon's friends considered him to be suffering from 'severe shock'. Perhaps later on self-protection dictated more distanced revisitings of such scarifying experience. These two poems are as close as Sassoon gets to 'realism'. And it is worth reiterating that such poems are in a minority. Even a dramatic narrative like 'Prelude: the Troops', which begins with a physical description of the trenches, soon lapses into a consolatory Romanticism in which dead soldiers are said to inhabit 'Valhalla'.

Less taxing to write, one imagines, were the satires which make up the bulk of Sassoon's output during this period. These poems rely on the technique Sassoon had learnt from Hardy's 'Satires of Circumstance', and which Sassoon had developed in 1916. The poems usually depend on fairly crude ironies which are rendered emphatic by a clinching punch line. Together with the less than sophisticated rhymes employed, this often has the effect of reducing the complexities of experience to a neat vignette which rather than creating an illusion of 'reality' signals high artifice. Anyone who is not a front-line soldier becomes a target for Sassoon's anger. Fathers, mothers, generals, politicians and the press take a hammering, and are all considered to be savagely complacent and cowardly. The violence of Sassoon's rage may be gauged from 'Fight to a Finish' which like 'Blighters' imagines soldiers exacting retribution upon their home-front 'enemies'. The situation is a welcome home parade for the troops attended by cheering crowds and 'yellow' press-men. The 'Fusiliers' are described fixing bayonets prior to engaging in the 'cushy' job of charging 'the mob', before advancing to 'clear those Junkers out of Parliament'.[97] Although we may sympathise with Sassoon's anger, we should not, I think, praise poems like this. Not only is the relish of violence distasteful, but the obviously undemocratic sentiments are chilling. By implication military values and virtues are imbued with a righteousness denied to everybody else. One might legitimately enquire what kind of civilian response Sassoon wished for. When one thinks of American and Australian troops returning from Vietnam who were embittered because they were not afforded rapturous civilian celebrations at their home coming, we further perceive the difficult implications of Sassoon's poem. Civilians are simply denied any proper response.

Even more disturbing perhaps are those poems which specifically target women, who are said to positively enjoy the suffering of their wounded heroes. The mysogyny in poems like 'Supreme Sacrifice', 'Glory of Women', and 'Their Frailty' finds an echo in Sassoon's diary where he writes of 'their [women's] gluttonous eyes' and proceeds, 'I think they love war, for all their lamenting over the sons and lovers.'[98] And again, 'Do not the women gloat secretly over the wounds of their lovers? Is there anything inwardly noble in savage sex instincts?'[99] It cannot be doubted that some women were enthusiasts for war,[100] but this is hardly the point. It is clear, I think, from these quotations that it was women's sexuality which troubled Sassoon. It is as if he projected his own self-loathing on to women, and sublimated his own sexual preferences by idealising the working-class 'lads' over whom he could wield some power in the trenches.

Sassoon's most interesting poems are those wherein such psychological problems are intimated. As I have already suggested, Sassoon was troubled whilst at Craiglockhart by the thought of his comrades still in France. And this concern is manifest in several poems written there, including 'Sick Leave', 'Banishment' and 'Autumn'. The first of these recalls the nightmares Sassoon suffered at Denmark Hill hospital and later at Craiglockhart. Whilst asleep the 'noiseless dead' are said to gather around him whispering 'Why are you here with all your watches ended?' The poem concludes with Sassoon's reaction to this, and another question:

In bitter safety I awake, unfriended;
And while the dawn begins with slashing rain
I think of the Battalion in the mud.
'When are you going out to them again?
Are they not still your brothers through our blood?'[101]

This is most obviously an expression of Sassoon's guilt feelings at having survived and being safe. But the lines have other, and rather more troubling implications. 'Safety' is paradoxically both 'bitter' and lonely, and Sassoon is implicitly summoned to make further sacrifice in the name of 'blood-brotherhood'. The feeling behind the poem is not far removed from that which generated the popular argument for the continuation of the war. Many felt that a negotiated peace would render meaningless the sacrifice of the troops thus far. We will recall that this was an idea also articulated by Rivers. The argument that sacrifice should beget further sacrifice is of course illogical and circular, but one can understand how easy it may have been to subscribe to in Sassoon's position. It is important now, however, to recognise the fatuity which made 'sacrifice' into a positive principle, and into a principle of love.

Guilt is the principal motivating emotion in 'Autumn' as well. Here in a rather conventional way, Sassoon likens his fallen comrades to the autumn leaves, 'Scattered in flocks of ruin'. But the point of the poem is encapsulated in the final couplet: 'O martyred youth and manhood overthrown,/The burden of your wrongs is on my head.'[102] The syntax of these lines makes it possible to interpret Sassoon's guilt as originating in both his role as someone who leads others to their death, as well as in his participation in the killing of young men. It is the former role which dominates 'Banishment'. The title of the poem is telling, suggesting as it does that the poet has been forcefully removed from his rightful place. And this is the burden of the opening line wherein the poet states that he has been 'banished from the patient men who fight'. The poem proceeds to extol these men who it is said, provoked 'pity' and 'pride' in the poet's heart. The lines constitute another celebration of the fighting men; they are, the poet says, 'arrayed in honour'. But their deaths on the battlefield led to the poet's 'mutinous' cry against 'those who sent them out into the night.' This gesture is now recognised as a failure and the poem concludes like this:

> Love drove me to rebel.
> Love drives me back to grope with them through hell;
> And in their tortured eyes I stand forgiven.[103]

These few lines succinctly express Sassoon's dilemma. He feels guilty if he is away from the trenches because this constitutes a betrayal of love and loyalty, and he is guilty if he is there for that involves him in the killing and violence. The only consolation remained the idea of a loving sacrifice.

The rest of Sassoon's military career may be summarised briefly. He rejoined the Welch Fusiliers in Litherland in December 1917. From there he went to Limerick before being posted to the 25th Battalion in Palestine. He spent March and April in the Middle East, a period of little incident, before his unit were sent back to the Western Front. Sassoon arrived in France in May, and having survived a flu epidemic which afflicted half of the men in the brigade, he eventually reached the front line in July. He was by this time an 'acting' Captain and was in charge of a company. Whilst returning from what seems to have been an entirely un-necessary patrol, Sassoon was shot in the head by one of his own men, who had mistaken the returning soldiers for Germans. The wound was relatively superficial but serious enough to necessitate Sassoon's evacuation to England where he remained on indefinite sick leave until his discharge on 11 March 1919, when he was still suffering ill-health as a result of wounds and his war experiences.

On resuming active service Sassoon, with the promise of physi-cal suffering in prospect, is soon recording a respite from mental torment. He records feeling 'peaceful' on more than one occa-sion,[104] although he now acknowledges that it is a peace gained by thoughtlessness. The nearer he got to battle the happier he became, and the more the war cast its spell over him. On arrival in France he records his feelings of 'confidence' and 'freedom from worry',[105] experiencing what he described as a 'St Martin's sum-mer of happy warrior youth'.[106] 'The nearer I get to the war', he wrote, 'the more I desire to share its terrors again.'[107] In Palestine Sassoon had lamented the lack of the 'tragic' and 'heroic'.[108] It was much easier to imagine such abstractions in France. And, true to form, Sassoon went in search of action. He engaged in several further acts of 'reckless' daring, before succumbing to his wound. It would be silly to suggest that Sassoon had suddenly lost all his negative feelings about the war – he had not. But there can be little doubt that there were aspects of it which continued to fascinate, attract and excite him. It is also undoubtedly true that apart from the excitement of 'playing the hero' with a disregard for his personal safety tantamount to a death wish, his other consolation was his sense of 'serving' the men under his command. Several diary entries point to this, none more so than that of 24 May which speaks of making sure his men got some tea: 'It is these little things, done for nameless soldiers, that make the war bearable.'[109]

In a more elevated celebration of 'nameless soldiers' Sassoon writes:

They have no smart uniforms, no bottles of hair oil, no secret information to make their conversations important and intriguing. Neither their photographs, nor those of their female relations, have ever appeared in the *Tatler*. They are a part of the huge dun-coloured mass of victims that passes across the shambles of war into the gloom of death where all ranks revert to private. But in their vast patience, in the simplicity of their anger and their mirth, they are as one soul. They are the tradition of human suffering, stripped of all its foolish decorations and ignoble strugglings for individual success and social advancement.[110]

What attracted Sassoon to the working class and ennobled them in his eyes was their serving and suffering. And if the troops demonstrated their capacity to do both, Sassoon was determined to match them.

One of the striking aspects of the diary entries for this last period of active service is that there is a new willingness to acknowledge the part played by his sexuality in his response to the men. It is possible that Rivers' 'treatment' had led to this self-recognition.[111] However this may be, it is certain that in describing the men 'leaning against each other with their arms round one another' he ascribes his emotion to his sexuality.[112] And in an even more telling entry he describes one Jim Lithwaite, a soldier whom Sassoon was kind to on more than one occasion. Sassoon writes of his 'love' for the man, and that 'there was a great deal of sex floating about in this particular effort'. The diary entry proceeds: 'No doubt he dreams about "saving my life". I wish I could save his.'[113] The idea of a noble sacrifice to 'save' one's friend is of course the 'Greater love' of which Christianity speaks. Both here and in several poems written during this period, Sassoon gets very close to admitting the sado-masochistic impulses which underwrite such definitions of 'love'. Immediately following the entry in his diary quoted above, there is a poem entitled 'Reward':

Months and weeks and days go past,
And my soldiers fall at last.
Months and weeks and days
Their ways must be my ways.
And evermore
Love guards the door.

From their eyes the gift I gain
Of grace that can subdue my pain.
From their eyes I hoard
  My reward.
O brothers in my striving, it were best
That I should share your rest.

Love is both the cause and the consolation for suffering. The poet must emulate the soldiers' suffering in order to be worthy of their love. Their sacrifice inspires Sassoon's. Any potential critique of the politics of the war is subordinated to the personal, emotional and erotic implications of suffering.

This is true of several other poems written during 1918, where Sassoon forges consolation from suffering. In 'Memory' it is the suffering of bereavement which is turned into celebration: 'For death has made me wise and bitter and strong;/And I am rich in all that I have lost.'[114] Similarly in 'Can I Forget', Sassoon pledges to remember a dying soldier from whose 'wrongs', the poet says, 'shall rise' the 'power and poignance' of his 'songs'. The poem concludes: 'And this shall comfort me until the end,/That I have been your captain and your friend.'[115] Poetry and love arise from suffering to offer 'comfort'. 'The Triumph', as its title implies, is even more affirmative, and more overtly sado-masochistic in its implications. The poem contrasts the poet's pre-war quest for beauty with his present terrible cognisance:

With death in the terrible flickering gloom of the fight
I was cruel and fierce with despair; I was naked and bound;
I was stricken: and Beauty returned through the shambles of night;
In the faces of men she returned; and their triumph I found.[116]

The poet presents himself as 'cruel and fierce', but also 'naked and bound'; he is both aggressor and victim, the dispenser of pain and the sufferer. And in the midst of the slaughter beauty emerges in the faces of men who, I take it, are triumphant in death. The Romantic equation of beauty with suffering reaches its terrible apotheosis.

The attitudes to suffering which Sassoon took into the war deriving from Christianity and Romanticism did not change, they merely intensified. 'Song-Books of the War', written in 1918, repeats ideas expressed in Sassoon's first 'war poem', 'Absolution', written in 1914. There is unconscious irony here, for in the later poem, Sassoon attempts to contrast innocence with experience. 'Song-Books of the War' imagines the response fifty years after the war of 'Adventurous lads' who, 'Reading a snatch of soldier song/Savage and jaunty, fierce and strong', will envy their elders 'dazzling times/When sacrifice absolved our earth.' The poem continues:

> Some ancient man with silver locks
> Will lift his weary face to say:
> 'War was a fiend who stopped our clocks
> Although we met him grim and gay.'
> And then he'll speak of Haig's last drive,
> Marvelling that any came alive
> Out of the shambles that men built
> And smashed, to cleanse the world of guilt.
> But the boys, with grin and sidelong glance,
> Will think, 'Poor grandad's day is done.'
> And dream of lads who fought in France
> And lived in time to share the fun.[117]

The problem in the poem is that the 'grim gaiety', and the 'savage and jaunty, fierce and strong' emotions of which Sassoon speaks, are precisely those most liable to provoke the 'Adventurous lads' to envy. And the absolution of the world by 'sacrifice', the cleansing of guilt in the slaughterhouse is also spoken of with little discernible irony. This curious poem predicts the problems with which I am striving. It is my contention that Sassoon's poems, for all their supposedly anti-war feeling, in fact express ideas and emotions which excite young and unwary readers, and covertly support war by providing positive consolations based on the idea that suffering is a good.

I have left discussion of what I take to be Sassoon's most moving poem to the last. This is a verse letter addressed to Robert Graves from Lancaster Gate Hospital after Sassoon had returned from the war for the last time. Although it is written in rhyming couplets, the poem expresses very raw emotions. It describes the troubled state of Sassoon's nerves with a neologism of which Joyce would have been proud: 'Sleeplessexasperuicide'; the place of 'sex' is tellingly central to the sleeplessness, exasperation, and suicidal feelings he is experiencing. The poem goes on to describe a visit from Rivers who is said to persuade Sassoon that he is 'a gallant and glorious lyrical soldjer' rather than the 'Worm that refuses to die'. But even Rivers cannot entirely suppress Sassoon's self-conflict. The poem moves to a close expressing again Sassoon's feelings of guilt for not being at the front with his troops. In the end it is to Rivers that he turns for 'help':

> O Rivers please take me. And make me
> Go back to the war till it break me.
> Some day my brain will go BANG,
> And they'll say what lovely faces were
> The soldier lads he sang
>
> Does this break your heart? What do I care?[118]

In the immediate aftermath of his return to England, and the armistice which followed some months later, Sassoon took some time to settle down. His protracted convalescence took him back into the world of aristocratic country houses and to his circle of literary friends in London. There followed a brief flirtation with Labour politics, and he continued for the next few years to consider himself a 'socialist'. But there is little evidence to suggest that his politics went beyond a rather patrician 'sympathy' for the 'poor' and the working class. Apart from this 'sympathy', which led him into arguments with family and friends, the most public manifestation of his politics was his acceptance in March 1919 of the literary editorship of the *Daily Herald*, the new mass-circulation paper with its 'Face towards the Future'.

Sassoon left his part-time job on the paper to undertake a poetry-reading tour of the United States which was conducted between February and August 1920. On his return from this excursion Sassoon reverted to his pre-war existence alternating between his literary life in London and his sporting life in the country. Although he felt in 1920 that his 'Labour sympathies' should 'preclude fox-hunting', the call of sport was rather stronger than Sassoon's conscience or political conviction. He returned, then, to, 'Inconsistency – double life – as usual – trying to be serious about life and work – buying a horse and dreaming of winning V.W.H. [Vale of White Horse] point-to-point.'[119] And the psychological difficulties of his war-time experience did not abate. The published diaries covering the years 1920–22 reveal a very troubled man indeed. His sexuality was a source of great anxiety to him. We learn that in late 1918 he began an affair with Gabriel Atkin which seems to have proceeded happily enough for about six months, and then to have caused Sassoon considerable irritation. On return from his American trip, Sassoon records a 'fresh start' with Gabriel, and the relationship certainly dragged on, not without difficulties, until the end of 1922. As late as 1926, Sassoon was still helping Gabriel financially.

That Sassoon's relationship with Gabriel was far from satisfactory is made quite clear in the diary. Gabriel is described as 'wholly pleasure loving',[120] as 'not a gentleman'[121] and, in a significant comparison with the men he served with in the war, as a 'cheap liqueur'.[122] We also hear over and over again of the 'cursed complication of sex',[123] the 'cursed nuisance of sex',[124] and of being 'very much harassed by sex-fevers'[125] or, 'continuously harassed by sex hungers'.[126] There is further, ample evidence that Sassoon feels guilty about his sexual orientation. He asks himself at one point whether it is his own fault that he is under 'this obsession of sex-cravings', and proceeds to speak of the 'spiritual sickness' that 'overshadows' him. His mind, he says, is 'diseased and distorted'; he is 'self-poisoned' and 'self-imprisoned'[127] He also speaks of the pleasure that he gains from '*conventional* things' because they are 'an antithesis' to his 'sexual secret'.[128] It is, I think, this guilt or self-hatred that generates the sado-masochistic element which is also clearly evident in Sassoon's relationship, not only with Gabriel but also with other men, one of whom he had an affair with in 1922.

In a state of 'nerves' and 'bad temper' Sassoon describes the 'lacerating' 'self-torturing condition' he experiences when he imagines himself to be 'too well understood' by Gabriel.[129] In similar language in another diary entry Sassoon speaks of his 'self-lacerating irritability' which he suspects is linked with his 'animal passions'.[130] There is also a reiteration of his desire for self-sacrifice, that emotion which, as we have seen, informs so much of his response to war. 7 April 1921 finds Sassoon experiencing 'those inward stirrings of unappeased nobility and self-sacrifice', and remarking how 'splendid' it would be to die for *something*.[131] Later the same year, remembering the war and the men with whom he fought, Sassoon wishes somewhat ambiguously, that he could 'find a moral equivalent to war', that he feels only 'half alive' and that part of him died with all his lost comrades.[132] The impulse towards suffering and self-punishment finds a more direct expression when Sassoon purchases and contemplates 'two photos of the martyrdom of San Lorenzo by G. Santacroce'. The picture, Sassoon says, 'has no interest except in its morbidly sexual appeal' to his 'sexually morbid mind'. Sassoon goes on in the same diary entry to quote a line from his own poem entitled 'Martyrdoms': 'I "glory with Lorenzo on his grid."'[133]

That Sassoon's psychology was not only masochistic, but also sadistic is evidenced in further diary entries. He writes, for instance, of an evening with Osbert Sitwell:

I suddenly realised that my attitude towards O is strongly sadistic. I saw, quite calmly, that my (supposed) stab at his feelings this afternoon aroused in me acute sexual feelings toward him . . . Does it help one – to 'realise' these things? . . . And is there anything in life which can be disconnected from this curse of sex?[134]

With reference to a love affair with 'P', Sassoon writes: 'I want to sting him into responsiveness by violent methods',[135] and records in another entry wishing to be 'unkind' to 'P', and wondering whether this affair will end in the same way as with Gabriel, in his 'being brutal'.[136]

Unlike his experience of suffering during the war, however, Sassoon found that he could not express his personal problems in either fiction or poetry. In 1921 and 1922 he continually records his sense of sterility, of having 'nothing to say',[137] and being 'dry as a biscuit'.[138] In one diary entry he dreams of writing a novel which will be 'one of the stepping stones across the raging (or lethargic) river of intolerance which divides creatures of [his] temperament from a free and unsecretive existence among their fellow men.'[139] One presumes that Sassoon's reticence, his sense of guilt and shame precluded his being able to fulfil or even begin this task.

For the rest of the 1920s Sassoon moved between London, the countryside, and Europe. He continued to write occasional poems, but did not embark upon a major literary project until 1926 when, in response to a suggestion by Edmund Gosse, he began writing *Memoirs of a Fox-Hunting Man*. This was the first of six autobiographical volumes that Sassoon published between 1928 and 1945, all dealing with his pre-war and war experiences. At the same time Sassoon finally settled down to live in the Wiltshire countryside. It is impossible and impractical to articulate the rest of Sassoon's biography in great detail. Suffice it to say that his letters of the late 1920s and early 1930s reveal another affair with a young man named Stephen Tennant, who suffered from tuberculosis, and whom Sassoon nursed for a time. The end of this relationship seems to have coincided with Sassoon's meeting and marriage to Hester Gatty. The couple were married in 1933 and went to live at Heytesbury House in Wiltshire. In September of the same year Sassoon was complaining to Ottoline Morell of feeling like a 'fly in a web' since he cannot escape 'the demon of his devotion' to Stephen.[140] Nevertheless, by the following year, writing to the same correspondent and referring to Wiltshire and Hester, Sassoon finds it almost unbelievable that he should live in such 'a perfect place, with such a perfect companion'.[141] Sassoon's marriage remained harmonious for about ten years. In 1936 a son was born, George, who was a source of comfort and delight to Sassoon for the rest of his life.

Towards the end of 1941 Sassoon separated from his wife, but he continued to see George regularly and Hester sporadically, although they seem to have fought a custody battle over their son in 1946. Between that year and his death in 1967 Sassoon remained in Wiltshire writing and playing cricket. The 1950s saw the crystallisation of his belief in Christianity. In the spring of 1953, he speaks in a letter of the Easter legend as being 'unsurpassable' and expresses the feeling that it is a 'fathomlessly powerful and dramatic story on which our salvation hangs'.[142] In 1957 he was formally admitted to the Roman Catholic Church. It was an entirely appropriate mental destination for a soldier poet who had sought and seen 'sacrifice' in war, who had imagined himself and others as Christ-like in their suffering, and who subscribed to the Romantic view that art was also dependent upon suffering and sacrifice. In 1960, at the age of seventy-four, Sassoon was still playing cricket with the help of a runner. The artist and the sportsman co-existed to the end.

Apart from his war poems, Sassoon's literary reputation depends upon the subsequent re-writing of his experiences in his six volumes of autobiography, and particularly on the three volumes which constitute *The Memoirs of George Sherston*: *Memoirs of a Fox-Hunting Man* (1928), *Memoirs of an Infantry Officer* (1930), and *Sherston's Progress* (1936). In these three intricately artful books, Sassoon adopts the persona of George Sherston to recreate the history of a 'simplified version of his outdoor self'. *Memoirs of a Fox-Hunting Man* takes us from schooldays to the trenches in Easter 1916. *Memoirs of an Infantry Officer* is an account of Sherston/Sassoon's soldiering until his protest and subsequent arrival at Craiglockhart. The final volume of the trilogy begins with an extended account of his relationship with Rivers at Craiglockhart and ends with Rivers' hospital visit to the wounded Sherston/Sassoon in 1918.

As I have already intimated, the trilogy formalises by its omissions the divide between Sassoon the sportsman and Sassoon the aesthete. George Sherston is a simplified version of Sassoon who has neither parents nor sex life, and moreover, is not interested in poetry much less a writer of it. Sassoon said of *Memoirs of a Fox-Hunting Man,* that the book was 'a recreative exercise [and] nothing more'; that he wished to keep his narration 'clear and unencumbered' and that the book should 'unroll like a scroll'.[143] That these aims were achieved is, I think, in large measure due to Sassoon's characterisation of himself as 'Sherston'. The whole tone and tenor of the trilogy depends upon Sherston's 'simplicity'. This is not the simplicity of the stupid, but implicitly that of the wise. The narrating voice of the elder 'Sherston' looks back at his younger self with a gentle irony which is not entirely uncritical but finally accepting. There is no room in this characterisation for literary, philosophical, or psychological sophistications. With tiresome regularity the narrator reminds the reader of his intellectual limitations, and in the end, I think, we are asked to rather admire these, as if too much thought might inhibit young George's 'getting of wisdom' and his gaining of 'manhood'.

We hear early on from the narrator in the first volume that 'there was an unmanly' element in young George's 'nature' which leads him into 'many blunders and secret humiliations.'[144] It is this 'element' as well as George's youthful egotism that is modified by his experiences of war. The elder George's (i.e. the narrator's) judgements upon his earlier self demonstrate that a successful educational journey has been undertaken. It is not until young Sherston's arrival at 'Slateford Hospital', however, and his meeting with Rivers in *Sherston's Progress* that we encounter the source of the narrator's enlightenment: 'I can only suggest that my definite approach to mental maturity began with my contact with the mind of Rivers.'[145] It is Rivers who has taught the narrator not to be egotistical by showing the young Sherston how ignorant he is, how little he knows of the wider picture of the war, how not to be 'conversationally dishonest'. It is Rivers who guides the young man to a realisation that his protest against the war is wrong-headed.[146] And when Sherston has re-joined the war his reactions to it are measured against what Rivers would think.[147]

At the end of *Sherston's Progress* young George is described in the hospital 'tearing [himself] to pieces and feeling miserable and frustrated'. This passage is as near as we get to mental anguish in the whole trilogy. Young George is 'in a muddle'. He feels guilty for leaving the battalion, guilty for surviving, and is full of self-remorse and bitterness. But this state of mind does not last long. The book and the trilogy conclude like this:

And then, unexpected and unannounced, Rivers came in and closed the door behind him. Quiet and alert, purposeful and unhesitating, he seemed to empty the room of everything that had needed exorcising.

My futile demons fled him – for his presence was a refutation of wrong-headedness. I knew then that I had been very lonely while I was at the War; I knew that I had a lot to learn, and that he was the only man who could help me.

Without a word he sat down by the bed; and his smile was benediction enough for all I'd been through. 'Oh, Rivers, I've had such a funny time since I saw you last!' I exclaimed. And I understood that this was what I'd been waiting for.[148]

The war enables Sherston to suffer, and Rivers enables Sherston to understand and accommodate that suffering into a 'balanced' view of himself and the war.

To anybody familiar with the diaries and the war poems, it is obvious that in the trilogy Sassoon is re-writing himself. All the passion, the heights and depths of emotion are erased in that later account, to be replaced by an urbane and ultimately very conservative 'understanding'. The direction of the re-writing is anti-heroic and rationalising. Many positive responses to the war on the part of young George, are turned by the narrator into 'defence mechanisms' or 'coping mechanisms', as if Sassoon feels the need to apologise for his past self. And the young Sherston's attitude to those whom Sassoon pilloried in his satirical poems – women, civilians, generals, and journalists – is much more balanced. Passionate anger has been erased, just as passionate affirmation of the war and of fighting is tempered.

Memoirs of an Infantry Officer, dealing as it does with the most concentrated period of Sassoon's active service, is full of examples of Sassoon re-writing his earlier reactions to combat. Every time Sherston goes into action we are told of the 'exhilaration', the 'wild exultation', the 'excitement' of the 'escapades'.[149] But such descriptions of his feelings are always moderated by the narrating voice 'normalising' these experiences with references to 'strained nerves' or reducing them to the familiar by ironic debunking. The young Sherston is judged 'An inflated fool'[150] for his eagerness to engage in patrolling. Having felt 'wild exultation' in another action, and having told us that he 'prided himself' upon having 'pulled off something rather heroic', the narrator steps in with: 'but when all was said and done it was only the sort of thing which people often did during a fire or a railway accident'.[151] In another episode when young George is enjoying himself in no man's land, this is quickly modified by being told that the young man was merely 'an interesting example of human egotism'.[152] In *Sherston's Progress*, recounting his final experiences of the trenches, we have this telling passage:

I was glad to be there, it seemed; and perhaps my thoughts for a moment revisited Slateford Hospital and were reminded of its unescapable atmosphere of humiliation. That was how active service used to hoodwink us. Wonderful moments in the War, we called them, and told people at home that after all we wouldn't have missed it for worlds. But it was only one's youngness, really, and the fact of being in a foreign country with a fresh mind. Not because of the War, but in spite of it, we felt such zest and fulfilment, and remembered it later on with nostalgic regret, forgetting the miseries and the grumblings, and how we longed for it to come to an end. Nevertheless, there I was, a living antithesis to the gloomier entries in my diary, and a physical retraction of my last year's protest against the 'political errors and insincerities for which the fighting men were being sacrificed'.[153]

Here Sassoon is covering all his bases. He cannot afford to admit to himself that there were aspects of the war that he enjoyed. It was his stated intention in the trilogy to provide an anti-war statement, so he is careful to try to erase or temper his enthusiasm for fighting. He also does not want to present the young George as 'heroic'. On the other hand he is anxious to assert that his experiences have not been futile – that he has learnt from his suffering. And, in recounting his adventurous exploits and the troops' response to these, George inevitably emerges with something of the hero about him.

We see in passages like this that the presentation of George Sherston as a 'simple' character masks the fact that his story is complicated by two levels of ambivalence. We have young George's contradictory reactions to his war experience described by a narrator who has a divided attitude towards his own past. Nowhere are the problems thus created, more evident than in that part of *Memoirs of an Infantry Officer* which deals with Sherston's protest against the war. The approach here to young Sherston's mental and emotional life is paradigmatic of Sassoon's procedure throughout the trilogy. We are *told* about mental anguish, but we are not shown it. The narrator's sometimes ironical, sometimes sympathetic voice, ensures that the relatively raw emotions we encounter in the poems and diary are smoothed and tempered. The reader has already been prepared for the narrator's attitude to the protest in an earlier statement in which the narrator tells us that he is 'no believer in wild denunciations of the war'.[154] It therefore comes as no surprise when we gain the very definite impression that the narrator disapproves of the actions of his younger self, and feels his protest to have lacked both insight and wisdom. The narrator endorses Rivers' attitude and a denunciation of a pacifist, McCamble, who dares to criticise Rivers and imply that the psychoanalyst is having a 'subtly disintegrating influence' on Sherston's pacifism.[155]

This consistent criticism of the young Sherston's protest by his elder counterpart only becomes problematic when we attempt to reconcile it with other positions taken up by the narrator, and with Sassoon's declared intentions with respect to the book. In a letter of 1936 Sassoon remarks that he wanted the trilogy to be 'propaganda for peace'.[156] The debunking of the young George's 'heroism', and the reductive rationalisations of his enjoyment of the war, are presumably part of this intention. Yet the most crucial gesture towards peace is debunked, and Rivers' view that the war was a necessary evil espoused. The narrator's ambivalence compounds the young Sherston's. At certain moments the younger and elder Sherston's attitudes even seem to coalesce. In this passage, for example, which occurs just as Sherston is about to make his protest, there seems no ironic detachment in the narrator's voice as he describes his difficulties in being assimilated into the 'Anti-War movement':

I couldn't quite believe that I had been assimilated. The reason for this feeling was their antipathy to everyone in a uniform. I was still wearing mine, and somehow I was unable to dislike being a Flintshire Fusilier. This little psychological dilemma now seems almost too delicate to be divulged. In their eyes, I suppose, there was no credit attached to the fact of having been at the front; but for me it had been a supremely important experience. I am obliged to admit that if these anti-war enthusiasts hadn't happened to be likeable I might have secretly despised them. Any man who had been on active service had an unfair advantage over those who hadn't. And the man who had really endured the War at its worst was everlastingly differentiated from everyone except his fellow soldiers.[157]

Here the narrator invests the war with significance for himself, and articulates his ultimate divide with civilians. The men who fought only have an unfair advantage, if some belief in military values is espoused. From a pacifist's point of view, it is the men who fought who are at a disadvantage.

It is crucial to assert that the trilogy does not represent 'propaganda for peace' much less an expression of pacifism. The books have been taken by subsequent critics as being 'anti-war', and yet much of them celebrates the event. How 'terrible' the war was, and some of its 'horrible' consequences are, of course, brought to the reader's attention. But there is no escaping the message that experiencing all this has been 'supremely important' and has been so because through this suffering George Sherston has learnt to become a 'better', 'wiser' person. It is a very conservative conclusion, made even more so by the repeated implication that individual protest with regard to international politics is both futile and wrong headed.

For someone who had ostensibly learnt to be less egotistical, Sassoon apparently still found himself a subject of much fascination as is evident from his penning of another three volumes of autobiography. These need not detain us long. Only one of them, *Siegfried's Journey,* deals with the war, and this in not much detail. Little is added to Sassoon's attitude towards the war here, except his admission of the 'complex advantages of being a soldier-poet'.[158] We are reminded that the war gave Sassoon his subject matter, and so increased his ambivalence towards action.

He wanted material for poems, and gained consolation from his increasing abilities and reputation as a poet. Apart from this, Sassoon's attitude towards his protest remains the same if not more vehement; it was a wrong-headed aberration of youth. Sassoon finds it difficult now to believe that a peace negotiated in 1917 'would have been permanent'. He continues, 'I share the general opinion that nothing on earth would have prevented a recurrence of Teutonic aggressiveness.'[159] That the war was supremely important to Sassoon is still quite clear, and his difficulty in escaping its thrall is both implicit and explicit.

Sassoon was brought up to believe that suffering was good and ennobling. Both Christianity and Romanticism assured him of this. The highest form of love, following Christ, was to die for one's friend. Not surprisingly this idealisation of sado-masochism, held a massive appeal to Sassoon who found that his society hated his sexual preferences; a hatred that he internalised and turned against himself. The war not only relieved him of boredom and gave him something to write about, but also provided a site for the expression and experience of sado-masochistic impulses. He became involved in a vicious circle of anger and guilt from which the only escape was death. This he unsuccessfully sought, both before and after his peace protest, which was another form of self-martyrdom. Having survived, he spent the rest of his life coming to terms with his experience through the accommodations of his autobiographies. Their uniformly comfortable and comforting tones, bespeak a need to render his life manageable. He stated of *Memoirs of a Fox-Hunting Man* that he wished to 'suppress his strong feelings'[160] in the book, and later said of *The Old Century* that he wished to outline his early life 'lightly and pleasantly'.[161] Rather than being books that speak out against war, they are books that accommodate that experience and make it manageable. Hence, I think, the massive popularity of the Sherston trilogy during the Second World War and since. Similarly, it is my contention, that the poems are not in any simple way anti-war. Too many of them find consolation in the suffering, too many of them celebrate sacrifice, for them to be an entirely convincing expression of anti-war sentiment. Sassoon never disentangled his attitude towards suffering or his feelings about the excitement and exhilaration of war. He also never came to terms with his sexuality. In a letter of 1949 he writes that the whole point of life is 'to try [and] rise above one's waist line'.[162] This denial of sexuality, together with his conversion to Catholicism reminds us of the power of the ideologies Sassoon inherited, and their appalling consequences. The creative and destructive potentialities of human beings are removed from their source in the human body and sited in the realms of the metaphysical, and so the massive sufferings of the war may be abstracted and turned into a positive principle which is supposed to 'teach' us. The history of the rest of this century suggests that on the contrary, suffering begets more suffering, and all we learn is what we do not learn.

Notes

1   D. Hibberd, *Owen the Poet,* London, 1986.
2   B. Bergonzi, *Heroes' Twilight,* London, (1965), 1980, pp. 92–108.
3   J. Silkin, *Out of Battle: the Poetry of the Great War,* London, 1972, pp. 132, 136–7, 145–6.
4   P. Fussell, *The Great War and Modern Memory,* London, 1975, (1977), pp. 82, 91ff and *passim.*
5   S. Sassoon, *The Old Century and Seven More Years,* London, 1938, p. 248.
6   Ibid., p. 15.
7   Ibid., p. 183.
8   Ibid., pp. 45–6.
9   Ibid., p. 50.
10 Ibid., p. 89.
11 Ibid., p. 148.
12 Ibid., p. 187.
13 S. Sassoon, *Siegfried's Journey,* London, (1945), 1982, p. 69.
14 Bergonzi, *Heroes' Twilight,* p. 92.
15 S. Sassoon, *The Weald of Youth,* London, 1942, p. 208.
16 Ibid., p. 214.
17 E. Carpenter, *The Intermediate Sex,* London, (1908), 1909, p. 27.
18 Ibid., p. 108 and *passim.*
19 Ibid., p. 128.
20 Ibid., p. 33.
21 Letter of S. Sassoon to E. Carpenter, July 27, 1911. MSS 386–179, Edward Carpenter Collection, Sheffield Public Library.
22 Sassoon, *The Weald of Youth,* p. 203.
23 Ibid., p. 269.

24 S. Sassoon, *The War Poems,* London, 1983, p. 15. Hereafter referred to as *TWP.*

25 S. Sassoon, *Diaries 1915–1918,* Rupert Hart-Davis, (ed.), London, 1983, p. 22.

26 Ibid., p. 25.

27 Ibid., p. 26.

28 Ibid.

29 Ibid., p. 33.

30 Ibid., p. 34.

31 Ibid., p. 35.

32 *TWP,* pp. 16–17.

33 See J.C. Dunn, *The War the Infantry Knew 1914–1919,* (1938), 1989, p. xxxviii, and R. Graves, *Goodbye to All That,* (1929) ,1960, p. 71.

34 *TWP,* p. 18.

35 Ibid., p. 22.

36 Ibid.

37 Our late-twentieth-century sensibility is likely to find somewhat risible phallic significations in both parts of this name. Sassoon lived in a more 'innocent' age. Given his various descriptions of his beloved, and the contemporary enthusiasm for all things chivalric, it is likely that he intended 'Tiltwood' to suggest a jousting knight.

38 S. Sassoon, *The Complete Memoirs of George Sherston,* (incorporating *Memoirs of a Fox-Hunting Man, Memoirs of an Infantry Officer* and *Sherston's Progress*) London, 1937, p. 241.

39 Ibid., p. 258.

40 Sassoon, *Diaries 1915–1918,* p. 45.

41 Ibid., p. 51.

42 Ibid., p. 52.

43 Ibid., p. 51.

44 Ibid., p. 53.

45 Quoted by G. Mosse, *Nationalism and Sexuality: Middle-Class Morality and Sexual Norms in Modern Europe,* Wisconsin, 1985, p. 44.

46 Sassoon, *Diaries 1915–1918,* p. 52.

47 Ibid., p. 59.

48 Ibid., p. 60 and *TWP,* p. 29.

49 Sassoon, *Diaries, 1915–1918,* p. 63.

50 *TWP,* pp. 31–5.

51 Ibid., pp. 36–8.

52 Sassoon, *Diaries 1915–1918,* p. 67.

53 Ibid., p. 72.

54 Ibid., p. 75.
55 He wrote approximately twenty-five war poems between July 1916 and February 1917.
56 *TWP*, p. 68.
57 Ibid., p. 49.
58 Ibid., p. 69.
59 Ibid., p. 60.
60 Ibid., p. 62.
61 Ibid., p. 61.
62 Sassoon, *Diaries 1915–18*, pp. 118–22.
63 Ibid., p. 124.
64 Ibid., p. 133.
65 Ibid., p. 151.
66 Ibid., p. 156.
67 Ibid., pp. 161–2.
68 *TWP*, p. 77.
69 Sassoon, *Diaries 1915–1918*, p. 171.
70 Ibid., p. 165.
71 Ibid., pp. 173–4.
72 R. Graves, *Goodbye to All That*, London, (1929), Harmondsworth,1960, p. 216.
73 Elaine Showalter in her book, *The Female Malady*, London, 1987, pp. 167–94, has written an account of Sassoon's treatment at Craiglockhart. Although I agree with the general direction of her arguments, there are some crucial differences in my approach. I think that Showalter accepts too readily Rivers' own theory that shell shock was the product of a tension between fear and duty. Her unwillingness to deal with Sassoon's homosexuality, and her arguments that shell shock was the expression of 'men's quarrels with the feminine element in their psyches' (p. 173) not only considerably simplifies Sassoon's dealings with Rivers but also implies an essentialism that I am anxious to avoid.
74 For a brief account of these see, E. Leed, *No Man's Land: Combat and Identity in World War I*, Cambridge, 1979, pp. 170–6.
75 M. Stone, 'Shellshock and the Psychologists', *The Anatomy of Madness*, vol. II, W. Bynum, R. Porter, M. Shepherd, (eds), London, 1985, p. 256.
76 Ibid.
77 W.H.R. Rivers, *Instinct and the Unconscious*, Cambridge , 1922, p. 205.
78 Quoted by Hibberd, *Owen the Poet*, p. 95.

79   Letter of R. Ross to E. Gosse, 19 July, 1917, in Sassoon, *Diaries 1915–1918*, pp. 181–2.
80   Ibid., p. 246.
81   Ibid., pp. 183–4.
82   S. Sassoon, *Siegfried's Journey*, p. 64.
83   S. Sassoon, *The Complete Memoirs of George Sherston*, p. 518.
84   P. Barker's recently published 'fictional' account of Sassoon at Craiglockhart in *Regeneration*, London, 1991, omits these tensions in Sassoon's relationship with Rivers.
85   J.S. Floyd, 'A Descriptive Account of Unpublished Letters of Siegfried Sassoon', PhD. thesis, University of Texas, 1972, p. 157.
86   Sassoon, *The Complete Memoirs of George Sherston*, pp. 521–2.
87   See Sassoon's letters in *Diaries 1915–1918*, pp. 183–98.
88   Ibid.
89   Ibid., p. 189.
90   Ibid., p. 191.
91   Sassoon, *The Complete Memoirs of George Sherston*, p. 523.
92   Floyd, 'A Descriptive Account of Unpublished Letters of Siegfried Sassoon', p. 158.
93   Sassoon, *The Complete Memoirs of George Sherston*, p. 541.
94   Sassoon, *Diaries 1915–1918*, pp. 193–4.
95   Sassoon, *The Complete Memoirs of George Sherston*, pp. 552–3.
96   R. Slobodin, *W.H. R. Rivers*, New York, 1978, pp. 58–73.
97   *TWP*, p. 96.
98   Sassoon, *Diaries 1915–1918*, p. 121.
99   Ibid., p. 175.
100 See C.M. Tylee, *The Great War and Women's Consciousness*, London, 1990.
101 *TWP*, p. 94.
102 Ibid., p. 109.
103 Ibid., p. 108.
104 Sassoon, *Diaries 1915–1918*, pp. 203, 252.
105 Ibid., p. 258.
106 Ibid., p. 261.
107 Ibid., p. 242.
108 Ibid., p. 218.
109 Ibid., p. 257.
110 Ibid., p. 243.
111 There is some evidence to suggest that Sassoon was troubled by his homosexuality whilst at Craiglockhart. See Hibberd, *Owen the Poet*, pp. 151 and 223.
112 Sassoon, *Diaries 1915–1918*, p. 242.

113 Ibid., p. 262.
114 *TWP*, p. 117.
115 Sassoon, *Diaries 1915–1918*, p. 278.
116 *TWP*, p. 127.
117 Ibid., p. 126.
118 Ibid., pp. 130–2.
119 S. Sassoon, *Diaries 1920–1922*, R. Hart-Davis, (ed.), London, 1981, p. 20.
120 Ibid., p. 71.
121 Ibid., p. 270.
122 Ibid., p. 74.
123 Ibid., p. 81.
124 Ibid., p. 86.
125 Ibid., p. 74.
126 Ibid., p. 154.
127 Ibid., p. 86.
128 Ibid., p. 136.
129 Ibid., p. 50.
130 Ibid., pp. 88–9.
131 Ibid., p. 57.
132 Ibid., p. 73.
133 Ibid., p. 280.
134 Ibid., p. 103.
135 Ibid., p. 225.
136 Ibid., p. 253.
137 Ibid., p. 74.
138 Ibid., p. 81.
139 Ibid., p. 53.
140 Floyd, *A Descriptive Account of Unpublished Letters of Siegfried Sassoon*, p. 224.
141 Ibid., p. 225.
142 Ibid., p. 306.
143 Ibid., p. 3.
144 Sassoon, *The Memoirs of George Sherston*, p. 17.
145 Ibid., p. 534.
146 Ibid., pp. 521–2, 534–5, 541–8.
147 Ibid., p. 646.
148 Ibid., p. 655.
149 Ibid., pp. 307, 329
150 Ibid., p. 302.
151 Ibid., p. 307.
152 Ibid., p. 329.
153 Ibid., p. 636.

154 Ibid., p. 425.
155 Ibid., pp. 532–3.
156 Floyd, *A Descriptive Account of Unpublished Letters of Siegfried Sassoon*, p. 332.
157 Sassoon, *The Complete Memoirs of George Sherston*, p. 483.
158 Sassoon, *Siegfried's Journey*, p. 69.
159 Ibid., p. 57.
160 Floyd, *A Descriptive Account of Unpublished Letters of Siegfried Sassoon*, p. 206.
161 Ibid., p. 31.
162 Ibid., p. 288.

4

Wilfred Owen

Wilfred Owen is the most famous and most praised of First World War poets. His name has become synonymous with 'war poetry' itself, and with the 'visionary compassion' which his work is said to express. Critics of the 1960s and 1970s take at face value Owen's own asseveration that 'the poetry is in the pity' and emphasise this aspect of his work. They find in these disturbing poems a humanist response to the horrors of modern warfare, and a debunking of imperialist notions of honour, glory, and patriotism, which is much to their (and our) political taste. Typical Victorian and Edwardian abstract afflatus is said to be replaced in Owen's poetry by 'realism'. Bernard Bergonzi says of Owen that, 'his absorption in the concrete realities of the front is complete',[1] whilst Jon Silkin argues that meeting Sassoon gave Owen 'the confidence to draw into his work a greater realism'.[2] Another critic goes so far as to speak of the 'straightforward reporting of experience' and the 'starkly realistic'[3] description to be found in Owen's poetry; this in spite of the obvious literariness of Owen's language and poetic form which both militate against any unproblematic, representationalist realism. In 1975, reviewing Jon Stallworthy's biography of the poet, Larkin hinted at the inadequacies of previous criticism, and prefigured more recent studies when he described somewhere behind Owen's poetry, 'a human problem that even after fifty years we are a long way from understanding'.[4] Since then, the most useful contribution to aiding our comprehension of this problem, and of Owen's work, has been made by Dominic Hibberd in a number of articles culminating in his book, *Owen the Poet*.[5]

Here Hibberd traces the development of Owen's 'poethood',

and shows through meticulous research and analysis the intertextuality of Owen's writing, and something of the fascinating relationship between the early love poems and the mature war poems. Full of insight as this is, Hibberd's view remains essentially Romantic and Humanist. Although some gestures are made in the direction of Owen's psychology, and in the direction of society's beliefs and mores, Hibberd's main concerns are *literary*. He is fascinated by what he calls Owen's 'peculiar imagination',[6] and by the 'strangeness and secrecy of his genius'.[7] The relationship between 'imagination' and 'reality' is manipulated by Hibberd to suggest that the war poems are rather more 'realistic' than the 'weird imaginings' of the pre-war work. Any 'unpleasantness' in Owen's poetry which might reflect badly on Owen from a bourgeois, liberal perspective is quickly relegated to the realms of the *literary* imagination, or to fantasy implicitly completely divorced from any 'reality'.[8] Owen's creative method is explained by quoting Wordsworth's Preface to the *Lyrical Ballads*,[9] and his 'true courage' is said to reside in his 'exposing his imagination to war experience as material for poetry'.[10] The 'task' of writing war poems based on 'war dreams' is described by Hibberd as 'both painful and dangerous'.[11] Owen then, remains very much the Romantic poet-hero in this book. And despite the greater complexity of Hibberd's approach compared with earlier critics, we hear again of 'realism' in the writing,[12] and Owen's own estimation of what he was doing and saying is repeated and endorsed. Thus a full chapter is devoted to 'The Pity of War', and in conclusion, Hibberd quotes from Owen's projected Preface and adds that Owen was 'true to his destined task of warning and pleading'.[13] What I wish to do in this chapter is to expose all this to further scrutiny and to interpret Hibberd's research from a different perspective. I want to return to the 'human problem' in Owen's work, and look again at his very complex reactions to the First World War in order to challenge the nature and role of 'pity' in his poetry, to re-evaluate his political stance, and where appropriate demonstrate the absence of anything approaching 'realism' in his work. All this will, as in previous chapters, emanate from a discussion of the place of suffering in Owen's life and oeuvre.

Harold Owen's memoirs, the *Collected Letters*, Stallworthy's biography, and Hibberd's book have made the ascertainable facts of Owen's life comparatively well known. It would be tedious to reproduce their work in detail here, yet it is, I think, worth looking again at various biographical aspects, since Owen's life can be 'read' (and written) in a variety of ways, and the reading of the life in my view has a crucial relationship to a reading of the poems. It is then, to a discussion of Owen's pre-war life that we now proceed.

Owen was born without the silver spoon that was so firmly placed into the mouth of Siegfried Sassoon. Nevertheless, his maternal grandfather had made enough money in business to build a very respectable, six-bedroom house in Oswestry, which was where Owen's parents, Tom and Susan, lived for the first years of their marriage, and where Wilfred was born in March, 1893. The first few years of Owen's life belong to the last years of the Owens' prosperity. In 1897 grandfather Shaw died leaving little but debts, and it became clear that the house would have to be sold. The family would now be obliged to live off Tom's relatively meagre earnings from his job as a clerk with the Great Western Railway. This burdensome financial situation was not eased by the fact that Wilfred already had a sister, Mary, born in 1895, and Susan Owen gave birth to another child, Harold, in September 1897. Colin Owen, the baby of the family, was born in 1900.

In 1897 the family moved from Shrewsbury to a terraced house in Wilmer Road, Birkenhead, a thoroughfare which Harold Owen describes as a 'long line of small, squalid, and near-slum dwellings'.[14] The family remained in Birkenhead until 1907, but they only remained at Wilmer Road a year, before moving in succession firstly to a semi-detached house in Elm Grove, and then to one situated in what Stallworthy describes as 'a slightly better-class locality'[15] at 51 Milton Road. Despite these peregrinations which clearly took the family away from working-class indigence towards at least lower-middle-class respectability, Harold Owen's account of these years is unremittingly gloomy. He speaks repeatedly of the 'perpetual struggle against poverty' and the 'threat of debt'[16] which weighed upon his mother and father, straining their relationship and thus affecting the children. Yet we are also given accounts of holidays in Ireland and Scarborough during these years, which bespeaks a family hardly on the breadline. From the perspective of the working class, the Owens cannot have been poor, but poverty, of course, is relative, and it seems likely that Harold Owen's account is coloured by the introjection of his parents' (and particularly his mother's) standards.

Susan Owen, it seems, was intent upon keeping up appearances which meant that her children were strictly segregated from their working-class neighbours. It also meant that the family, against the wishes of Mr. Owen, lived at the limit of their means, leaving no money available to cultivate a social circle amongst the Birkenhead bourgeoisie. Harold Owen records that this rendered the family 'classless'.[17] But they were not so much without class, as massively class conscious. They were in the position of 'not belonging' to the working class, and aspiring towards the middle to upper middle class. The lower middle class is viewed as an immensely uncomfortable, not to say unviable station. Wilfred cannot have escaped the influence of such attitudes, and they must have encouraged him to regard himself as one set apart. As we shall see, he also inherited a certain snobbishness which owes something to these years and to his mother's aspirations.

That money was not the only source of tension within the Owen family is further attested to by Harold Owen, who writes that at this time his parents found it 'difficult to agree upon major or minor points of any sort'.[18] Despite a genuine affection between the pair, Tom and Susan Owen seem to have been an ill-assorted couple. He loved an active, outdoor life, and pined for his youthful days of adventure when he had sailed before the mast to India, and worked there for some years. He also enjoyed cricket, and was possessed of a fine singing voice which he put to good use at concerts in the Seaman's Mission in Liverpool. It is said that he knew 'an almost endless range of songs which included nearly all the Gilbert and Sullivan works and many excerpts from serious opera'.[19] What Susan Owen made of Gilbert and Sullivan can only be guessed at, but suffice it to say that she was a devoutly religious evangelical Christian, who read her Bible daily and who was active in both the Temperance Society, and the British and Foreign Bible Society. Presumably she preferred her husband to sing hymns in church rather than regale sailors with light opera. Susan disapproved of her husband's nautical enthusiasms, and her physical enervation contrasted sharply with his athleticism. No doubt these differences of interest and temperament were initially a source of attraction between them, but under the strain of raising a family in less than ideal circumstances, they became the grounds for arguments in which the children, predictably, became the subject of disagreement.

Wilfred, being the first born, was the initial focus of dissension. Tom wished to encourage his son in those active, physical pursuits he so admired, perhaps envisaging for Wilfred the career of a sea captain which he would have liked for himself. But Susan Owen disapproved of all this, and formed a bond with her eldest son that only his early death could break. They were excessively close, with Susan encouraging Wilfred's introspective, scholarly ambitions, and leading him as she hoped, towards a career in the Church. Mary, who was a sickly child, also remained very close to her mother, though this caused less friction than Wilfred's case because of the difference in expectations then accepted as a result of her gender. Her schooling and career, sadly, do not seem to have figured much in the Owens' concerns. Furthermore, being a girl, and fragile as well, precluded her it seems from many of her father's interests, excursions, and ambitions. With Harold and Colin it was different. They developed an alliance with their father, in symmetrical reaction to the elder two children. Harold was particularly close to Tom, and at least to some extent fulfilled his father's wishes by going to sea at the age of sixteen.

These family dynamics were not, of course, as simple and absolute as they have been drawn above. Harold Owen is anxious to assure us that his father loved all the children dearly. Nevertheless, Wilfred's very close relationship to his mother, and difficult, rather estranged relationship with his father are, I think, significant in all that follows, particularly in Owen developing an image of himself as not a 'normal, manly, fellow'.[20] One of the immediate consequences in Birkenhead was that Wilfred was given preferential treatment in the matter of his education. In 1899 he was sent to the preparatory department of the Birkenhead Institute, and in 1901 began in the junior division of that school. In the complex class system of English Edwardian education, this grammar school lay somewhere, appropriately in the middle, between the elevated heights of the great public schools, and the depths of the free board schools. Harold Owen was consigned to the latter. Wilfred helped by a natural aptitude, and fuelled with his mother's ambition for him, made the most of his opportunity, and soon became an avid scholar often working long into the night over his books.

Unlike Brooke and Sassoon then, Owen did not suffer a public school; his education was less 'Classical'. But if he missed the peculiar psychological pressures that adolescents suffered in boarding schools, there was no shortage of stifling influences at home. As well as encouraging his scholarship, Susan Owen rigorously encouraged his religiosity. She taught him to emulate her daily Bible reading, and as Dominic Hibberd has observed, in 1903 'she pursued an especially serious course of Bible study with him, apparently in answer to some trouble that he was passing through.'[21] Hibberd goes on to quote various texts which are underlined in Susan Owen's Bible. They are marked with Wilfred's name and some of them are dated February 1903. Amongst these are: 'If we suffer, we shall also reign with him' (2 Timothy 2:12), and 'Satan hath desired to have you . . .But I have prayed for thee.' (Luke 22: 31–2). So at the age of ten, Wilfred was reading the second chapter of 2 Timothy, in which St. Paul exhorts Timothy to 'endure hardness as a good soldier of Jesus Christ', to 'shun profane and vain babblings', and to 'flee also youthful lusts'. He was also being taught that Satan was not above desiring power over little boys, and that to suffer was to be good. In the following years the intensity of this religious teaching did not abate; Mrs Owen was intent upon encouraging a Christian vocation.[22] The effect of this upon Owen's developing sexuality must have been profound. Much later Owen was to chastise his mother for keeping him in ignorance of sexual facts, but as an adolescent he was clearly taught that any sexual feelings were shameful and sinful. As I have remarked in previous chapters, the glorification of suffering offered by Christianity is concomitant with its advocacy of sexual repression and the cultivation of negative attitudes towards sexuality. Thus suffering begets suffering in an endless round.

That such a cycle was operative in the Owen family can be further demonstrated by considering Susan Owen's neurotic health problems. After the birth of Colin we are told that Susan Owen's health 'deteriorated rather seriously' although 'no specific physical disease' could be diagnosed. She had little energy and was massively hypochondriacal, symptoms which were, perhaps, the corollary of the self-sacrifice which she held up as an ideal. Hypochondria has connections with sado-masochism in that it not only entails a will to suffer, but also tends to impose suffering upon others. It seems axiomatic that those who sacrifice themselves, often demand that others be sacrificed also. And certainly this seems to have been the dynamic at work in the Owen family. Harold writes feelingly of rejecting his mother's exhortations concerning the 'absolute need always to practice' self-sacrifice. For his sister, it was not so easy:

My mother . . .had inculcated into the little girl such a powerful sense of duty and the need for filial devotion that it amounted to a form of self-sacrifice, an expression which my mother was inordinately fond of using . . .[Mary] accepted the doctrine only too easily and as a consequence became obsessed with an unnatural and far too adult sense of responsibility towards my mother's comforts and well-being, a sense which was later to develop into a self-effacing devotion of service to her, and much later still to turn to a nursing dedication, all of which left so little time to her for the cultivation of herself.[23]

As we know, Wilfred's ultimate self-sacrifice was to take a different form, but there can be little doubt that his mother's teaching was not lost upon him. By the time he was fourteen, his letters are demonstrating not only a solicitous concern for his mother's ailments, but also an equal concern for his own. At the same time, he was developing his interest in poetry and the example of Keats was always before him. The will to suffer, thus took on a further dimension; suffering even to death was the way of Romantic art. Again, Harold shrewdly remarks upon this connection:

his over eagerness to entertain the suggestion of death sprang from a concern for and an unhealthy absorption in his own state of health. This was beginning to grip him dangerously . . .Keats was ever-present in his mind, . . . I know that Wilfred was beginning to be convinced . . .that high attainment and the expected period of life were impossible to combine, and he was inclined when working well to fear it denoted early death; and when feeling robust and healthy to fear that this was a signal of lack of talent and a negation of all his hopes for literary achievement.[24]

It is hardly surprising then, that Owen's first surviving poems are fraught with sado-masochistic images. But before we look at these, we need to sketch in the rest of Owen's early life.

Unlike Harold, Wilfred seems to have been relatively happy at Birkenhead largely due to his enjoyment of school and of his relationship with his mother. Certainly the few published letters dating from this period evince little but cheerfulness expressed in a precociously articulate English. In 1907 the family left Birkenhead and went to Shrewsbury, where Wilfred attended the fee-paying technical school whilst Harold went to the board school again. Wilfred did well at this school, particularly in French and English. He read Spenser, Keats and Shakespeare under the careful tutelage of Miss Wright, the English mistress who did so much to develop Owen's interest in poetry. In the following years he also developed an interest in geology, botany and archaeology, which were also to be of importance in his later work.

After leaving school, Owen spent some time in 1911 as a temporary pupil teacher whilst he studied for his University of London matriculation exams. The school work proved heavier than he had expected, and this may have contributed to the fact that although he passed the matriculation exam, he did not achieve the pass with honours which he apparently needed in order to enable him to embark upon a degree. All through the early part of the year Owen and his family had been fretting about his future. At one stage he speaks of 'indecision rapidly turning into distraction'.[25] The immediate answer on failing to gain entrance to university was provided by a churchman friend of the family, who suggested that Wilfred should go as a lay assistant to a vicar who would give time and help for study, in return for Wilfred's work around the parish. Accordingly such a position was found with the Reverend Wigan, vicar of Dunsden, a small parish on the outskirts of Reading close to where Susan Owen's sister, Emma Gunston, lived with her family.

By the time Wilfred took up this position he had already written the first of his surviving poems. There are three poems dating from 1910–11 all of which are heavily influenced by Keats. 'To Poesy' is an ardent expression of Owen's desire that the muse should grace him with a secret kiss, 'far from men's gaze'. As Stallworthy has noted, the poem owes much to Keats's 'The Fall of Hyperion'. It is a youthful supplication torn between hope and fear, self-aggrandisement and self-deprecation. 'Written in a Wood, September 1910' is a remembrance of Keats's death, and expresses a determination yet to 'see fair Keats, and hear his lyre', whilst 'Sonnet' pays further homage being 'Written at Teignmouth on a Pilgrimage to Keats's house'. In verse clogged with lush adjectives and heavy with nineteenth-century afflatus, Owen celebrates the 'Mystic Doom' of his beloved subject. The sestet provides a final paean in which the poet apostrophises nature to mourn the loss of the poet. There is a positive relish of pain here:

> Eternally may sad waves wail his death,
> Choke in their grief 'mongst rocks where he has lain,
> Or heave in silence, yearning with hushed breath,
> While mournfully trail the slow-moved mists and rain,
> And softly the small drops slide from weeping trees,
> Quivering in anguish to the sobbing breeze.[26]

Two years later, Owen was still writing of being 'in love' with Keats.[27] And in the 'yearning', 'quivering', 'sobbing' of this poem we may detect the sublimated sexuality which is a large part of his response to the 'dead youth'.

Wilfred spent from October 1911 to February 1913 at Dunsden. It was an intensely unhappy time for him which culminated in mental and physical breakdown. There were several reasons for this. As the poems discussed above might suggest, Owen's earlier religious enthusiasms were now being 'spilled' into Romantic art. Love for Keats seems to have overtaken love for Christ. The conflict thus engendered involved more than a simple intellectual tension between art and religion. We will recall Susan Owen's ambitions for her son; she had by no means relinquished the hope that he would become a clergyman. A relative estrangement from his father, together with his mother's religiosity and her passionate love for him, conspired to repress and oppress the development of Owen's sexuality as well as to complicate the issue of his allegiance to poetry or to the church. Whilst he was at Dunsden there is plenty of evidence to suggest that he was sexually very confused, and that art was ranged with sensuality against religion in his mind. He was in the position of trying to free himself from the influence of his mother and of the church in order to give his sexuality and art free expression. But the tensions here were fraught with guilt, and although he could eventually boast that he had 'murdered his false creed'[28] (i.e. Christianity), the sexual and emotional problems centred upon his mother were much less tractable, and were only partially solved at the time of his death. It is worth looking at his Dunsden experience in some detail, as it provides considerable insight into the psychology which produced a rash of pre-war poems.

Among Owen's duties at the vicarage were visiting the sick and poor, and running the church youth group. These activities led him to experience relationships which, rather than strengthening his Christian faith, had implications at variance with strict evangelical doctrine. He had not been long at Dunsden before he developed what Stallworthy has called 'an adolescent crush' upon a boy from the youth club named Vivian Rampton. Owen went for walks and had tea with the boy, 'unbeknown to the Parish . . .and the vicarage in particular'.[29] There is speculation that this relationship was the cause of the final 'furore' at the vicarage in January 1913, which precipitated Owen's departure. However this may be, it is certain that in March 1912 there was romance in Owen's life, and Rampton was not its only source.

Owen found himself revising his prejudices against working-class young men. The sons of ploughmen, he discovers, are not all 'round vacant eyes and mouth and intellects to correspond'. On the contrary he finds them possessed of '(sometimes) fine features, and (somehow) nice manners'. He goes on to say that he wishes he could enlarge upon his experiences and the 'thoughts they engender'.[30] If he had risked further articulation, I suspect he would have been led in similar directions to Edward Carpenter's idealisations of working-class men. Certainly there is passion in Owen's description of giving tea to another young ploughman whom he describes as 'an Ambrose'.[31] And at the Keswick evangelical convention of July 1912, Owen was struck by a 'Northumberland lad', whom he perceived as a paragon of Christian virtue: 'The watching of his conduct, conversation, expression of countenance during meetings, bids fair to speak louder to my soul than the thunderings of twenty latter day Prophets from their rostra upon these everlasting hills.'[32]

Owen goes on to say that the 'scar-backed mining lad' represents Christianity in action, and that 'no profane word' passes his lips 'tho pricked with piercing pain and surrounded by the grossest human mud that ever sank to a pit's bottom'.

Passion and compassion become indistinguishable here, and both are given distinctly literary expression. 'Pain' is noticeably the occasion for particular linguistic relish. Rather than instigating Christian charity, Owen's observations are the catalyst for sensuous composition. We may observe the same phenomenon in Owen's description of his visits to the sick and poor. Having indulged in a particularly vivid description of one such visit in a letter to his sister, he goes on to ask, as if he is not quite sure himself, 'Why am I telling you these dreadful things'. The answer he gives himself and Mary, is one he will repeat again later in a different context: he is, he says, trying to 'educate' his sister in the 'Book of Life'.[33] It is an open question whether life and its victims, or the Book are uppermost in Owen's thoughts. Certainly suffering and literature are rarely separated in his mind. He was delighted, for instance, to discover that Shelley also often visited the sick and the poor, thereby vindicating Owen in his activities, as well as confirming Shelley as one who wrote 'marvellous verse' from a 'lovely' life.[34]

Elsewhere a consumptive child becomes the occasion of a rhetorical flourish learnt from Dickens. Following a description of 'poor Violet' and her destitute family we have this expostulatory imitation: 'This, I suppose, is only a typical *case*; one of many *Cases*! O hard word! How it savours of rigid, frigid professionalism! How it suggests smooth and polished, formal, labelled, mechanical callousness!'[35] If the influence of Dickens is covert here, it is made overt in a now famous letter wherein Owen seeks to ally himself with the 'British School of revolt and reconstruction' as exemplified by 'Burns, Shelley, Byron, Wordsworth, Coleridge and Tennyson.' These and other writers have formed in Owen's mind a formidable opposition to the Revd Wigan:

I am increasingly liberalising and liberating my thought, spite of the Vicar's strong Conservatism. And when he paws his beard, and wonders whether £10 is too high a price for new curtains for the dining room, . . . then the fires smoulder; I could shake hands with Mrs. Dilber who stole Scrooge's Bed-Curtains; and was affronted that old Joe was surprised, or questioned her right! From what I hear straight from the tight-pursed lips of wolfish ploughmen in their cottages, I might say there is material ready for another revolution. Perhaps men will *strike*, not with absence from work; but with arms at work. Am I for or against upheaval? I know not; I am not happy in these thoughts; yet they press upon me. I am happier when I go to '*distribute dole*

> To poor sick people, richer in His eyes,
> Who ransomed us, and haler too than I.'

These lines I quote, have haunted me incessantly.[36]

The idea of political agitation by members of the working class makes Owen nervous in a typically middle class way. He is much happier with the idea of distributing dole to the sick who are yet healthier than he is. Suffering, illness, and literature are inextricably bound together in Owen's psyche. It is no wonder then that Tennyson's lines 'haunted' him, as his letters from Dunsden are punctuated with reports of his own ill health.

From February 1912 until he left Dunsden a year later in a state of mental and physical collapse, Owen regularly complained of feeling unwell. There are attacks of indigestion, feelings of 'unwonted' depression, intimations of 'morbidity of temperament', headache and nausea. The consolation for all this was that he could describe himself to his mother in July as 'an invalid and a poet'. After the Keswick convention, which clearly helped to bring the tensions in Owen's position to the fore, Owen spent a few days at home before returning to Dunsden feeling 'flabby and unstable'. Inevitably, this leads him to 'set down some verses.' He records at the same time a 'feeling of pent-up grief' which is 'not altogether an unpleasant feeling, but so strange and unusual'.[37] A few days later on 14 August, he speaks of falling off his bicycle and grazing his knuckles. This seemingly trivial incident provokes the following:

I was washing some of the dirt out of the wound, & had applied some of my Carbolic Ointment, when sudden twilight seemed to fall upon the world, an horror of great darkness closed around me – strange noises and a sensation of swimming underwater overtooked [sic] me, and in fact I fell into a regular syncope. I did not fall down however, nor yet lose all consciousness; but the semi-blindness, and the chill were frightful. . .

O it was a blissful moment when the lights were turned up again in my head! And the sensation of quickening circulation and warmth was like the Return of Spring for deliciousness. I found myself indeed in an icy sweat and of a really beautiful and romantic pallor. Half an hour later I had tea, and was keenly hungry.[38]

This is not the end of the account, every detail of the recovery is told. There is a morbid relish and self-dramatisation here; Owen's imagination is as much moved by his own suffering as it is by that of other people.

The fascination with his physical condition manifest here, has a corollary in Owen's psyche. From August until the final debacle in January, Owen consistently reports to his mother upon the state of his nerves. Reading Rossetti's *Life of Keats* becomes an occasion for Owen to admit that he has 'more than once turned hot and cold and trembly over the first haemorrhage scene'. Still speaking of Keats, he continues:

But I never guessed till now the frightful travail of his soul towards Death; never came so near laying hold of the ghastly horror of his mind at this time. Rossetti guided my groping hand right into the wound, and I touched, for one moment the incandescent Heart of Keats.[39]

Religious ecstasy has become literary ecstasy, and like the former, the latter seems to be predicated upon sado-masochistic sexuality. Pleasure is gained from probing wounds, which in turn give access to the beloved's 'heart'.

A month later, Owen further discusses his nerves, assuring his mother that he has a 'tingling capacity for pleasure on occasion', but that this is purchased at the price of having 'nerves exquisitely responsive to painful sensation'.[40] One imagines that 'tingling pleasure' might sound somewhat dangerous to the Puritanical Susan Owen, and that she found pain somewhat safer. For his part, there is little enough evidence in the letters of any pleasure except in pain. A few days later he is experiencing a 'dervishy vertigo',[41] and in December he variously reports that his nerves are in 'a shocking state', that his 'breast is continually "too full"'[42] and that he is 'weak as water about the "nerves"'.[43] He went home to Shrewsbury for Christmas, and shortly after returning to Dunsden, on 4 January 1913, he wrote the following letter to his mother. It has been savagely edited by Harold Owen,[44] so that the first page is missing as is a further crucial half-page, leaving us to guess, rather than know exactly what occurred:

The furor [*several words missing*] now abated in the Vicarage, thank Mnemosyne; but I hope that I, who 'discovered' him something over a year ago, may [*half page missing*] but the Vicar's presence (taciturn instead of wontedly gay) symbolic of my stern Destiny, sat heavy on my soul the night . . .

Murder will out, and I have murdered my false creed. If a true one exists, I shall find it. If not, adieu to the still falser creeds that hold the hearts of nearly all my fellow men.

Escape from this hotbed of religion I now long for more than I could ever have conceived a year and three months ago . . .

To leave Dunsden will mean a terrible bust-up; but I have no intention of sneaking away by smuggling my reasons down the backstairs. I will vanish in thunder and lightning, if I go at all.[45]

The consensus so far is that the 'discovered' person alluded to here is Vivian Rampton. However this may be, it is implicit in Owen's subsequent record of various interviews with the Vicar, that the Revd Wigan felt that if Owen were to remain at Dunsden he would have to give up the idea of writing verse, and that he would have to forego contact with the village children. These conditions were unacceptable to Owen and he left Dunsden in early February.

On returning home, Owen immediately fell ill with 'congestion of the lungs', and was avidly nursed by his mother. Six months earlier Owen had written to his 'most sweet among mothers': 'O how do I stand (yes and sit, lie, kneel and walk, too) in need of some physical caress from you.'[46] His illness clearly enabled him to obtain such succour and to escape from his religious and sexual dilemmas. Rather than being distressed and censorious, considering that Wilfred had abandoned all thought of a career in the Church, Susan Owen was manoeuvred into the position of supporter and nurse. She even collaborated with Owen's literary ambitions to the extent of believing his illness to be the onset of TB. It wasn't. Nevertheless 1913 found Owen an 'invalid and a poet', rather than a priest or a lover.

The poems from this period, as might be expected, express the conflicts we have been looking at so far, with more intensity and less restraint than in the letters. There are three poems, 'Lines Written on My Nineteenth Birthday', 'Supposed Confessions of a Secondrate Sensitive Mind in Dejection' and 'The Dread of Falling into Naught' which explore Owen's sado-masochistic emotions. The first of these was written on the occasion of a dyspepsic attack. Both the origins of this poem, and its portentousness are apt to be amusing. Nevertheless the psychology it reveals is significant. Owen questions in the poem why it is that he is experiencing 'Pain today?' Answering his own question he avers that this is his 'rightful share'. And in so suffering he attracts the ministrations of friends, yet misses the eyes and voice of his mother whose 'portrait' he 'oft kisses'. All this leads to the scribbling of 'these few lines', and to the following conclusion:

> For there have been revealed to me
> Heart-secrets since the coming of this day,
> Making me thankful for its thorn-paved way.

Among them this: 'No joy is comparable
Unto the *Melting* – soft and gradual –
Of Torture's needles in the flesh. To sail
Smoothly from out the abysmal anguish-jail
And tread the placid plains of *normal ease*
Is sweeter far, I deem, than all the glees
Which we may catch by mounting higher still
Into the dangerous air where actual Bliss doth thrill.'[47]

Pain and release from pain are favourably compared with the dangerous air of 'actual Bliss'. Torture is preferred to sexual orgasm. The frustration of Eros leads to a hymn of pain which is immediately dispatched in a letter to his mother, thereby ensuring her vicarious suffering as well – masochism thus leading to sadism.

Both 'Supposed Confessions of a Secondrate Sensitive Mind in Dejection' (the title of which may be thought painful enough) and 'The Fear of Falling into Naught', figure conflicts which can be directly attributed to Owen's relationship with his mother. In the former poem 'Despondency' is personified as a Medusa figure whom the poet is powerless to resist and who gives rise to violent, sado-masochistic dreams. But she also indirectly gives rise to poetry. 'Despondency' has much in common with Owen's mother. He both craved her caress, but knew he should not. Furthermore, she is the agent of his sexual repression, teaching him to hate his own sexual feelings, thereby giving rise to the sado-masochism which characterises their relationship, and which characterises the dreams he suffered from at Dunsden. Some time after leaving the vicarage he wrote that his nights there were 'terrible to be borne'.[48] But out of these dreams, and out of the conflict between his mother and his sexual feelings arose the poems that Owen so wished to write. A similar complex of ideas and emotions is expressed in 'The Dread of Falling into Naught' which was written in September 1912. Here there is a movement from a fear of 'falling into naught' to a positive wish for the same. What is frightening to the poet is a separation from nature which is variously figured as an old ailing woman, and as 'mother-earth'. But 'Poetry' leads him back to the comforts of the maternal breast where he is seemingly content to expire. The poem prefigures Owen's flight from Dunsden towards the maternal bosom which is at once comforting, but also threatening. The 'fear of falling into naught' is both the fear of separation from his mother and the fear of over-attachment to her.

As well as these dramatisations of psychological tension modelled on those of Keats and Shelley, Owen wrote several poems and fragments at Dunsden which deal with another aspect of his difficulties: his relationship with children. Some of these are addressed to a female child, probably his 'favourite' Milly Montague or the consumptive Violet Franklin, others have more obvious relevance to Vivian Rampton. The former poems are the more complex, as they struggle to articulate passionate yet chaste emotions which are predicated upon the child's 'innocence'. Two fragments, "Tis but love's shadow' and 'I heard low sobbing as I passed her door' seem to be exercises working towards the completed 'Impromptu' which was written in January 1913, and constitutes a hymn to a child's 'sinless' affections. The poem asserts that 'Mother and Bretheren, Teachers, Holy Guides' who in the past have been dear to him, will not understand his 'last woe', there is only one who will:

> I once had hopes of heaven, whereon I slept and smiled,
> But a cold hand awoke me from that dream.
>
> Only thy youth, fair child, thy beauty, joy, and youth,
> Can give me all I want, heart-ease and rest.
>
> Though thou art ignorant of what dark books may hold,
> Or darker pages of real human life
>
> Yet thou art not too young, too holy-innocent,
> To pity one in pain for human sin.[49]

Owen goes on to implore the child to hold his face in her hands, and to open her 'infinite vast eyes' upon him, so that his 'life' will 'melt out into their depth', and he can 'die away' content to live in the 'memory of her mind', to 'lie casketed' in her head. Here, as in the fragments, it is as if Owen feels guilty about his erotic impulses and so self-consciously sublimates them into a chaste and salving relationship with an innocent girl child. Comparisons with Brooke's cult of youth exemplified by his admiration for *Peter Pan*, and his obsessions with 'cleanliness' help to demonstrate that Owen's feelings were not quite so unusual as they might sound today.

In other poems, however, Owen strives to combat his guilt

feelings and to celebrate Eros. The best example of this is to be found in 'The Time was Aeon', a poem begun at Dunsden, but not finally completed until the summer of 1915. The poem begins by asserting that the experience to be recounted is 'not a dream,/But true resumption of experienced things'. Owen goes on in melodramatic fashion to paint a scene of 'vast deformity' which is nevertheless 'made lovely by pervasion of the spirit'. A 'Presence there' creates 'low rich music' transforming the 'sordid'. We are soon vouchsafed that this malignant place is the world and that the name of the 'unapparent spirit' is 'An evil Angel's'. Paradoxically the name of the 'regnant Presence' is 'the Flesh':

> It bore the naked likeness of a boy
> Flawlessly moulded, fine exceedingly,
> Beautiful unsurpassably – so much
> More portraiture were fond futility
> For even thought is not long possible,
> Becoming too soon passion: and meseemed
> His outline changed, from beauty unto beauty,
> As change the contours of slim, sleeping clouds.[50]

There are several more lines of this celebration before Owen metamorphoses the 'Flesh' back into a 'statue' which resembles 'strong music' opposed to the 'huge disorder of the place'. But he then goes on to describe those who revile the art and homoerotic passion which are clearly represented by this fleshly statue:

> Then watched I how there ran towards that way
> A multitude of railers, hot with hate,
> And maddened by the voice of a small Jew
> Who cried with a loud voice, saying 'Away!
> Away with him!' and 'Crucify him! Him,
> With the affections and the lusts thereof.'

Here Owen conflates a text from St Paul's Epistle to the Galatians, with the Gospels' account of the crowd baying for Christ's crucifixion. One of the effects of this is to equate Christ with the 'affections and the lusts', with sensuality, sexuality and art. A Romantic view of Christ thus triumphs over an evangelical one. And it is not difficult to perceive how small a step Owen had to take in order to see the soldier 'lads' dying on the Western Front as Christ-like figures, apt subjects for art.

But we should beware of reading 'The Time was Aeon' as a

completely unequivocal renunciation of evangelical Christianity, in the way that both Welland and Hibberd prefer. There are still traces of Owen's guilty ambivalence about the 'flesh' in this poem. We are told for instance that the 'flesh' constitutes an 'evil name'. And notwithstanding the hymn to the boy's beauty which is the emotional centre of the poem, Owen's transformation of the flesh into 'statue' and 'music' still bespeaks a difficulty with the flesh as flesh. If we bear this in mind, the final lines of the poem may also be read in a less than straightforward way. St Paul's assertion 'they that are Christ's have crucified the flesh with the affections and lusts' is based on the central metaphor of Christianity, i.e. that physical crucifixion leads to spiritual salvation. In Christianity the crucifixion is a good, despite the hatred that engendered it. The Romantic transformation of this metaphor suggests that the crucifixion of the artist is a good, since it engenders art. Something of this lingers in Owen's poem. It is possible to feel that he would still 'crucify' the 'affections and the lusts' for art, if not for Christ.

Owen remained ill until April 1913. After convalescing in Torquay for a time, he decided to sit for the Reading University scholarship exams in May. He failed to gain a scholarship, and in August he seems to have suffered something of a relapse to his health in the form of a bronchial attack. Both mother and son were convinced that this was incipient TB despite the doctor's assurances to the contrary. Nevertheless, the doctor agreed that to winter in France would do Wilfred no harm. This plan accorded well with his own wishes, and in September he set off for the Berlitz English School in Bordeaux where he had gained part-time employment as a teacher. Owen spent the best part of the next two years in France doing his best to further the 'liberalising and liberating' that had begun at Dunsden. At first he was unhappy in France, and by November 1913 he was ill again. This time with gastro-enteritis. In a long letter to his mother marked 'PRIVATE' (an injunction he was to repeat later in several of his letters from the Western Front) he enthusiastically detailed his sufferings and enquired after his mother's, since she had been having trouble with toothache.[51] Health (or perhaps more accurately sickness) dominates much of the correspondence for the next few months, but gradually Owen's spirits seem to have revived, although his mother's interminable 'headaches' continued for the duration of his stay in France.

One cause of her troubles was evidently a fear that 'Baby Wulfie'[52] might fall in love. In a letter of February 1914 Owen seems to be responding to some enquiry of his mother's when he embarks upon a gentle remonstrance. He has, he says, never been 'so absolutely free of "heart-trouble" within these ten years past'. He continues:

This will no doubt give you immense satisfaction. But it *should* not. . . You ought not to discourage too hard.

If you knew what hands have been laid on my arm, in the night, along the Bordeaux streets, or what eyes play upon me in the restaurant where I daily eat, methinks you would wish that the star and adoration of my life had risen; or would quickly rise.

But never fear: thank Home, and Poetry, and the FORCE behind both. And rejoice with me that a calmer time has come for me; and that fifty blandishments cannot move me like ten notes of a violin or a line from Keats.

All women, without exception, *annoy* me, and the mercenaries . . .I utterly detest; more indeed than as a charitable being, I ought.[53]

There are glimmerings of a new self-consciousness here. Whilst Mrs. Owen is still implicitly acknowledged as the 'FORCE' behind his poetry which in turn keeps him chaste, there is also a recognition that her attitude to his love life is damaging. He is also dimly aware that his attitude to women is not entirely laudable. He further admonishes his mother for having kept him in ignorance of matters sexual: 'If you never had any revelations to make to me at fourteen' he says, 'I shall have no confession now I am 21. At least none such as must make me blush and weep and you grow pale.'[54]

That Owen was free of 'heart trouble' may have as much to do with the distance that he had put between himself and his mother, as it had with being disentangled from his 'protégés' in Dunsden. More certain is the fact that Owen was still struggling to come to terms with his sexuality. As we have seen from the Dunsden experience, he was impassioned by young male beauty, but there is also some evidence to suggest that young women were also beginning to attract him. For instance, in a letter to his sister of April 1914, Owen describes an outing with some friends on which occasion he met the Poitu family, including their sixteen-year-old daughter, Henriette. She is described by Owen as 'a superb specimen of human beauty', who at the dinner table reduced him to sitting 'like an Egyptian piece of Statuary, hands on knees, staring apparently into space; but seeing well enough to count how often the marvellous eyes looked in my direction.' Owen was not, however, rendered completely powerless by Henriette. In the afternoon there was a walk, with he and Henriette 'arm-in-arm', and he 'could scarcely have been happier'. The memory, he says, will remain sweet to him because he 'took no *advantage* of that young and ardent nature'. He returned home to pen 'fifty lines of poetry in as many minutes'.[55] Dominic Hibberd has tentatively identified these as part of the 'Perseus' fragments to which he has done more than justice. All that I would wish to add here is that the confusion in the poem as to the gender of the beloved, may not be merely Owen trying to 'disguise' his homosexuality, but rather an expression of genuine bisexual feelings.

In June 1914 Owen was invited by 'an elegant Parisian pupil of his, Mme Léger' to accompany her and her family to the Pyrenees for the summer months in the capacity of a private tutor. Owen gleefully accepted this proposition, as the work at the Berlitz school had been extremely arduous. He was also pleased as he seemed to be gaining an entrée into social circles which had remained closed to him in England. Just as much as his mother wished, Owen hungered to escape his lower-middle-class origins. On arrival in France he told his friends and acquaintances that he came from an aristocratic family, and now he was introduced into the lives of the wealthy. Mme Léger ran an interior decorating business in Paris and Bordeaux, whilst Monsieur had abandoned engineering for a career in the theatre. He was now retired and was considerably older than his wife. Mme Léger developed an attraction both mental and physical to Owen who was at pains to reassure his mother that all was well, that Mme had not been on the stage, and that he, Wilfred, did not give 'two pins' for Madame's *coquetterie*.[56] Indeed he seems to have been as much interested in Madame's eleven-year-old daughter, Nénette, as he was with the older woman. He speaks at length of the child in several letters, but remarks that he is 'alas or happily, who shall say? – too old to be in love'[57] with her.

Owen arrived in Bagnères-de-Bigorre for his stay with the Légers at the end of July. A few days later the war began and made 'a great stir'. 'Nobody', reported Owen, 'is very gay'.[58] Nobody, that was, except Owen. A few days after writing the above he declares himself to be 'immensely happy and famously well'.[59] And he seems to have continued in this state of mind for the rest of his stay. One of the contributing factors in his ongoing contentment was the friendship that he developed at this time with Laurent Tailhade. Tailhade was fifty-nine, a poet of the Decadence 'who had been at the centre of Parisian artistic society in its most famous period'.[60] On their second meeting Tailhade greeted Owen 'like a lover' and positively 'slobbered' over him.[61] Like many other aesthetes of the decadence Tailhade seems to have had a penchant for young men. He also relished the sado-masochism which is such a striking feature of the period's writing, and himself penned an essay on masochism. He also introduced Owen to Flaubert, and it was the grotesqueries of *La Tentation de Saint-Antoine* and *Salammbo* that attracted both Tailhade and his young disciple.

In October Mme Léger left France for a business trip to Canada. She had invited Owen to join her, but he predictably enough remained prudent and turned down this offer. Instead Owen got a job as a tutor to two boys, Johnny and Bobby de la Touche, living in Merignac just outside Bordeaux. Eventually they were supposed to be going to England to attend a public school, but difficulties with Channel crossings delayed this, as it also delayed Owen's return to England. In the event it does not seem that he was over-anxious to leave France. It was not until May 1915 that he travelled to England to despatch some errands for one M Peyronnet, a scent manufacturer who had offered Owen work. Wilfred only remained in England for a few weeks before returning to Bordeaux. He eventually returned to England again in September 1915, accompanying the de la Touche boys and seeing them off to school before going on to Shrewsbury.

In the meantime Owen continued his 'course in the University of Life'. By January 1915, he says, he has already taken this course, and gained diplomas 'sealed with many secret seals'.[62] There are rumours that Owen had his first truly sexual experiences in Bordeaux. Perhaps he was encouraged in these by Tailhade. Certainly the elder poet will have done little to discourage the idea that poetry was allied to homosexuality and a trembling sensibility. Robert Graves, not always the most reliable witness in these matters, says that Wilfred Owen told him in 1918 that he had 'picked up young men in Bordeaux but never overcome guilt feelings sufficiently for any lasting relationship'.[63] Having carefully negotiated the advances of Mme Léger, and the different attractions of Nénette, Owen living alone again in Bordeaux certainly sought out the company of young men. The full extent of his sexual experience, however, cannot be accurately gauged.What can be remarked is that in the 1915 letters there is a lack of commentary about his own health. His mother's ailments, however, still drew regular remarks from him, and in February he 'celebrated' the anniversary of the onset of pneumonia two years previously, by remembering his mother's ministrations to him at that time. These memories give rise to 'a sweet anguish, an ecstasy, (very difficult to describe, but something like the effect of a great music)'.[64] Despite enjoying himself with the Légers, with Tailhade, and in Bordeaux, and despite their liberating influences, Owen was still far from settling the psychological problems that had beset him at Dunsden.

The few poems Owen wrote during his time in France testify to this. As Hibberd has noted the 'Perseus' fragments are full of evidence of sexual confusion and of sado-masochistic imagery.[65] 'Long ages past in Egypt' is similarly violent. The poem is addressed to a deity who is 'the last fulfilment/Of all the wicked, and of all the beautiful', and furthermore is 'the face reflected in a mirror/Of wild desire, of pain, of bitter pleasure'. Desire is equated with sinfulness, pain with pleasure. And no wonder, since the deity in question, who has a 'face fairer than a flower', rejoices in murder:

> But with a little knife so wantonly
> Thou slewest women and thy pining lovers,
> And on thy lips the stain of crimson blood,
> And on thy brow the pallor of their death.[66]

D.S.R. Welland has noted that the 'real motivation behind the poem seems to have been only a surfeit of Swinburne and Wilde, as is apparent from the heavily accented alliteration, the reliance on a naively-employed sensuous imagery'.[67] That Owen was at this time falling under the influence of Decadent writers, French as well as English, cannot be questioned. But the point, I think, is that Owen's psychology dictated a very strong reaction to this reading matter. He was drawn to it because it was expressing conflicts which he was experiencing. The violent deity addressed in the poem may owe something to Wilde's 'The Sphinx', but equally it may have to do with the 'phantasms' that made his nights 'horrible to be borne' during the Dunsden crisis.

All was not, however, horror and nightmare. Between August and October 1914 Owen wrote a celebration of Nénette Léger's 'loveliness' in a poem entitled 'The Sleeping Beauty'. The burden of the poem is that she is too young to be awoken, and he cannot play the role of Prince Charming:

> So back I drew from that Princess,
> Because it was too soon, and not my part,
> To start voluptuous pulses in her heart,
> And kiss her to the world of consciousness.[68]

If he felt thus constrained with Nénette, he seems to have felt less so with the male subject of an 'Impromptu' composed about a year later in Bordeaux. The opening of the poem has affinities with his later celebration of loving comradeship, 'Greater Love'. Here, however, Owen remains gentle and celebratory; violence is for the moment banished:

> Now, let me feel the softness of thy hand –
> For it is softer than the breasts of girls,
> And warmer than the pillows of their cheeks,
> And richer than the fullness of their eyes,
> And stronger than the ardour of their hearts.[69]

Another two stanzas continue this extravagant praise of the beloveds 'hand', before a further three are devoted to the child's eyes which are said to 'bless' the poet 'with a bliss unguessed of God'.

Owen's writings were not abundant at this time, as he remarked to his mother in February 1915: 'All winter, all last year and longer I have read no poetry, nor thought poetically.'[70] And although this does not seem to have been literally the case, it is not far removed from the truth. This is, I think, of some significance in dealing, as I now wish to, with Owen's response to the war. Hibberd has written that Owen's 'early responses to the crisis were characteristic of the period, with little trace of either originality or scepticism'.[71] He has further opined that what made Owen finally decide to volunteer was 'the simple conviction that Germany had to be resisted and that calls for reinforcements could not be ignored after the Gallipoli losses'.[72] I do not agree with

Hibberd upon these matters. Owen's political response may have been unremarkably conservative, but his personal responses to the conflict were anything but conventional. The fact that he waited so long to volunteer is in itself surely worth some discussion. And the letters he wrote from Bordeaux, Bagnères and Merignac during the first year of the war enable us to trace his changing attitudes closely, and they are sufficiently idiosyncratic to be discussed in some detail.

A few days after the beginning of hostilities Owen boastfully wrote to his younger brother Colin that, 'After all my years of playing soldiers, and then of reading History, I have almost a mania to be in the East, to see fighting, and to serve. For I like to think this is the last War of the World!'[73] This was his first and last conventional response. Owen's 'mania' either passed very quickly, or was a fabrication of braggadocio made to impress his little boy-scouting brother. For later in the same month he speaks of his happiness, before admitting that the war affects him 'less than it ought'. He is, he says, adopting the 'perfect English custom of dealing with an offender': ignoring him. Owen feels his own life 'all the more precious . . .in the presence of this deflowering of Europe' and coolly suggests that 'the guns will effect a little useful weeding'. In a similarly unabashed manner he continues: 'I regret the mortality of the English regulars less than that of the French, Belgian, or even Russian or German armies: because the former are all Tommy Atkins, poor fellows, while the continental armies are inclusive of the finest brains and temperaments of the land.'[74] This is very much Owen the aspiring aristocrat in whom compassion is conspicuously absent. And it is surely misleading to suggest that such attitudes were 'characteristic of the period'. The numbers of volunteers who came forward in the autumn of 1914 surely gives the lie to this idea.

In December he broaches the subject of his role in the war again. Speaking of the *Daily Mail*'s attack on the 'duties shirked by English young men', Owen confesses to feeling some 'shame' but, 'while those ten thousand lusty louts go on playing football I shall go on playing with my little axiom: that my life is worth more than my death to Englishmen'.[75] The massively unfeeling and superior attitude to the working class here sits uneasily with those critics who have tried to make Owen a champion of the left. He is convinced at this stage that his potential as a poet is sufficient reason to stay free of the war. As time went on, however, he suffered further prickings of conscience. These were allayed in a different manner. It is not his value as a potential poet that salves, but the sufferings of his recent past. His conscience, he says, 'is easily cleared by the recollection of certain happenings'[76] in his past. And again two months later he writes: 'I could not bear to draw comparisons with the life of the trenches and mine; unless I felt in a manner to have suffered my share of life. And I feel I have.'[77]

This is perhaps signal of the depths of mental anguish the Dunsden experience had cost him, otherwise the comparison between his nervous collapse and the slaughter and sufferings of trench warfare seem curiously ill conceived. It can and has been argued that Owen at this stage was as blissfully ignorant of the brutal realities of war as were many other non-combatant civilians. But this is not the case. In a letter pre-dating the last two quoted he describes to his brother in elaborate detail, embellished with pencil drawings, the horrific wounds he has witnessed on a visit to the local hospital in Bordeaux with 'the Doctor Sauvaitre'. There is a relish in this communication, reminiscent of letters concerning his own and his mother's health problems. Owen dwells upon the 'crushed shinbone' which 'the doctor had to twist . . . and push . . . like a piston to get out the pus'. Further details include a knee with a hole through it, and 'a head into which a ball had entered and come out again'. The pencil drawings are large and graphic, complete with diagrammatic arrows and in one case, a label pointing to a foot covered in 'dirt and blood'. Following all this Owen says to his brother, who was then serving in the Merchant Navy under the threat of submarine attack, 'I deliberately tell you all this to educate you to the actualities of the war.' And, most curiously concludes that, 'I was not much upset by the morning at the hospital; and this is a striking proof of my health'.[78]

Apart from demonstrating that Owen had at least some inkling as to the 'actualities' of war some twelve months before he enlisted, this letter I think, is also very illuminating with respect to Owen's psychology and its attendant emotional confusions. There is clearly a pressure to communicate what he has seen, yet an almost boastful expression of how little moved he has been by this encounter. And the ostensible motivation to educate his brother strikes one as a rationalisation rather than as a convincing imperative directing the utterance. Like his earlier letter from Dunsden 'educating' his sister about the 'dreadful things' in the village, we feel Owen's ambivalent fascination with suffering, before we are convinced by his pedagogic ambition. In both letters we are not far removed from some of the procedures of his war poems, where all manner of sufferings are rendered in close detail in order to 'educate' a supposedly ignorant civilian population.

In 1914, however, Owen *was* happy and healthy enough, not to rush headlong towards the sufferings of the trenches. It was not until June 1915 that he seriously began to consider enlisting. He was at this time still privately tutoring in France, but the future was unsettled and uncertain. Peyronnet had spoken of Owen representing his affairs in the east, but the Dardanelles campaign had intervened. Owen found himself in a position which had caused his family (and particularly his father) great concern for several years. He was, as he admitted, without a footing in life, with only his ambition to be a poet giving him a precarious toehold. On 20 June he wrote to his mother that if the Dardanelles campaign was not successfully concluded by September, then he would join up. He goes on to say that he hopes things in the Dardanelles will 'last out as long as the war, which will be through the winter', because he now does 'most *intensely want to fight*'.[79] What has brought on this bellicose ambition is not entirely clear. The pressure of conscience will have played a part, as will the lack of viable alternatives. But a more powerful and pertinent motivation was at work. On the last day of June he wrote again to his mother and remarked thinking much about Hilaire Belloc. As well as adding to Owen's 'appreciation of travel', Belloc had evidently struck a more resounding chord:

Another thing: was it not Belloc's great forefinger which pointed out to me this passage of De Vigny: *If any man despairs of becoming a Poet, let him carry his pack and march in the ranks* [sic].

Now I don't despair of *becoming* a Poet: 'Before Abraham was, I am' so to speak . . .

Will you set about finding the address of the 'Artists' Rifles', as this is the Corps which offers commissions to 'gentlemen returning from abroad'.[80]

Taken together with the fact that his time in France had not been terribly productive for his poetry, this is surely very revealing. Owen implicitly expresses the hope that warfare will make him into a poet, and his use of Christ's words to describe himself *qua* poet obliquely identifies the figure of the writer with the suffering martyr. In deciding for suffering, however, Owen was not going to give away his social pretensions; he is not going to 'march in the ranks', but join a corps for 'gentlemen'.

Despite some little vacillation, Owen's enthusiasm to participate in the war rapidly developed. And in July we find him conceiving of war in connection with literature. He speaks of visiting the 'battlefield of Castillon where, in 1453, Talbot Earl of Shrewsbury suffered the defeat which lost Guienne and Bordeaux to the English forever'. Owen continues:

I can't understand it, but this battlefield will interest me as much as the field of the Marne; and I am reading a tale of the Punic Wars with more interest than the Communiques. There is only one cure for me! I am already quaking at the idea of Parade; and yawning with the boredom of it. *Now if I could make it a real, live adventure, a real, old adventure, by flinging myself into Italy?*[81]

The thought of fighting had clearly captured Owen's imagination, and the unstated conclusion of the conditional phrase here is surely to do with his poetry. If he can make it a 'real adventure' yet and 'old' one (the paradox is telling) he may be able to create his own literature from the experience. From his role as 'Poet' initially being used as a reason to keep from the war, it has now become, I think, a major reason for his going.

Owen enlisted in the Artists' Rifles on 21 October 1915. There followed a period of fourteen months training, before joining the 2nd Battalion of the Manchester Regiment in France at the beginning of January 1917. This initial period in the army seems, on the whole, to have been a happy time for Owen. The busy routines and physical demands of army life left little time for introspection. He did, however, pause to wonder at the incongruity between 'preparing to lay down our lives for another, the highest moral act possible' and the 'jostle of discipline and jest.'[82] Already he is conceiving of his service in terms of passive sacrifice and suffering, rather than dwelling on the active implications of being trained to kill his fellow human beings; it is an attitude which will carry over into some of his most famous war poems. But for now he is enjoying the swank of the army, the military glamour of bugles and drums. The few poems he has time to write do not push his preoccupations much further. Predictably he is still troubled by his sexuality. In 'Palinode', as Stallworthy notes, Owen hints 'at a sexual awakening' which has somehow 'poisoned' the poet.[83] Sexual pleasure and desire are implicitly guilty in 'It was a navy boy, so prim, so trim' where an encounter with a beautiful youth can be spoken of and celebrated, because the said young man is devoted to his mother, and lies beyond the poet's projected advances.

Written in a more decadent manner are three sonnets, 'Storm', 'Music', and 'Purple', all poems that turn upon the guilty pleasures, the sado-masochistic enjoyments, of love. In 'Storm' the act of love is likened to a lightning bolt being attracted to a tree. The poet 'draws the brilliant danger, tremulous, bowed'. The destructive power is then celebrated: 'And happier were it if my sap consume;/Glorious will shine the opening of my heart.' The 'gods, whose beauty is death' will laugh in approval. Erotic love is imaged as violently destructive, rather than gently creative. In 'Music' the 'symphony' of love implicitly includes violins which give expression to the poet's 'sorrows and thirsting sins', whilst 'Purple' concludes with a Swinburnian image of Venus, 'whose rose skin/Mauve-marbled, purples Eros' mouth for sacred sin.' The violence implicit in the bleeding mouth, the oxymoron of the close, the emotional tensions which these images imply, were soon to have an application upon the Western Front. And in another sonnet probably drafted at about the same time as these, Owen addresses Eros in a poem which specifically equates erotic love with the idea of sacrifice:

> In that I loved you, Love, I worshipped you;
> In that I worshipped well, I sacrificed.
> All of most worth I bound and burned and slew:
> The innocent small things, fair friends and Christ.[84]

The poem goes on to record how Love nevertheless departs, leaving the poet to 'stare upon the ash of all I burned'. As Stallworthy suggests, the poem seems to relate to Owen's Dunsden experience. What is significant for my purposes is the idea of an erotic 'greater love' that leads the poet not only to indulge in self-sacrifice, but also in the sacrifice of others. The pertinence of this to the way he viewed his experience on the Somme hardly requires further comment.

Before his first experience of the front line, on 1 January 1917, Owen wrote to his mother from France. Despite some physical discomforts, his mood was ebullient:

This morning I was hit! We were bombing and a fragment from somewhere hit my thumb knuckle. I coaxed out 1 drop of blood. Alas! no more!!

There is a fine heroic feeling about being in France, and I am in perfect spirits. A tinge of excitement is about me, but excitement is always necessary to my happiness.[85]

However flippant this description of a training exercise might be, the excited sense of heroism and the thrill of danger are clearly expressed. There is also something of that by now familiar interest in his own wounds; to suffer is, perhaps, as essential to military virtue as it is to heroic acts of love, or literary heroism. Ten days later Owen is describing a tour of the trenches which his regiment is soon to occupy. He speaks of his party being shelled and goes on: 'I tell you these things because *afterwards* they will sound less exciting. If I leave all my exploits for recitation after the war without mentioning them now, they will be appearing bomb-shell-bastic.' The same letter concludes: 'Have no anxiety. I cannot do a better thing or be in a righter place. Yet I am not sainted therefore, and so I beg you to annoy . . . [sic], for my wicked pleasure.'[86] Once more there is exhilaration here and also a sense of self-righteousness about his situation. Although the tone of the closing sentence is again playful, the choice of the word 'sainted' is telling. The figure of the martyr lurks behind the prose, and it is one that Owen is both attracted to and gratified by. That he feels it necessary to justify his narrative is like earlier occasions we have noted when Owen was describing difficult experiences; he perhaps felt that he was more interested and excited by his subject matter than he ought to have been.

As we might expect, Owen's first taste of action did not ease this dilemma. Owen 'can see no reason for deceiving' his mother as he proceeds in a letter of 16 January to describe in great detail his own and his comrades sufferings as they held a 'dug-out' in no man's land. 'It was', he says, 'Seventh Hell'. Neither pity nor self-pity direct the utterance; rather there is simply a need to tell, to share the emotional burden of what has been undergone. The letter concludes like this:

I allow myself to tell you all these things because *I am never going back to this awful post*. It is the worst the Manchesters have ever held; and we are going back for a rest . . .

In conclusion, I must say that if there is any power whom the Soldiery execrate more than another it is that of our distinguished countryman.

You may pass it on via Owen, Owen.

Don't pass round these sheets but have portions typed for Leslie etc.[87]

This is the first note of Owen's much celebrated 'protest' against the war, and an exceedingly self-conscious sound it makes. The soldiers 'cursing' of Lloyd George is to be made public, as are certain 'other portions' of the letter at the discretion of his mother. In referring to himself as 'Owen, Owen', he is identifying himself with Owen Glendower, thereby both giving himself the elevated status of a national hero[88] who can authoritatively challenge Lloyd George and, at the same time, depersonalising his experience.

Three days later he writes home again, and reverts to a description of no man's land and the trenches. His writing is drenched in Biblical and literary metaphors. No man's land is the 'eternal place of gnashing of teeth', it is worse than the 'Slough of Despond' and the 'fires of Sodom and Gamorrah'. It is 'pock-marked like a body of foulest diseases and its odour is the breath of cancer'. This is very much the voice of 'Owen, Owen'. The letter concludes:

Now I have let myself tell you more facts than I should, in the exuberance of having already done *'a Bit'*.

The people of England needn't hope. They must agitate. But they are not yet agitated even. Let them imagine 50 strong men trembling as with ague for 50 hours![89]

Many of the unresolved dilemmas, the emotional complexities of Owen's war poems are prefigured here, as are the corresponding difficulties for the reader. Owen himself again betrays uncertainty as to what should or should not be said and why. The reason for his highly metaphoric, notably non-realistic descriptions is given as 'exuberance'. But then we have the need for protest expressed in an oddly bathetic image of fifty men trembling with illness. The point that Owen evades throughout the letter is that men were slaughtering each other. Nevertheless, the horrors of the war as described earlier in the letter implicitly authenticate Owen's position and provide a basis for protest. The paradox is that protest against the war depends upon participation in it.

Following this first taste of action, Owen spent two months out of the line. In February 1917 he was posted to take a course for transport officers, and in March shortly after re-joining his battalion, he concussed himself having fallen into a ruined cellar, and was hospitalised at the 13th Casualty Clearing Station (CCS). In April he was involved in action again, this time in the vicinity of Savy Wood. The 2nd Manchesters were engaged for twelve days. In order to reach the wood the battalion had advanced through a terrific barrage which Owen later described in a letter to his brother:

The sensations of going over the top are about as exhilarating as those dreams of falling over a precipice, when you see the rocks at the bottom surging up to you. I woke up without being squashed. Some didn't. There was an extraordinary exultation in the act of slowly walking forward showing ourselves openly . . .

Then we were caught in a Tornado of shells. The various 'waves' were all broken up and we carried on like a crowd moving off a cricket field. When I looked back and saw the ground all crawling and wormy with wounded bodies, I felt no horror at all but only an immense exultation at having got through the Barrage.[90]

Exultation and exhilaration, however, were short lived, and the following twelve days were to be replete with horrors which culminated in his being blown up on a railway embankment and virtually buried alive. After the previous incidents in the dug-out and cellar, this was the third time Owen had been trapped underground. As Hibberd points out, that Owen suffered peace time fears of paralysis and drowning can only have intensified the awfulness of this experience.[91]

A week after surviving his days in the line, Owen was observed by his commanding officer to be behaving strangely, and was ordered to report to the medical officer who found him to be shaky and tremulous with a confused memory, and so sent him down the line to the 13th CCS. It was from here that he wrote to his sister that it was not the Bosche that had worked him up nor the explosives, but living so long by his brother officer, 'who lay not only near by, but in various places around and about'.[92] As in the Dunsden days, he spared his relatives nothing of his sufferings. Nevertheless, Owen reassures both his mother and his sister that he has not had a breakdown, but is merely avoiding one, and on 4 May can record feeling 'a great calm happiness'.[93] But just how calm Owen was, must be open to question since he was evacuated to England by a psychologist who prided himself upon being able to return 70 per cent of his patients to the trenches after only a fortnight's treatment.[94]

Owen arrived at Craiglockhart War Hospital on 26 June – about a month before Sassoon. He remained there until the end of October and then after a period of leave was put on light duties with the 5th Battalion at Scarborough. From there he moved to Ripon in March 1918 until being passed fit for general service in June. He returned to Scarborough and went out to France again in August. It was during this year that he wrote the war poems for which he has become so celebrated. Before discussing these, it is helpful to look at the way in which Owen was treated at Craiglockhart in order to understand as nearly as we can his state of mind whilst writing the poems.

Owen was lucky in his doctor, Arthur Brock, who like W.H. Rivers, was in the vanguard of his profession, and had devised his own method of treating patients which he called 'ergotherapy'. Brock's ideas are set forth in his post-war book *Health and Conduct* and in a number of articles, one of the most important being tellingly entitled, 'The Re-Education of the Adult'. The book and articles are a curious mixture of forward-thinking sociology, and backward-looking Puritanism. Following Geddes (who may have been indebted to Marx for this idea) Brock took the central problem of modern man to be his alienation from his environment. Thus, much of Brock's work constitutes an attack on the modern industrial city. Rightly, I think, he took war psychology to be an 'acute exacerbation of a more or less chronic or sub-acute condition' from which society had been suffering long before World War I. It is in the diagnosis of the 'condition' that I part company with Dr. Brock. During the war, he says, 'all the evil tendencies of pre-war psychology become more marked'. These 'evil' tendencies encapsulate not only alienation from the environment, but also a 'personal or organismal' problem: 'weakness of morale'.[95] The latter may follow directly from the former according to Dr. Brock, but the patient may have a predisposition to weak morale, thus explaining why every soldier did not suffer from nervous disorder.

We may, then, applaud Brock for his thoughts on alienation, and his largely humanitarian attitudes to the treatment of both city hooligans and sufferers from war neurosis. But in my view, the severe moral attitudes which are part of his belief system severely vitiate his theories and his practice as a shell-shock doctor. He could, for example, look upon the carnage of the Western Front in entirely conventional Edwardian terms. In *Health and Conduct* Brock writes of the 'superhuman sanity', and the 'moral energy', displayed in acts of superhuman self-abnegation. He also makes mention of the 'noble dead';[96] an idea that both Owen and Sassoon found bitterly risible. But it is Brock's attitude to suffering which I find most pertinent for it could only reinforce Owen in his attitude. Brock clearly believed that suffering and self-abnegation constitute a good, and as an obvious corollary thought that an unwillingness to suffer constituted 'evil'. Such beliefs are incompatible with an anti-war stance, since war provokes suffering and enables those supreme acts of self-abnegation so admired by Brock. But war is also the perfect site for the expression of sadism and masochism. Looked at in these terms war becomes not the expression of superhuman sanity, but of an all too human insanity.

But to return to Brock and his methods of treatment. He addressed himself to both environmental and personal issues. He argued that men suffering from war neurosis suffered from ergophobia; because their experience of the war environment was so horrific they endured an alienating and disintegrating effect, which left them with what Brock called an 'abhorrence' for the 'whole battle of life': they have become frightened of making an effort. This ergophobia (a fancy word for work-shy) had in Brock's view to be treated by 'ergotherapy', the aim of which was to reintegrate the patient to his environment. Patients were sent out of the hospital to observe their surroundings both scientifically and culturally. Various officers were given the task of dealing with specific aspects of the environment: amateur geologists, meteorologists, zoologists and botanists roamed round Slateford and Edinburgh, reporting their findings back to the Field Club that Brock had founded. Having undergone this preliminary stage, patients were further encouraged to act upon their environment, by pursuing the practice of arts and crafts, engineering, gardening and agricultural projects.

Together with this approach to the natural environment, Brock instituted a programme designed to integrate his patients with the social and civic environment. Patients were encouraged to become involved with family, neighbourhood, and city in a graduated programme of reintegration. One of the problems that Brock does not address in his writings is precisely how integrating officers suffering from nervous anxiety into Edinburgh society, was to make them better able to come to terms with or face again the battlefields of the Western Front: a question that I am at a loss to answer. Similarly, the practice of such benign arts as rug making, wood carving, basket weaving and pottery painting seem soothing in a rather soporific way, and make an awful and ironic contrast to the savage activities and experiences that the men were trying to come to terms with.

But there was yet another aspect of Brock's programme, which more specifically addressed itself to these problems. 'To any scheme of character reconstruction', he says, 'renunciation must of course play its part. The patient must impose from within his own discipline.' Brock continues:

The neurasthenic patient must learn to do without things. He must impose a certain amount of stoic discipline upon himself. If he does not narrowly scrutinise his own daily acts, there is a danger that the ground gained by 'ergotherapy' may be unwittingly lost again from day to day by minor self-indulgences.

As a concrete example of the kind of stoicism *a petit pied* which I recommend to many of my patients I may mention the taking of a cold bath or swim before breakfast. The man who will *keep this up* for some weeks in the middle of winter is not likely to quail before the successive tests which will come later.[97]

The relatively harmless whimsies of ergotherapy were then to be bolstered by some stern encouragements towards self-punishment, so that the anxious officers could once again more happily embrace the rigours of a 'noble' death.

This is precisely what happened to Owen. At Craiglockhart he joined in ergotherapeutic exercises with a will. Before the war he had been a keen amateur naturalist, and was interested in geology. So it comes as no surprise to find that Owen was a founding member of Brock's Field Club to which he gave a highly successful paper on the entertaining subject of 'Do Plants Think'. Owen also took part in amateur dramatics and edited the hospital magazine *The Hydra* which was another brainchild of Brock's. Other therapeutic activities included learning German, doing a little teaching in an Edinburgh school, and making a copper bowl. He was also swimming daily, and in any hours spared from this hectic round of activities, he was writing his poems. He seems to have been kept relatively cheerful during the daylight hours by constantly having his thoughts directed away from the war, but at night he was a 'sick man' suffering from sleeplessness and bellicose dreams.[98] Perhaps for Owen, part of the stoical self-discipline advocated by Brock was the translation of these dreams into poetry; a confrontation with the horrors of his psyche which Brock's overt therapies seemed to ignore if not exacerbate. Certainly the poems are replete with 'all the arts of hurting'.

Two poems which are not strictly speaking war poems, but were revised and finished during Owen's time at Craiglockhart, serve as a useful introduction to some of the central concerns of the war poems. Both 'How do I love Thee' and 'The Poet in Pain' express the central place that suffering has in Owen's emotional life and world view. The first of these sonnets, it is thought was begun at the 13th Casualty Clearing Station, before Owen was evacuated to England. The octet laments that the poet cannot woo the beloved in any conventional ways, implicitly because this is the love that dare not speak its name. This is confirmed in the final four lines:

> But I do love thee even as Shakespeare loved,
> Most gently wild, and desperately for ever,
> Full-hearted, grave, and manfully in vain,
> With thought, high pain, and ever vaster pain.[99]

It is tempting to suggest that the subject of this poem was one of the soldier 'lads' celebrated elsewhere in somewhat less personal terms in Owen's work. However this may be, it is clear that love and pain are virtually synonymous, just as art and pain are in the second sonnet, 'The Poet in Pain'. Here Owen argues that there are some who write of pain, but have never suffered any, and that there are sufferers who are sometimes silent. Owen, the poet, goes on:

> If therefore my remorseless ache
> Be needful to proof-test upon my flesh
> The thoughts I think, and in words bleeding-fresh
> Teach me for speechless sufferers to plain,

I would not quench it.[100]

Self-flagellation is here defended and turned into altruism. Like Sassoon, Owen was comforted by the thought that his poems were speaking for the inarticulate soldiery. But also like Sassoon, the relationship between private feeling and public gesture is by no means straightforward in the poems themselves.

Paradigmatic of this problem, and central I think to under-standing the problems at the heart of Owen's war poems, is 'Apologia Pro Poemate Meo'. It is thought that this poem was written in response to a letter from Robert Graves who urged Owen to 'cheer up and write more optimistically' on the grounds that 'a poet should have a spirit above wars.' The 'spirit' that Owen expresses in this poem is not 'above' wars, but intimately and inextricably involved with them. The first seven stanzas of this poem constitute a passionate celebration of war:

> I, too, saw God through mud,-
> The mud that cracked on cheeks when wretches smiled.
> War brought more glory to their eyes than blood,
> And gave their laughs more glee than shakes a child.
>
> Merry it was to laugh there -
> Where death becomes absurd and life absurder.
> For power was on us as we slashed bones bare
> Not to feel sickness or remorse of murder.[101]

The poet goes on to record having 'dropped off fear', having 'witnessed exultation' and having 'made fellowships-/Untold of happy lovers in old songs'. This love is 'wound with war's hard wire whose stakes are strong' and 'bound with the bandage of the arm that drips'. The poet has also perceived 'beauty', 'music' and 'peace where shell-storms spouted reddest spate'. Always there is ambivalence in the record of these pleasures since they arise out of pain, but this should not blind us to the reality of the celebra-tion. The poem is, for the most part, a sado-masochistic hymn. But following from this, the poem concludes with the following lines addressed to a civilian audience:

> Nevertheless, except you share
> With them in hell the sorrowful dark of hell,
> Whose world is but the trembling of a flare
> And heaven but as the highway for a shell,

You shall not hear their mirth:
  You shall not come to think them well content
  By any jest of mine. These men are worth
  Your tears. You are not worth their merriment.

This 'apology' for his 'protest' poems is very telling. Having
expressed the glory, power, exultation, love and beauty of warfare,
Owen then attempts to subvert his own utterance with respect to
an imagined audience. The poem shifts from private feelings to
public morality. The audience are not 'allowed' to hear the soldiers' mirth (despite Owen's vivid description of it), because we
have not experienced the 'sorrowful dark of hell' upon which the
soldiers' 'merriment' is predicated. To shed tears is our only
proper role; we have to suffer like the troops in order to be
'worthy'. It has been said that Owen was 'trying to convey the
horror and pity of war to home-front readers'. And this is, I think,
how he saw his public role. But it is one fraught with unresolved
tensions and difficulties. Apart from the unwarranted presumption
that the homefront was *en masse* entirely and unfeelingly ignorant
of the 'horrors' of war, there is the more troublesome problem that
Owen is suing for peace whilst at the same time finding positive
value, even 'love' and 'glory' in the fighting. In 'Apologia Pro
Poemate Meo' the audience is implicitly despised for being non-
combatant. In a curious way the poem is an invitation to fight,
rather than a plea for peace.

Owen was, I think, in a similar situation to Sassoon whom he
met at Craiglockhart. There were aspects of the war that both of
them found exciting, stimulating and emotionally fulfilling, but
this gave rise to massive guilt feelings. One way of exculpating
this, to some extent at least, was to write poems which attempted
to 'protest' on behalf of their 'inarticulate' comrades at the front.
'Apologia Pro Poemate Meo' is interestingly similar in its procedures to the two letters I have quoted earlier wherein Owen
purports to 'educate' his sister and brother. In both letters, suffering is dwelt upon in great and loving detail, before the final
rationalising address to the audience. This is surely true of this
poem. Indeed, it could be argued that the soldiers in his command
took the place of his 'children' and ploughmen at Dunsden. We
notice in the early stanzas of the poem, how the soldiers are
implicitly Christ-like, and also how they have 'more glee than

shakes a child'. And just as he wrote of the 'sufferings' of children and ploughmen so he writes of the soldiers' suffering. His libidinous passions, Eros and art, are fulfilled by his relationship with his men. The difference between his experiences at Dunsden and those on the Western Front was the degree of violence and suffering involved, and that whilst he was suffering himself at the war, he was also the cause of violent suffering to others. At Dunsden, his passions which he considered illicit caused him guilt. In the war, those illicit passions were given further rein, and the corresponding guilt feelings must have been all the stronger. It was no wonder he wished to feel on occasion that he was taking the high moral ground.

Before we look at some of the famous 'protest poems' though, there are other poems which demonstrate that his 'Apologia' is not the only one of Owen's poems to celebrate aspects of warfare. 'Has Your Soul Sipped' and 'I saw his round mouth's crimson' are perhaps the most Decadent (in every sense of that word) of Owen's war poems. The first of these was written at Craiglockhart, the other a little later in Scarborough. 'Has your soul sipped' begins with the question, 'Has your soul sipped/Of the sweetness of all sweets', and goes on to assert that he, the poet, has been 'witness/Of a strange sweetness/All fancy surpassing'. There follow six stanzas in which the poet's experience is said to be sweeter than various other possibilities; sweeter than love's nectar, for instance, or sweeter than death. Sweeter too than 'proud wounds' or the 'sweet murder' of the 'martyr/Smiling at God'. Sweeter to the poet than all these things is,

> . . . that smile,
> Faint as a wan, worn myth',
> Faint and exceeding small,
> On a boy's murdered mouth.

> Though from his throat
> The life-tide leaps
> There was no threat
> On his lips.

> But with the bitter blood
> And the death-smell
> All his life's sweetness bled

Into a smile.[102]

The 'wan, worn myth' Owen has in mind might be that of the beautiful, much beloved youth Adonis, who also met with a violent death. Certainly the beauty Owen perceives here has its origins in erotic feeling. Significantly the youth is like Owen's habitual presentation of the soldier; he is a passive victim rather than an active participant in fighting. There is 'no threat' on the lips of this youth, even though he is murdered. Sacrifice is celebrated, but for aesthetic and erotic reasons, rather than religious or spiritual ones. The poem represents a further extension of Owen's shift of allegiance from Christ to Keats.

This is also true of the following poem wherein the poet's observation of a dying man becomes an aesthetic experience with decidedly erotic overtones:

> I saw his round mouth's crimson deepen as it fell,
>   Like a sun, in his last deep hour;
> Watched the magnificent recession of farewell,
>   Clouding, half gleam, half glower,
> And a last splendour burn the heavens of his cheek.
>   And in his eyes
> The cold stars lighting very old and bleak,
>   In different skies.[103]

This draws on the whole tradition of Romanticism, and particularly the late-Victorian fondness for sunsets. It certainly provides a telling antidote to those who would seek to further Owen's reputation as a 'realistic' war poet.

If these two poems provide examples of Owen's aesthetic/erotic response to war they nevertheless lack the complexity of 'Apologia' because they do not attempt to moralise or 'teach' from their perception. 'Greater Love', by contrast, develops those stanzas of 'Apologia' which compare the love between soldiers to heterosexual erotic love. As the title implies, Owen finds the former 'Greater' than the latter, because more sacrifice and suffering are involved. The love of the dying soldiers is described as 'pure' and above erotic passion, yet the language in which their dying is described is nothing if not sensual. The poem begins with the assertion that 'Red lips are not so red/ As the stained stones kissed by the English dead' and goes on to apostrophise, 'O, Love, your eyes lose lure/When I behold eyes blinded in my stead!' The next stanza continues:

> Your slender attitude
>   Trembles not exquisite like limbs knife-skewed,
> Rolling and rolling there
>   Where God seems not to care;
> Till the fierce love they bear
>   Cramps them in death's extreme decrepitude.[104]

The pronoun here is directed against women, in a morbidly sensual description which prefers violence and death to the creativity of Eros. The poem ends in a similar way to 'Apologia' with the poet turning ever more strongly against his audience. The difference is that here the audience is implicitly, but specifically female:

> Heart, you were never hot
>   Nor large, nor full like hearts made great with shot;
> And though your hand be pale,
> Paler are all which trail
> Your cross through flame and hail:
>   Weep, you may weep, for you may touch them not.

As Jon Stallworthy has pointed out, the last line of the poem echoes Christ's words to Mary Magdalene as they are reported in John's Gospel. This, together with the title (also taken from John's Gospel) seems to place the poem within the ambit of Christianity. But Owen's love is not simply spiritual, and Christ is not Christ, but any number of soldier 'lads'. The mysogyny implicit in the final lines, only serves to render emphatic the point that Owen in this poem is writing homoerotic celebration rather than 'visionary compassion'. I do not wish to imply that these two emotions are necessarily mutually exclusive. What is troubling in Owen's work is that the celebration of love between men takes place in a context of massive violence; war in the poems is the source of that love, and directly or indirectly legitimates its expression.

The poems we have looked at so far might be considered by some to be atypical of Owen's war poems. Certainly they give expression to a complexity of response that is absent in some of the more overtly didactic poems. But even in the latter it is possible to perceive Owen's private feelings intruding upon the ostensible public point of the poems. 'Le Christianisme' and 'At a Calvary Near the Ancre' show something of Sassoon's influence on Owen in so far as they are written in a leaner, less mellifluous style than some of Owen's earlier work and they attempt to make their religious and political points through the application of relatively crude ironies. In its first stanza 'Le Christianisme' uses a metaphor of the physical destruction of a church building to express Owen's sense of the moral turpitude of the established church. The second and concluding stanza focuses upon a piece of statuary that has somehow so far escaped:

> One Virgin still immaculate
> > Smiles on for war to flatter her.
> She's halo'd with an old tin hat,
> > But a piece of hell will batter her.[105]

This is not just about Owen's reaction to Christianity. One feels that Owen here is violently indicting all women for what he supposes to be their support of the war. Like Sassoon, he is responsible for propagating an aggressive vision of women during the war which at its best may be deemed an inaccurate half truth, at worst mysogynistic.

'At a Calvary Near the Ancre' takes up the theme assayed in 'Greater Love', but with more overtly didactic punch. Soldiers take the role of Christ whilst priests and politicians play the parts of the Biblical scribes and pharisees:

> The scribes on all the people shove
> > And bawl allegiance to the state,
> But they who love the greater love
> > Lay down their life; they do not hate.[106]

In this stanza Owen castigates the reasons for fighting, but not the fighting itself. He locates value in the latter, but not the former. Fighting is the means to a glorious suffering, to the 'greater love' of martyrdom and to homoerotic solidarity. We perceive that Owen's political perceptions are completely at odds with his private feelings. The critique of nationalism in the stanza above is rendered meaningless by the lines that follow. If fighting is the means to an exalted spiritual suffering, as Owen states here, it hardly matters *why* one is fighting. Owen's public poems of 'pity' and 'protest' are weakened by this unresolved dilemma.

More of Owen's poems written at Craiglockhart, Scarborough and Ripon before he went back to France again, bear witness to this. In poems like 'The Dead-Beat', 'The Letter', 'The Chances' and 'Dulce Et Decorum Est', again the influence of Sassoon is apparent. The poems constitute neat constructions of situational irony rendered in either rhyming couplets or an ABAB/CDCD rhyme scheme. These procedures sometimes result in a tendency towards the glib and certainly militates against arguments for the poems' realism. Owen also (and this is particularly true of 'The Letter' and 'The Chances') though bravely attempting to write in the language of the private soldiers, is never very comfortable with the demotic, forcing it into poetic form and thereby sacrificing authenticity for didactic punch. This gives the poems an unremitting air of artificiality, the apotheosis of which might be discerned in the closing lines of the octet in 'The Chances', where 'cushy' is made to rhyme embarrassingly with 'mushy'. More crucial to my argument than these technical reservations, however, is the response these poems seem to be asking for. Owen is ostensibly detailing suffering in order to provoke a reaction of pity and indignation. The victims of war he portrays are implicitly innocent. We are told of men dying, we do not hear of the same men killing. Owen divests the individual soldiers of responsibility, his target being the politicians and the people back home who do not 'understand'. In other words the guilt of the audience is taken for granted, whilst any moral responsibility the soldier might bear is excised.

'Dulce Et Decorum Est' is justly regarded as one of Owen's finest didactic poems and, with less perspicacity celebrated for its 'realism'. Not only its poetic form, but also the introduction of nightmare images force the poem away from simple notions of realism. The gassed soldier's eyes 'writhe' in his 'hanging face' like a 'devil's sick of sin'. 'Devils' clearly have no place in the arena of the reality principle. But for a moment, through this image which might have its source in Owen's own 'bellicose dreams', he hints at the guilt and responsibility of the 'victim'. As the poem continues, however, the focus, and with it implicitly the blame, is shifted as Owen directs his utterance outwards to make his public point. If we, the audience, had seen such terrible suffering we,

> . . . would not tell with such high zest
> To children ardent for some desperate glory,
> The old Lie: Dulce et decorum est
> Pro patria mori.[107]

This needed to be said in 1917 in a way it does not need to be said now. The poem is undoubtedly powerful, and to deflate the rhetoric of imperialism is clearly salutary. But now, if we are not to react with complacent self-satisfaction, safe in the knowledge that we do not tell our children 'old lies' we are, I think, obliged to recognise the tendency in a poem like this to substitute different kinds of glorification and heroism for those being satirised. The poem seeks pity for its victims, but also tacitly asks for our admiration of the sufferings endured. And it is highly significant that these sufferings are not only those of the gassed soldiers, but also Owen the poet's. Indeed the conclusion of the poem is predicated with a series of conditional clauses which relate directly to the poet: 'If in some smothering dreams you too could pace' . . . 'If you could hear with every jolt' . . .'you would not tell' etc. The wisdom of the poem stems from the sufferings endured by the poet. Suffering authenticates the morality, and we are asked to admire this and those who have so suffered; Owen becomes the hero of his own poem, and suffering is glorified as the means to wisdom. The 'Greater love' which absolves soldiers from responsibility for causing suffering, whilst elevating their experience in proportion to the sufferings endured, needs to be called into question.

It could be argued that in a poem like 'Disabled' Owen moves in this direction. The poem seems to me one of his finest in so far as it treats of the motivations of many young men for volunteering. They are seen to have acted with a careless volition, and through carefully modulated sensuality Owen uncovers the tragic irony of the young soldier whose militaristic ideas of 'manliness' have been reduced to impotency. But even here, where the pity of war, and the pity of the attraction of war to some young men is powerfully rendered, at the close of the poem Owen places his presumed audience in an untenable position:

> Some cheered him home, but not as crowds cheer Goal.
> Only a solemn man who brought him fruits
> *Thanked* him; and then inquired about his soul.

> Now, he will spend a few sick years in institutes,
> And do what things the rules consider wise,
> And take whatever pity they may dole.
> Tonight he noticed how the women's eyes

Passed from him to the strong men that were whole.
How cold and late it is! Why don't they come
And put him into bed? Why don't they come?[108]

Irony is directed to expose the response of the home front as entirely inadequate to the soldier's tragedy. Both the well intentioned gesture of the do-gooder, and the pity 'doled' will be of no benefit. One sees the point all too well. Nevertheless the poem leaves the reader in an uncomfortable limbo because real 'pity' by implication seems to be the preserve of the fighters, if not of Owen himself. Behind the utterance lies the assumption that in order to 'understand', in order to really pity, one has to go out and experience the fighting.

Owen wrote in a letter from the 13th CCS that he was a 'conscientious objector with a very seared conscience'.[109] He later wrote from Craiglockhart, 'I hate washy pacifists as temperamentally as I hate whiskied prussianists.'[110] The latter phrase explains the former, and both illuminate the problems in so many of his war poems. We, as an audience are asked to pity, but we are also implicitly told that we *can't* either understand or pity unless we too go and fight. Thus anti-war poems become in subtle ways war poems in quite a different sense from that accepted by the myth of First War writing. Owen is not a pacifist and his poems are not either.

'Insensibility' is a poem which expresses the paradoxes of Owen's 'protest' poems most clearly. Here Owen seeks to ironically contrast the justifiable 'insensibility' of the troops with the unjustifiable 'insensibility' of the home front. But this is not all the poem articulates. Between the insensibility of both 'men' and civilians is the sensibility of 'Owen Owen', officer and poet:

Happy are men who yet before they are killed
Can let their veins run cold.
Whom no compassion fleers
Or makes their feet
Sore on the alleys cobbled with their brothers.
The front line withers.
But they are troops who fade, not flowers,
For poets' tearful fooling:
Men, gaps for filling:
Losses, who might have fought
Longer; but no one bothers.[111]

Despite his rhetorical gesture about 'poet's tearful fooling', there is a tendency here for Owen to again become the hero of his own poem: it is at least implicit that he has 'Compassion' and is 'bothered'. The poem continues through section II, III, and IV, to elaborate upon the 'fortunate' soldiers who have 'ceased feeling', 'lost imagination', whose minds were 'never trained'; they are not susceptible to the horrors that Owen has to endure. Of course the poem is indicating the appalling experiences that cause the soldiers' insensibility, and these are such that even people like himself have an excuse for following suit:

> We wise, who with a thought besmirch
> Blood over all our soul,
> How should we see our task
> But through his blunt and lashless eyes?
> Alive, he is not vital overmuch;
> Dying, not mortal overmuch;
> Nor sad, nor proud,
> Nor curious at all.
> He cannot tell
> Old men's placidity from his.

Although again Owen is pointing towards the grievous circumstances which have occasioned the soldiers plight, it is difficult to avoid the massive condescension he displays towards the private soldiers. The poet's self-pity turns to self-congratulation here. He has already demonstrated his 'sensibility' and does so again here with his argument that the 'wise' (like himself) are entirely justified in aspiring to the insensibility of the 'others' under the circumstances. We note regretfully that Owen's snobbery judges the soldiers, upon whose behalf he sees himself speaking, as implicitly stupid ('unwise'). Despite this aberration, Owen continues to argue that what cannot be justified, is the position of those at home:

> But cursed are dullards whom no cannon stuns,
> That they should be as stones.
> Wretched are they, and mean
> With paucity that never was simplicity.
> By choice they made themselves immune
> To pity and whatever moans in man
> Before the last sea and the hapless stars;
> Whatever mourns when many leave these shores;
> Whatever shares

The eternal reciprocity of tears.

The effect of these grandiloquent gestures is to elevate the soldiers' experience indiscriminately at the expense of all non-combatants. The crux of this final verse paragraph is in the line which begins 'By choice', which neatly sidesteps the issue that he, and many of his fellow soldiers, volunteered. According to Owen, fighting and killing gives the soldiers the right to be insensible, and also gives them (particularly those who remain 'sensible' like Owen) the prerogative of 'pity', 'mourning' and the 'eternal reciprocity of tears'. The poem assumes an enormous moral rectitude which its arguments cannot sustain.

Owen's poems of 1917 and early 1918 embody the conflicts which were surely contributory to the severity of his shellshock neurosis. He has a love–hate relationship with the war and this ambivalence extends to every facet of his response. On the one hand he wished to 'educate' the home-front as to the horrors of trench warfare, but on the other he consistently portrayed the home-front as incapable of learning. And the horrors of trench warfare had an undeniable fascination for him. He was fond of quoting from Rabindranath Tagore, 'What I have seen is unsurpassable'.[112] The soldiers with whom he served were figures of homoerotic beauty, whose passive suffering is at once lamented and enjoyed. They are also, occasionally, 'insensible' killers, but they are denied moral responsibility for this. To be a soldier is to be 'manly' but is also to risk emasculation (c.f. 'Disabled'). Owen is both proud and guilty that he has served. The pride in his own suffering, and the way that this is rationalised into an educative function via his poems has already been touched upon. And the poems also act as a palliative for any guilt he felt at exercising violence. They become the rationale for being 'a conscientious objector with a very seared conscience'.

It seems highly unlikely that Brock's 'ergotherapy' did anything to resolve these tensions, and Owen's war nightmares continued after he had left Craiglockhart. However advanced Brock's views were, like Rivers, he could ultimately only view shell shock as a 'failure' that had to be made good.[113] The strongly Puritanical emphasis of 'ergotherapy' could only have reinforced such ideas, and doubtless Owen shared them. And like Sassoon, whose example was always before him, Owen is soon convinced that he must go out to France again. Writing to his mother on New Year's Eve 1917, Owen wrote:

I go out of this year a Poet, my dear Mother, as which I did not enter it. I am held peer by the Georgians; I am a poet's poet.

I am started. The tugs have left me; I feel the great swelling of the open sea taking my galleon.[114]

This is heady stuff and plainly Owen, despite all his experience of the Western Front, had lost none of the Romantic image of himself as a poet with a capital P. What had secured his position with the Georgians was his relationship with Sassoon whom Owen hero-worshipped. There is no evidence of any sexual relationship between them, and indeed Sassoon seems to have taken a somewhat cool and condescending view of Owen, nevertheless as Hibberd has remarked, Sassoon not only inspired Owen's technical development as a poet, he also introduced him to the London literary circles centred upon Robbie Ross. As I have noticed in the previous chapter, there was a strong homosexual element to these, and it seems highly likely that Sassoon and Owen discussed their sexual orientation, and possibly the ideas of Edward Carpenter at Craiglockhart.[115] That Owen gained much of confidence from all this is without question. He refers to Sassoon as 'Keats + Christ + Elijah + my Colonel + my father-confessor + Amenophis IV in profile'.[116] Although there is facetiousness here, the 'dispassionate' love Owen had for Sassoon and the influence of the latter can be easily gauged by considering how important to Owen's life Christ and Keats had been.

By the time Owen wrote this letter Sassoon had made his decision to return to active service, and although Owen was still not fit to emulate his hero, he had already made up his mind that this was the proper course. The letter quoted above continues to recall what he was doing, seeing and feeling on new year's eve of the previous year. He recalls the 'incomprehensible look' on the faces of the men in the base camp at Etaples. It is a look that cannot be seen in England or in any battle. He concludes: 'It will never be painted, and no actor will ever seize it. And to describe it, I think I must go back and be with them.'[117] Like his earlier decision to volunteer, Owen's motivations for wishing to return to France are involved with an increasing sense of his destiny as 'Poet'. Thanks to Sassoon's introductions, Owen was feted by some of the leading literary figures in London, and his work was beginning to be recognised. He could not be unaware that the war had given rise to his finest poetry. To follow Sassoon's example, go out again, and as he later put it, 'help these boys . . . indirectly, by watching their sufferings that I may speak of them as well as a pleader can',[118] was clearly what he wished to do. Owen wrote in another letter: 'I am much gladder to be going out again than afraid. I shall be better able to cry my outcry, playing my part.'[119]

To 'plead', to 'cry his outcry', is the moral justification for his return to the war. But it is a highly irrational, personal justification. Apart from anything else it presumes that writing poetry was an effective means of 'pleading;' or 'crying one's outcry'. In the immediate political situation of 1917–18 this was not true. Very few poems of Owen's were published during the war, and it was interestingly enough, not until the 1930s that his work gained much serious notice. The greatest contemporary protest against the war was coming, as it always had, from the left-wing pacifists, some of whom had been imprisoned for their trouble. But as we have seen, and again like Sassoon, 'temperamentally' Owen 'hated' pacifists.

Going back to France ensured Owen more suffering, and more material for his poems. He was content to be there. What he did not wish to make public was this contentment. His private reaction to the war became ever more divorced from his public reaction to it. The following extracts from several letters, written during his second time on active service in France, makes this abundantly clear:

Serenity Shelley never dreamed of crowns me.[120]

Tell them, [Harold and Colin Owen] and them only, how peculiarly unreluctant I am to be back here.[121]

Do not inform friends & relations that I pass my hours reading, sleeping, conversing, & gathering roses from bewildered gardens. But so it is . . .[122]

. . . may your peace be as divine as mine is tonight.[123]

Do not (as I afore-mentioned) undeceive the world which thinks I'm having a bad time.[124]

It past the limits of my Abhorrence. I lost all earthly faculties and fought like an angel . . .I only shot one man with my revolver (at about thirty yards); The rest I took with a smile.[125]

I live between the extremes of gross materialism – feeding savagely and sleeping doggishly – and of high spirituality – suffering & sacrificing.[126]

It should be noted that the last two letters quoted above are addressed to Owen's mother and marked 'Strictly Private' and 'Not for circulation as a whole', respectively.

I think it is highly likely that Owen was not fully aware of his ambivalent attitude to suffering, and certainly it seems to me that his public 'protest poems' mask or partially mask their origins and motivations. But interestingly in two late poems, 'Strange Meeting' and 'Spring Offensive' there is evidence to suggest that Owen was beginning to battle with what he himself called 'the inwardness of war'.[127] Indeed in another letter to his mother written as early as August 1917 he writes: 'There is a mote in many eyes, often no other than a tear. It is this: That men are laying down their lives for a friend. I say it is a mote; a distorted view to hold in a general way.'[128] Here there seems to be a consciousness that the Christian text sentimentalises and Romantically justifies mass slaughter: being blown apart by a 5.9 shell in the name of the British, French or German Empire is not adequately analysed by 'Greater Love'.

'Strange Meeting' expresses the glimmerings of a different vision. It has hitherto puzzled and fascinated critics because it expresses deeply contradictory positions which are never reconciled. The poem portrays a Romantic dream vision of hell wherein two of the living dead converse. They are soldiers. One suggests that 'here is no cause to mourn', and the reply to this contention constitutes the rest of the poem:

'None,' said that other, 'save the undone years,
The hopelessness. Whatever hope is yours,
Was my life also; I went hunting wild
After the wildest beauty in the world,
Which lies not calm in eyes, or braided hair,
But mocks the steady running of the hour,
And if it grieves, grieves richlier than here.
For by my glee might many men have laughed,
And of my weeping something had been left,
Which must die now. I mean the truth untold,
The pity of war, the pity war distilled.
Now men will go content with what we spoiled'[129]

The 'wildest beauty in the world' pertains to art. The dead soldier is also a poet. He laments that his grief and joy have not been transmuted into what Yeats called 'the artifice of eternity'. The 'truth' about war is located in the 'pity' it 'distilled'. But this will now be left unspoken since the poet has been killed.

All this is coherent as far as it goes. But as the poem proceeds the protagonist articulates a different position asserting that when alive he had the 'courage', 'mystery', 'wisdom' and 'mastery' to miss 'the march of this retreating world' and 'would' have played a different role:

> Then when much blood had clogged their chariot-wheels
> I would go up and wash them from sweet wells,
> Even with truths that lie too deep for taint.
> I would have poured my spirit without stint
> But not through wounds; not on the cess of war.
> Foreheads of men have bled where no wounds were.

Since the poem makes clear that the speaker has been killed in action, the assertion of 'courage' and 'mastery' to miss the world's retreat into war, has something of a hollow ring to it. But this is perhaps intentional irony. It is possible that Owen had a vague echo of a biblical text in his head when he wrote of having 'mastery'. In 2 Timothy, Chapter 2, (mentioned earlier because Mrs Owen marked a verse therein with the word 'Wilfred'), speaking of 'a good soldier in Christ' we have the following verse: 'And if a man also strive for mastery, *yet* is he not crowned, except he strive lawfully.' The point would seem to be that the speaker has misused his gifts in the service of war. The lines above imply that if he had his time again he would not fight. This contradicts the earlier lament, however, for there it is implicit that the poet's art has a direct relationship to the 'truth untold', the 'pity' of war. The persona, like Owen, is caught between wishing he had been a pacifist, and yet perceiving in warfare the materials of 'truthful' poetry. It is also entirely significant that even whilst articulating the pacifist position, the speaker implies that he still would have adopted a Christ-like martyrdom in order to 'pour his spirit', in order to write. The reference to Christ praying in the Garden of Gethesemene, 'Foreheads have bled where no wounds were', comes from Luke, Chapter 22 – the other reference in Mrs. Owen's Bible marked 'Wilfred'. It is as if Owen, as well as dealing

with his personal attitude to war is also grappling with the whole
question of the role of Christianity in the war; of what it means
to be 'a good soldier in Christ'.

If he had no sure answer to this conundrum, it is not to be
expected that the conclusion of the poem will yield any unproblematic reading. The speaker continues from the lines above:

I am the enemy you killed, my friend.
I knew you in this dark: for so you frowned
Yesterday through me as you jabbed and killed.
I parried; but my hands were loath and cold.
Let us sleep now . . .

Hibberd has discussed this at length, and pointed out its relationship to Oscar Wilde's lines from the 'Ballad of Reading Gaol': 'Yet
each man kills the thing he loves . . .some do it with a bitter look
. . .The brave man with a sword.' As Hibberd remarks, the
ambiguity of 'frowned through' is crucial to properly understanding the stanza.[130] Here is the ultimate expression of a love–
hate relationship: the enemy is also a beloved. The 'other' is both
the poet's double and a German. The point is thus made that in
killing another person, something within yourself dies. Furthermore Owen has realised that to lay down one's life for a friend in
war, is intimately related to killing other potential lovers. In the
poem, the soldiers meet, recognise, and in the end, sleep. What has
intervened is not a creative exchange of erotic love, but remembrance of a mutually destructive act of violence. Although the
poem has not resolved the problem of the relationship between
suffering and creativity, it does in these final lines move some way
towards a critique of sado-masochism.

But 'Spring Offensive', the last poem that Owen was working
on before he died, demonstrates that he was a long way from
resolving the conflicts in his reactions to warfare. The poem
describes an attack. We see the soldiers before, during, and after
the action. All three stages are deeply Romanticised. When the
'little word' for the attack is spoken there are 'No alarms/Of
bugles, no high flags, no clamorous haste, – Only a lift and flare
of eyes that faced/The sun'. The 'lift and flare of eyes' is surely as
much an image of Romantic heroism as the missing 'alarms',
'bugles' and 'flags'. The subsequent slaughter is described thus:

. . . And instantly the whole sky burned

> With fury against them; earth set sudden cups
> In thousands for their blood; and the green slope
> Chasmed and deepened sheer to infinite space.[131]

What is striking about this is just how *unrealistic* it is. Owen
avoids, as he does in so many of his poems, the crucial fact that
men were killing men; the earth and sky are not the perpetrators,
but accessories to the murder. The crux of the poem which lies in
the final stanza, brings us little closer to 'reality'. A rhetoric of
exaggeration echoes the extremity of the experience it describes,
and leads to a final unanswered rhetorical question:

> But what say such as from existence' brink
> Ventured but drave too swift to sink,
> The few who rushed in the body to enter hell,
> And there out-fiending all its fiends and flames
> With superhuman inhumanities,
> Long-famous glories, immemorial shames –
> And crawling slowly back, have by degrees
> Regained cool peaceful air in wonder –
> Why speak not they of comrades that went under?

There is a sense of the soldier's volition here, often elided in other
of Owen's poems, as they 'rush' to their death. But the lines are
fraught with paradox. It is the inability to resolve the tensions
between 'superhuman inhumanities', 'glory' and 'shame', which
implicitly answers the final rhetorical question. The survivors are
filled with wonder and with guilt; feelings impossible of resolution
or synthesis. Therefore they are silent about their dead comrades.
But beyond this is the further irony that Owen *does* speak of those
who have 'gone under' and the appropriate question is, to what
purpose? On the one hand the poem seeks to express the emotional conflicts engendered by warfare, but on the other, the
language of the poem tends to rescue human nature from indictment. Men are no longer men, they are 'fiends'; inhumanities
become 'superhuman'. Although the poem goes further than some
of his earlier work in directly giving voice to the ambivalent 'glory'
and 'shame' Owen perceived in warfare, it still implicitly resists a
bald recognition of the violence man is capable of, and tends to
elevate this on to another plane of experience. Owen wishes to
retrieve or preserve a notion of 'humanity' which excludes the
human potential for massive brutality.

'What I have seen is unsurpassable'. There is in this remark a sense of celebration which I think is crucial in attempting to understand the significance of Owen's work. For he not only criticised warfare, he also celebrated, even glorified it because it is the site of suffering and of love. In his work, war is seen as appalling, but it is this very quality which engenders the loving sacrifice of the men. Critics have wished to see Owen as a humanist, a courageous political spokesman, and above all a poet of pity and compassion. I have attempted to show that his emotional and psychological development was such that he suffered, and in his own and other people's suffering located supreme value. Owen could not be a pacifist because he perceived too much value in the suffering that the violence engendered. His political position was never very lucidly articulated, and his letters give every indication of being uninterested in the wider political issues which the war might be said to have raised. He does not seem to have had the elementary grasp of politics possessed by Sassoon. His attitude to his men can hardly be claimed as an index of his feelings for the oppressed. Owen aspired to the aristocracy of art, and wrote of his men as 'inferiors' who were different in kind to himself. His erotic interest could certainly cross class barriers, but his political beliefs remained conservative. As for the 'poetry in the pity', let it first be said that Owen's poetry is very much in the poetry. Secondly, it needs to be urged that whatever pity there is in these poems is not of the sentimental, humanist kind that is taught in our High Schools. Passion and compassion are one in these poems. Owen's erotic impulses may be glimpsed behind most of what he wrote. And this again, is why he cannot and should not be seen as an entirely anti-war poet. The war was the place that legitimised love between men, and for this Owen could not disavow it. The suffering he endured in England before the war was largely to do with the difficulties of his sexual orientation in a society that outlawed homosexuality. Love and suffering became synonymous for Owen, and in the war he found the apotheosis of both. In his last letter home before he was killed on 4 November 1918, he concludes:

I hope you are as warm as I am; as serene in your room as I am here; and that you think of me never in bed as resignedly as I think of you always in bed. Of this I am certain you could not be visited by a band of friends half so fine as surround me here.[132]

This is a fitting conclusion for Owen; he is the love poet of the war, finding 'serenity' amidst the shambles. And it is this that I have sought to illuminate. The 'Human Problem' in Owen's poetry lies in those depths of the mind, not yet fully understood where, as Freud put it, the battle of 'Eros' and 'Thanatos', the creative and the destructive principles, is constantly waged. That Owen had to go to war in order to find serenity in love is as sound an indictment of nineteenth-century ideologies as there could be. Christianity, Romanticism, capitalism created Owen's values, and though he was struggling against some of the dominant ideologies of his day, in the end his work falls back upon them, and ultimately elevates the place of suffering into a place of love.

Notes

1 B. Bergonzi, *Heroes' Twilight: a Study of the Literature of the Great War,* London, (1965), 1980, p. 128.
2 J. Silkin, *Out of Battle,* London, 1972, p. 208.
3 S. Backman, *Tradition Transformed,* Lund, 1979, pp. 37 and 64.
4 P. Larkin, 'The Real Wilfred', *Encounter* 44, 1975, p. 81.
5 D. Hibberd, *Owen the Poet,* London, 1986.
6 Ibid., p. 13.
7 Ibid., p. 192.
8 Ibid., pp. 68–9 and *passim.*
9 Ibid., pp. 136–9.
10 Ibid., p. 115.
11 Ibid., p. 138.
12 Ibid., p. 129.
13 Ibid., pp. 136–149.
14 H. Owen, *Journey From Obscurity: Memoirs of the Owen Family,* vol. I, London, 1963, p. 19.
15 J. Stallworthy, *Wilfred Owen: A Biography,* London, 1974, p. 14
16 Owen, *Journey From Obscurity,* vol. I, p. 21.
17 Ibid., p. 62.
18 Ibid., p. 39.
19 Ibid., p. 40.
20 W. Owen, *Collected Letters,* H. Owen and J. Bell, (eds.), London, 1967, p. 150. This text hereafter will be referred to as *CL.*
21 Hibberd, *Owen the Poet,* p. 6.
22 By the time he was fourteen, Wilfred was quoting scriptural texts in letters to his mother, and it is at about this time that 'Wilfred's

Church' conducted family evensong. In this ritual, Wilfred 'aided and encouraged' by his mother would arrange the sitting-room into a church, and clad in the vestments she had made him, would conduct a full evening service complete with sermon. See Owen, *Journey From Obscurity*, vol. I, pp. 150–1.

23   Owen, *Journey From Obscurity*, vol. I., p. 120.
24   Ibid., pp. 161–2.
25   *CL*, p. 70.
26   W. Owen, *The Complete Poems and Fragments*, J. Stallworthy, (ed.), vol I, London, 1983, p. 10. This volume is hereafter referred to as *CPF*.
27   *CL*, p. 187.
28   Ibid., p. 175.
29   Ibid., pp. 119–20.
30   Ibid., p. 109.
30   Ibid., p. 122.
32   Ibid., p. 151
33   Ibid., p. 95.
34   Ibid., p. 106.
35   Ibid., p. 126.
36   Ibid., p. 131.
37   Ibid., p. 152.
38   Ibid., pp. 153–4.
39   Ibid., pp. 160–1.
40   Ibid., p. 167.
41   Ibid., p. 169.
42   Ibid., p. 171.
43   Ibid., p. 172.
44   Harold Owen 'edited' the letters by using ink, rubber, and pencil upon the originals to excise certain words, phrases and short passages. In cases that he thought particularly 'dangerous' to Owen's reputation, scissors were used to delete passages. See the editors' Introduction to *CL*,p. 5.
45   *CL*, pp. 174–5.
46   Ibid., p. 137.
47   *CPF*, vol. I., p. 12.
48   *CL*, p. 536.
49   *CPF*, vol. I, pp. 61–2.
50   Ibid., pp. 73–4.
51   *CL*, pp. 204–6.
52   Ibid., p. 213.
53   Ibid., p. 234.
54   The excisions from these sentences in *CL* p. 234, have been made

good by Hibberd, *Owen the Poet*, p. 34.
55 *CL*, pp. 242–5.
56 Ibid., pp. 278–80.
57 Ibid., p. 280.
58 Ibid., p. 272.
59 Ibid., p. 273.
60 Hibberd, *Owen the Poet*, p. 30.
61 *CL*, p. 282.
62 Ibid., p. 316.
63 Hibberd, *Owen the Poet*, p. 199.
64 *CL*, p. 322.
65 Hibberd, *Owen the Poet*, pp. 42–54.
66 *CPF*, p. 70.
67 Ibid.
68 Ibid., p. 104.
69 Ibid., p. 76.
70 *CL*, p. 322.
71 Hibberd, *Owen the Poet*, p. 57.
72 Ibid., p. 58.
73 *CL*, p. 274.
74 Ibid., p. 282.
75 Ibid., p. 300.
76 Ibid., p. 311.
77 Ibid., p. 320.
78 Ibid., pp. 284–6.
79 Ibid., p. 341.
80 Ibid., p. 342.
81 Ibid., p. 348.
82 Ibid., p. 387.
83 *CPF*, pp. 77–8.
84 Ibid., p. 115.
85 *CL*, p. 421.
86 Ibid., pp. 425–7.
87 Ibid., pp. 427–8.
88 Owen was very proud of his Welsh ancestry. See Stallworthy, *Wilfred Owen*, pp. 3–4, 57.
89 *CL*, p. 429.
90 Ibid., p. 458.
91 Hibberd, *Owen the Poet*, p. 75.
92 *CL*, p. 456.
93 Ibid., p. 454.
94 Hibberd, *Owen the Poet*, p. 77.
95 A. Brock, *Health and Conduct*, London, 1923, pp. 136–8.

96   Ibid., p. 136.
97   A. Brock, 'The Re-Education of the Adult', *Sociological Review*, vol. 10, summer 1918, p. 36.
98   *CL*, p. 480.
99   *CPF*, vol. I, p. 86.
100 Ibid., p. 111.
101 Ibid., pp. 124–5.
102 Ibid., pp. 90–1.
103 Ibid., p. 123.
104 Ibid., p. 166.
105 Ibid., p. 126.
106 Ibid., p. 134.
107 Ibid., p. 140.
108 Ibid., p. 175–7.
109 *CL*, p. 461.
110 Ibid., p. 498.
111 *CPF*, p. 145–6.
112 *CL*, note 1, p. 430 and See Stallworthy, *Wilfred Owen*, p. 159.
113 Brock, *Health and Conduct*, pp. 136–48.
114 *CL*, p. 521.
115 Hibberd, *Owen the Poet*, pp. 117, 150–1.
116 *CL*, p. 505.
117 Ibid., p. 521.
118 Ibid., p. 580.
119 Ibid., p. 568.
120 Ibid., p. 571.
121 Ibid., p. 574.
122 Ibid., p. 575.
123 Ibid., p. 576.
124 Ibid.
125 Ibid., p. 580.
126 Ibid., p. 584.
127 Ibid., p. 543.
128 Ibid., p. 484.
129 *CPF*, p. 148.
130 Hibberd, *Owen the Poet*, pp. 171–2.
131 *CPF*, p. 192–3.
132 *CL*, p. 591.

5

Robert Graves

We have dealt so far with the three most famous and most mythologised of English First War poets, and I have been at pains to demonstrate the way in which received ideologies, Christianity, imperialism, Romanticism worked together in their lives to foster certain attitudes to sexuality and to suffering which in turn affected the way that they wrote about the war. In doing this, I have been concerned with hitherto unexplored similarities in the life and work of these writers. This pattern continues as I turn lastly to Graves, a close friend of Sassoon's, an admiring acquaintance of Owen's, and privy to the London literary circle centred upon Edward Marsh and Robbie Ross in which Brooke was such an eminent pre-war figure. Unlike the friends of his early manhood, however, Graves's reputation now is not first and foremost as a war poet. In a fantastically prolific literary career which continued productively until 1975, Graves wrote an enormous number of books encompassing poetry, novels and non fiction, such that he has an illustrious name in all these forms, and for writings which, ostensibly at least, have nothing whatsoever to do with the First World War. Nevertheless, *Goodbye to All That* (1929), remains one of the 'undoubted English autobiographical masterpieces'[1] to emanate from that conflict and in 1988 a new edition of his *Poems About War*[2] was published. In this chapter I will deal with Graves's war poetry, and with *Goodbye to All That*. I touch briefly upon some of his immediately post-war poetry, where it seems related to his experiences of the war, and conclude with a discussion of the lasting effects of his war experience upon his career after 1929. But following the model of my previous chapters, it is to Graves's early life that we must first turn.

Robert von Ranke Graves was born in 1895; he was nine years younger than Sassoon, eight years younger than Brooke, and two years younger than Owen. Unlike these other poets, Graves was precisely of an age to finish his final term at school in July 1914, and volunteer for the war a month later. But his youth did not mean that he escaped the typical rigours of an Edwardian childhood. Indeed his parents, Alfred and Amalie, were relatively well advanced in years by the time Robert was born, and old-fashioned proprieties were very much the order of the day at home. Alfred Perceval Graves was forty-nine in 1895 and had embarked upon his second marriage some four years earlier. He was of Anglo-Irish descent, but spent all of his working life in England, first as a teacher and then as an inspector of schools. He had five children by his first marriage, and five by his second, of whom Robert was the middle child. Apart from this brave fecundity, and the obvious obligations it entailed, Alfred also found time to pursue a literary career as a writer of poetry and song. His second wife was the 'saintly' Amalie von Ranke the daughter of a Norwegian mother and a German father whose uncle was the great historian Leopold von Ranke. Amy was thirty-four when she brought to her marriage not only a considerable fortune but also a devout Puritanism. The latter served to reinvigorate Alfred's rather less strict religious attitudes, and on his marriage he signed the pledge at his bride's behest.[3]

Robert then, was brought up in a deeply religious household. As well as reading to her children from the Bible, and making them learn hymns, Amy also 'told her children "stories about inventors and doctors who gave their lives for the suffering and poor boys who struggled to the top of the tree, and saintly men who made examples of themselves"'.[4] As a young boy, Robert was 'devoted' to his mother and she bred in him an obsession with purity and virtue, together with a concomitant terror of hellfire and damnation. Graves recalls that his early religious indoctrination also induced in him a 'sexual embarrassment' from which [he] found it very difficult to free [himself].[5]

Along with this early Christian education, went a sensitive awareness of class. At the age of four and a half, Robert contracted scarlet fever and could not be nursed at home. He was sent to a public fever hospital where he was placed in a ward with 'twenty little proletarians, and only one bourgeois child' besides himself. On returning home he found that his newly acquired accent 'was deplored', and that his fellow-sufferers had been 'very vulgar'. A year later he met again one of the boys who had been in the ward, and this caused a painful revelation:

. . . I suddenly realised with my first shudder of gentility that two sorts of Christians existed – ourselves, and the lower classes . . . I had thought of 'Master' and 'Miss' merely as vocative prefixes used for addressing other people's children; but now I found that the servants were the lower classes, and that we were 'ourselves'.

I accepted this class separation as naturally as I accepted religious dogma, and did not finally discard it until nearly twenty years later.[6]

The orthodoxies implied by 'class separation' and 'religious dogma' were aspects of a wider political conservatism which accepted imperialism as part of the natural order. Graves recalls in the first edition of his autobiography that his early childhood was 'clouded' by the Boer War. His mother's diary records the 'great gloom' that lay over the household during the siege of Ladysmith, and their was often 'great tension at the breakfast table' between Alfred, and his eldest son, Philip, who dared to 'openly support the Boers'.[7] Robert may have begun to question some aspects of belligerent imperialism during his last years at Charterhouse, but these did not prevent him from volunteering to fight, and it was not until well after the end of the war, that Graves conquered his assumptions about class and 'gentility'. As we shall see, the effect of religious dogma upon his sexuality was to have profound, and it could be argued, life-long consequences for Graves's development.

If home influences were extremely strong, it is not to be thought that formal education did not also play a part in equipping Graves with the ideologies of an English 'gentleman'. Between 1902 and 1908 he attended several different schools where he suffered a variety of tortures whilst at the same time learning classics, rugger, and 'how to keep a straight bat at cricket'.[8] He also found the sexual shyness learned from his mother was further exacerbated. Graves recalls the horror he felt at one school where the boys were made to bathe naked in an open-air bath. He was, he says, 'overcome with horror' at the sight, and observing one of the older boys, particularly disturbed to learn that hair grew 'all over' mature bodies. Perhaps worse than this was Graves's encounter with the headmaster's daughter who with a friend had attempted to find out the secrets of male anatomy by attacking Graves and 'exploring down [his] shirt neck'. This caused Robert to 'sweat with terror' whenever he met them. Graves's own commentary upon his schoolboy reactions to members of the opposite sex is telling:

In English preparatory and public schools romance is necessarily homosexual. The opposite sex is despised and treated as something obscene. Many boys never recover from this perversion. For every one born homosexual, at least ten permanent pseudo-homosexuals are made by the public-school system: nine of these ten as honourably chaste and sentimental as I was.[9]

We will have more to say about Graves's attitudes towards homosexuality, and his distinction here between 'real' and 'pseudo' homosexuality, later on. For now it is enough to notice that he is in no doubt as to the contribution made by his 'education' to his sexual difficulties. Equally revolted by adult male bodies, as he was terrified by young girls, it is not suprising that Graves remained, at least for now and some time to come, 'chaste and sentimental'.

Graves's experience of school was not improved by his attendance at Charterhouse from 1909 to 1914. He had a loathesome time. Not only had his parents encouraged his Puritanism, they had also given him every encouragement to develop his sensitivities in the direction of poetry. Such proclivities did not form a happy part of the 'public-school spirit', which Graves later described as fundamentally 'evil'. Scholarship was despised as games were worshipped, and anybody perceived as 'different' was systematically bullied and terrorised. The scholarly Graves who hated bawdy humour, and 'filth' in all its forms, whose middle name was German, and who was not so affluent as most of the other boys at the school, was a natural target for the 'hearties'. Things went from bad to worse in his second year when a doctor decided that Robert should not play football because of a heart condition. It was at this point according to his own story, that he began to feign madness, an idea he gained from '*The Book of Kings,* where David had "scrabbled on the prison wall"'.[10] He also began to write poetry seriously which, he says, was considered by his house as 'further proof of insanity'. But there was a positive side to his creative endeavours. They illicited an invitation to join the school poetry society, which had only seven members, most of whom were older than Graves. This afforded him friendship as well as much-needed advice as to how to deal with the 'bloody barbarians'.[11] A boy named Raymond Rodakowski, a year senior to Graves and from a different house, who had also been tormented because of his Polish surname, suggested that learning to box was the answer to being bullied; it was the way to beat the football 'bloods' at their own game. Accordingly, Graves began boxing 'seriously and savagely'.

Graves says that he loved Raymond since the older boy recognised him as 'a good poet, and a good person'. Towards the end of his second year, approaching his sixteenth birthday, the two boys boxed each other in the annual boxing and gymnastic display. Describing this event in his autobiography in 1929 Graves comments: 'There is a lot of sex feeling in boxing – the dual play, the reciprocity, the pain not felt as pain . . . We were out neither to hurt nor win, though we hit each other hard.'[12] The equation of sex, and pain is one that Graves continued to make and fathom for the rest of his life. But here, in this context, it introduces us to the subject of romance, friendship, and sexuality as Graves experienced them at school; a subject complicated not only by Graves's own accounts of these matters, but also by his subsequent biographers' treatment of them. Let us, first of all, continue the narrative according to Graves. His relationship with Rodakowski is said to be 'comradely' rather than 'amorous', and was interrupted by a disagreement about religion. Graves had looked forward to his confirmation as 'a spiritual climax', and had prepared himself for it with all the seriousness that his mother could have wished for, and that this anticipation implies. But the event proved anti-climactic and Graves took up his disappointment with Rodakowski. The older boy almost teasingly boasted of his own atheism and rationalism. Graves was both shocked and dismayed. Putting 'religion and [his] chances of salvation before human love', he broke with his friend completely, and although there was later some attempt to patch the relationship, the two boys remained cool and distant for the rest of their time at Charterhouse.[13]

But in Graves's fourth year, when he was in the sixth form, he 'fell in love' with a boy three years younger than himself, one G.H. Johnstone who is referred to as 'Dick' in *Goodbye to All That,* and 'Peter' in Graves's letters. This relationship continued until 1917, and was of great comfort to Graves whilst he was serving in France during 1915 and 1916. The end of the relationship occurred when Graves realised with great shock that 'Peter' had been convicted of soliciting a corporal in a Canadian regiment stationed near Charterhouse. That this precipitated a crisis in Graves's life is indicative of the nature of the relationship: it was essentially chaste and idealistic. In his autobigraphy, Graves describes his beloved as 'exceptionally intelligent and fine-spirited',[14] and in a letter of 1915 'Peter' is described as a 'radiant and unusual creature', 'a poet long before I'll ever be', who is 'still wholesome-minded and clean-living'.[15] The emphasis here upon 'moral' purity is continued when Graves goes on to agree with his old headmaster's distinction between the 'amorous' and the erotic:

Yet I agree with Rendall's distinction between 'amorousness' (by which he meant a sentimental falling in love with younger boys) and eroticism, or adolescent lust. The intimacy that frequently took place was very seldom between an elder boy and the object of his affection – that would have spoiled the romantic illusion – but almost always between boys of the same age who were not in love, and used each other as convenient sex-instruments. So the atmosphere was always heavy with romance of a conventional early-Victorian type, complicated by cynicism and foulness.[16]

It is worth reminding ourselves that this was first written when Graves was thirty-four and allowed to remain when he revised the book at the age of sixty-two. The Puritanical divorce of love and lust, of mind and body implicit in the distinction between the 'amorous' and the 'erotic' is endorsed by Graves, and is testament to the long-standing psychological effects of his education and upbringing. The quotation above concludes with the articulation of a position close to that advocated by the public schools, and which I spoke of with respect to Rupert Brooke, wherein the idealistic love of David and Jonathan is encouraged whilst physical expressions of love were regarded as 'beastly'.

In *Goodbye to All That* Graves offers us nice distinctions between his 'comradely' feelings for Raymond, his amorous feelings for 'Peter', and 'eroticism' or 'lust' which he does not admit to experiencing. He was, he says, 'unconscious of any sexual desire for Dick'. Certainly anything to do with the sexual seems to have simply disgusted the young Graves, and so it is likely that his own such feelings were savagely repressed. But however 'unconscious' Graves was (and possibly remained) of 'desire', it seems to me impossible to distinguish between the 'comradely' and the 'amorous' without pre-supposing some kind of sexual attraction in the latter which is absent in the former. But feelings of fear, guilt, and self-disgust have intruded upon frank dealings with this. Graves's homophobia in later life serves to confirm this supposition. In a letter of the 1940s, Graves wrote the following summation of his feelings about Wilfred Owen: 'Owen was a weakling really; I liked him but there was that passive homosexual streak in him which is even more disgusting than the active streak in Auden.'[17] In his letters of 1917–18 to and about Owen, Graves shows none of this animosity. It seems that as he grew older, he became increasingly threatened by aspects of his own past, and consequently grew vehemently 'manly' and heterosexual.

Graves's biographers deal with the issue of his 'homosexuality' variously. Richard Graves uses his great uncle's own language to deal with the problem. Robert, he says, 'like many young men' had gone through a 'pseudo-homosexual phase', but later found that his 'natural instincts were heterosexual'.[18] This of course begs the question as to what constitutes 'real' as opposed to 'pseudo' homosexuality, as well as leaving the implication that Graves's feelings as a young man were 'unnatural'. The latter idea becomes manifestly problematic when one considers Graves's own admission that he 'felt difficulty in adjusting [himself] to the experience of woman love'.[19] This does not sound to me like the remark of one overcome with 'natural', 'instinctual' passion.

Martin Seymour-Smith's approach is more complicated, and is, one suspects, coloured by his friendship with Graves and his knowledge of Graves's own attitude to these matters. Smith opines that both the 'homosexual practices' and 'idealistic "pure" love' which 'flourish at British public schools' is not 'really "homosexuality"' but rather 'a phase through which the majority of boys naturally pass'.[20] He later argues that Graves was heterosexual, unlike Sassoon and Owen who are described as having 'true homosexuality', as if it were a medical condition rather than a mode of being. Seymour-Smith goes on to argue that Graves, 'because of his awkward innocence, and his ignorance of sex' was incapable as a young man of distinguishing between love and friendship, but he was 'never homosexual'. He was, however, according to Smith, frightened both at school and afterwards 'that he might be', and that he would discover himself 'incapable of loving women'.[21] Seymour-Smith's pronouncements, like those of both Robert and Richard Graves, carry the implication that they *know* what 'true' or 'real' homosexuality constitutes. But none of them attempt to define the word at all, or to clarify what they mean by it.

Graves and his biographers are certain, however, that Robert was 'really' heterosexual. They are very anxious to divorce the young man's feelings from the word 'homosexual' or, in Smith's case, even from the word 'homoerotic'.[22] This seems to me to be needlessly defensive, illogical, and in the final analysis panders to the prejudices which did (and do) so much to ensure the kinds of difficulties that the writers in this book encountered with their sexual development and feelings. It is, I think, more helpful to consider Graves's experience using the interactive model outlined in an earlier chapter which suggests that we form our sexuality, along with our self-image largely as a result of social interactions. Using such a model, we can suggest that at Charterhouse, Graves, though confused and frightened by sexuality, began to identify himself with the 'Intermediate Sex' outlined by Edward Carpenter in his book of that title. Like Sassoon, Graves wrote to Carpenter about his feelings. The letter is dated 30 May 1914, and is from Charterhouse. It has been ignored by Graves's biographers. It begins as follows:

I am deeply indebted to you for *Iolaus* and *The Intermediate Sex* which have absolutely taken the scales from my eyes and caused me immense elation. You have provided a quite convincing explanation for all the problems, doubts and suspicions that I have been troubled by in my outlook on sex, and I see everything clearly.[23]

Iolaus was Carpenter's 'Anthology of Friendship' which included Phaedrus's speech, Michelangelo's sonnets, Tennyson's *In Memoriam,* Whitman's 'Leaves of Grass' and many other poems and essays about homosexuality. We have already had occasion to discuss the *Intermediate Sex,* and it is to various aspects of this book that Graves addresses himself in the rest of his letter. For instance, he suggests that the 'boy troop of Ulster' in the Cuchulan Saga constitute an additional 'Theban band' to those discussed by

Carpenter; it is says Graves 'another account of blood brother-hood.'

Graves proceeds to a discussion of the 'Urning' tendency in the poet, Richard Middleton. Graves cites various poems in which he claims that Middleton wanted 'to confess his love for a boy', but 'puts the words into the mouth of a childless woman or a girl.' These, he says, are 'old evasions which I have often myself employed'. Love between boys at Charterhouse forms the subject of the rest of the letter, and predictably enough what concerns Graves is the difference between lust and love, together with the 'damnable conspiracy of silence and suppression' practised by the school authorities. On the former subject, he has this to say:

This house at Charterhouse has emerged at last from a long period of vice . . . I know at least twelve in a house who have the courage of their conviction . . . That yields a very high percentage. People are always confiding their affairs to me so I am in a position to state that the mutual attractions are the purest and most inspiring factors in school life. They are quite spontaneous in nearly every case and not due to either force of example or to beastliness. In houses where immorality is rife, for instance this house four years ago, fellows who had contracted dirty habits practised them not on the boy whom they loved but on some third person whom they didn't mind wronging.[24]

Like Carpenter, the Puritanical Graves is anxious to idealise homosexual love, and is outraged that the school does not sufficiently recognise the reality and nobility of such affection. This accords well with Graves's account in *Goodbye to All That* where he describes defending his love for 'Dick' when taken to task by the headmaster. Graves writes of 'lecturing' his headmaster 'loftily' on the 'advantage of friendship between elder and younger boys, citing Plato, the Greek poets, Shakespeare, Michelangelo, and others, who had felt as I did.'[25] The headmaster took no further action. Perhaps he would have been less reassured to know that the most likely source for Graves's citations was Carpenter's *Iolaus*.

The distinction between 'real' and 'pseudo' homosexuality seems to me then, irrelevant to an understanding of Graves's feelings as a schoolboy. He thought of himself as an 'Urning' or chaste homosexual in Carpenter's terms. And, Seymour-Smith's contention that Graves simply confused love and friendship is surely denied by Graves's own account of his relationship with

'Dick' in *Goodbye to All That*. Despite the emphasis on chastity in this account, Graves also tells the following story which is predicated upon the physical attraction involved in the relationship. The choirmaster apparently warned Graves about exchanging 'glances' with Dick in chapel. This infuriated Graves whose anger was further inflamed when he was told that the choirmaster had been seen kissing Dick on a choir treat. Graves writes that he went 'quite mad', and immediately challenged the choirmaster who resigned as a result of Graves's threats to 'expose' a scandal. Graves reflects tellingly upon this incident that, 'No doubt my sense of moral outrage concealed a murderous jealousy.'[26] One cannot but agree with this self-assessment, and its implication of submerged physical desire.

If most of the masters at Charterhouse were uncongenial to Graves and unsympathetic to his relationship with 'Dick', there was one who was not and who befriended the young poet. George Mallory, who gained fame when he was lost attempting to climb Everest, lent Graves books and took him on rock-climbing expeditions during school vacations. He also introduced Graves to that powerful figure in Georgian poetry, Edward Marsh. When Graves left school in July 1914 it was only 'Dick' and Mallory that he regretted. A month later war was declared, and Graves volunteered for a commission, despite the fact that he had recently been one of only six boys who had opposed a motion at the Charterhouse Debating Society urging 'that this house is in favour of compulsory military service.' He had also tilted against militarism by resigning from the school Officers' Training Corps the year before he left. That he was so quick to volunteer is then worthy of some comment. Graves's own explanation of his behaviour alludes to his dread of going up to Oxford, to his outrage at the violation of Belgian neutrality, to his belief (shared with most of the population) that the war would be over quickly, and to his notion that all the fighting would be done by regulars. These reasonings are repeated by Graves's biographers, with Seymour-Smith's added assertion that the young man felt 'compromised by his German blood'.[27]

All this is cogent, but we may also speculate that the promise of Romance played a part in Graves's decision. It is quite clear that Graves agreed with Carpenter's idealisations of 'blood brotherhood' and 'comradely sacrifice'.[28] What better way of experiencing such things than to volunteer for the army? Certainly, soldiering offered more in this way than going to Oxford, which Graves viewed as merely a continuation of the miseries of Charterhouse. Soldiering also enabled a perpetuation of the balance Graves struck at school between traditional 'manly' pursuits like boxing or rock-climbing and the artistic aspirations which Carpenter had taught him to associate with his homosexual tendency. Graves was in a similar situation to Sassoon; becoming a soldier provided an opportunity for vigorous physical pursuits which could then become the subject of poetry.

Some evidence that matters military could hold the promise of Romance for Graves is offered by a poem written before he left Charterhouse. 'The Dying Knight and the Fauns' describes the poet's 'dreams of yesternight' in which he observes his 'blood brother great in fight/ . . . lying, slowly dying'. Amidst some bucolic evocation, the fauns are introduced grinning 'in wonder through the branches'. The rest of the poem constitutes their appreciation of the 'knight'. They,

> Wonder at his radiant fairness,
> At his dinted, shattered harness,
> With uncouth and bestial sounds,
> Knowing naught of war or wounds:
> But the crimson life-blood oozes
> And makes roses of the daisies,
> Purple carpets of the mosses –
> Softly now his spirit passes
> As the bee forsakes the lily,
> As the berry leaves the holly;
> But the fauns still think him living,
> And with bay leaves they are weaving
> Crowns to deck him. Well they may!
> He was worthy of the Bay.[29]

Seymour-Smith has argued that Graves's 'involvement in the homoerotic tradition is non-existent',[30] and certainly the influence of Swinburne, Wilde, or any of the other late-nineteenth-century Decadents is not apparent here or elsewhere. This may be because Graves's Puritanical attitudes were so strong that the sensuousness of these writers repelled him, or it may be simply that no one introduced him to their writings. In 1915 Graves wrote to Eddie Marsh about the factors that had combined to produce his 'ob-

solete technique'. These included the great preponderance of the
'classical' over the modern in his education, but perhaps more
importantly there was the influence of his father: 'He was hand in
glove with Tennyson and Ruskin and that lot and has been trying
to mould me in the outworn tradition, and tho' I have struggled
hard against this . . . the old Adam is always cropping up
unnoticed . . .'[31]

In 'The Dying Knight and the Fauns' we can certainly observe
the accuracy of Graves's diagnosis. The Victorian interest in me-
dieval chivalry combines with the classical 'Fauns' to produce a
very strange, but psychologically interesting combination. And
despite his distance from the Decadents, at the centre of the poem
is the by now familiar image of the sacrificed youth whose aesthetic appeal resides not merely, or even principally, in his own
physique but crucially in his spilt life-blood. Significantly, this
blood in Graves's poem turns the pretty but innocuous daisies into
the red roses of love. The poem is essentially homoerotic and
sado-masochistic. We might also notice that in keeping with the
other writers I have dealt with, the young Graves implies that
dying in battle is more 'civilised' than the expression of Eros. The
fauns allow Graves to covertly express his sexual interest. Their
'uncouth and bestial sounds' know nothing of 'wounds and war';
what they do know about by implication and association is matters sexual. That they crown the dead knight with the bays,
interestingly connects the erotic with the poetic. The knight is
Apollonian, with all that this implies of physical grandeur, but the
bays are also of course associated with poetry. The poem then
expresses an interesting complex of feelings in which Graves does
battle with his own Puritanism. At the end of the poem the knight
is safely dead, sacrificed, so that the poet can celebrate his chaste
'blood-brotherhood', but meanwhile the fauns are celebrating life,
sexuality, and poetry.

Other poems written at Charterhouse and just afterwards, included in Graves's first volume, *Over the Brazier* (1916), express
various aspects of this conflict, in which the Puritanical is never
defeated. The most obvious example of this is in 'Oh, and Oh!'
which starts like other of his contemporaneous poems in a nursery
rhyme vein asserting that the 'world's a muddle'. But this soon
gives way to a dramatic change of tone, and we are treated to the
following condemnation with its revulsion from various kinds of

'dirt':

>   Down dirty streets in stench and smoke
>   The pale townsfolk
>   Crawl and kiss and cuddle
>   In doorways hug and huddle;
>   Loutish he
>   And sluttish she
>   In loathsome love together press
>   And unbelievable ugliness.[32]

There is evidence to suggest that this was written shortly after Graves had joined the army in 1914 when he was posted to Lancaster.[33] Certainly the environs of the poem would suggest as much. For Graves the squalor of the surroundings becomes one with what he takes to be the 'squalor' of heterosexual love. Extremely unpleasant class prejudices are allied with moral and religious 'education' to produce this extraordinarily virulent condemnation of erotic, heterosexual love. The poem continues to imagine the couples involved as 'spiders' spinning a loathesome web from which he is aloof. Nevertheless the poet is 'angry' and 'feverish', his love is 'sick' because 'Far away lives [his] darling.' The slightly buried implication is that the world is muddled to allow the heterosexual 'ugliness' described above, whilst he is pining for the beauty and chastity of his (homosexual) beloved. We are forcibly reminded of Brooke imagining his generation escaping the 'little emptiness of love' and going to war like 'swimmers into cleanness leaping'. It can come as no surprise that as a young man Graves admired Brooke's poems.

George Mallory had introduced Graves not only to Eddie Marsh, but also to the work of the Georgian poets whose careers were sponsored by that quiet impresario. And there is more than a hint of Brooke's influence in the rhymed octosyllabics of 'Youth and Folly', a poem which, as its title suggests, attempts to celebrate a theme dear to Brooke's heart. Graves wrote the poem following a Charterhouse sermon which advised the boys of the awfulness of life, and chastised them for being too 'jolly' to understand the 'folly' of their lives. Graves's protest is to compose a rollicking poem which purports to 'celebrate the Gods of Mirth/And Love and Youth and Springing Earth'. Much follows concerning Pan and Bacchus, but one feels, as so often with Brooke, that Graves protests too much, and that this revelry is far more wishful than actual. The close of the poem, however ironic in intent, returns us to the reality of Graves's intellectual and emotional conflict:

> Then I realize and start
> And curse my arrogant young heart,
> Bind it over to confess
> Its horrible ungodliness,
> Set myself penances, and sigh
> That I was born in sin, and try
> To find the whole world vanity.[34]

That this is not mere self-irony, is signalled by Graves's return to a religious theme in the most famous of his early poems, 'In the Wilderness'. Here the Pre-Raphaelite flavour of 'The Dying Knight and the Fauns' is recaptured, as Graves conflates the Old Testament story of the scapegoat with the New Testament account of Christ's sojourn in the wilderness.

The bulk of the poem constitutes an extremely sympathetic portrait of Christ's 'gentle' endurance of suffering, and his teachings to both 'lost desert folk' and various birds and animals. The scapegoat, Christ's 'Comrade, with ragged coat', is introduced in the closing lines, and is described in such a way as to inevitably call to mind Holman Hunt's painting:

> Gaunt ribs – poor innocent –
> Bleeding foot, burning throat,
> The guileless old scape-goat;
> For forty nights and days
> Followed in Jesus' ways,
> Sure guard behind Him kept,
> Tears like a lover wept.[35]

As John Vickery has remarked, there is an identification here between the scapegoat and Christ. Both are innocent sufferers for other peoples' sins.[36] But there are interesting differences between the two figures aswell. Christ is imaged as powerful and in control; the scapegoat is not. The scapegoat guards and follows and suffers for love; he is a figure not unlike an idealised 'Christian soldier'. And, although this poem appears in the 'Charterhouse' section of *Over the Brazier,* it seems likely that it was written just after joining the army in 1914, as Graves's own edition of this book is annotated to the effect that the 'scapegoat' was suggested by the regimental mascot of the Royal Welch Fusiliers.[37] This only compounds the temptation to read the poem as an autobiographical metaphor concerning his own situation; he has volunteered to sacrifice himself as a true soldier and Christian.

Graves has carefully concealed any youthful, religious or Romantic idealism from his account of volunteering for the army in *Goodbye to All That*, preferring instead to dwell upon pragmatism. But it is impossible to read the poems we have discussed so far, or those that follow, without perceiving that idealism there must have been. In his first months in the army, however, there was little enough to fuel any visionary enthusiasm, for after three weeks training he was sent on detachment to look after a rugged bunch of Welsh Reservists who were guarding German internees in Lancaster. Graves was soon fretting to be removed from this mundane posting, and began to develop an impatience to be at the war. But his forbearance was to be tested further, for it was not until May 1915 that he arrived at Le Havre.

Graves had a relatively easy introduction to trench warfare. In mid May he was attached to the Second Welsh Regiment who were then occupying trenches near Cambrin. These, Graves found to be congenial, describing them in a letter home as 'palaces . . . wonderful places'.[38] The next two months were spent in and out of the front line, alternating between Cambrin and the more 'sensational' trenches amongst the Cuinchy brickstacks. Here he experienced the effects of shelling, trench mortars, and sniping, but there were no major offensives and little patrolling by either side. At the end of July he was re-united with the Royal Welch Fusiliers, joining their 2nd Battalion at Laventie. It was here that he first had the dangerous and nerve-straining experience of patrolling no man's land. After a particularly troubling experience towards the end of August, Graves went home on leave, but was back in France by mid September in time to take part in his first major engagement.

This was the 'bloody balls-up' otherwise known as the Battle of Loos which began on 25 September. Between that date and 3 October Graves got no more than eight hours sleep, although again he seems to have been relatively lucky in so far as his company was not called upon during this time to go over the top. At least twice they were prepared to attack, only to have the orders rescinded at the last moment. Nevertheless, these ten days provided enough terrifying experience to shake Graves's nerve and confidence. Not only had he been obliged to deal with the inevitable tensions of leading his men under fire, and of imminently facing combat, but also he was nightly involved in bringing in the dead and wounded from no man's land. He saw some dreadful sights before the battalion were moved back to re-group and recover.

Following this period Graves was attached to the battalion sappers safely behind the front line, and there he remained until the end of November, when he was sent to join the 1st Battalion as a captain at Locon near Festubert. It was at this time that Graves met and befriended both Siegfried Sassoon and David Thomas. December and January were spent in training, and then Graves was sent to Harfleur as an instructor, before his next spell of trench duty which began (and ended) in March 1916. We will recall that it was on 18 March 1916 that David Thomas was killed in the Fricourt trenches. Although Graves was not as close to Thomas as was Sassoon, he nevertheless felt David's death keenly, and his nerves were adversely affected again. Graves was saved from a 'general nervous collapse' by a period of leave, which was elongated by the painful necessity of an operation on his nose. Thanks to this, Graves spent nearly three months in England, and was in the country to celebrate the publication of his first volume, *Over the Brazier*, in May.

Graves's reactions to his first tours at the front were predictably complex, wavering between the devil-my-care and darker intimations. His letters prior to the Battle of Loos are, for the most part, cheerful enough. In May 1915, he writes to Eddie Marsh commiserating upon the death of Rupert Brooke, and boasting of not being frightened at all in the trenches, and of remaining undisturbed by violent artillery duels.[39] Likewise to his father, a little later, there is more than a hint of braggadocio:

the first excitement of the baptism of fire soon wears off, and the joys of sniping fat Germans, though sweet, are seldom long-lived. There is a ripple of machine-gun fire to and fro like a garden spray and the snippy sniper gets snapped.

You can't imagine how dull everything is here: nothing but a perpetual field day, mostly aimless pottering.[40]

The overt sadism encapsulated in the brief 'sweet' joys of sniping Germans, has as its masochistic corollary the reciprocal suffering entailed in the endurance of the machine-gun. The crisp, almost playful onomatopoeia with which the sniper is despatched, together with the ambivalent image of the 'garden spray' (spraying the garden is usually a positive action) suggests that Graves consciously or not welcomes these just desserts.

But elsewhere a different note is sounded in which Graves seems to be aware of the psychological temptations to extol suffering. In a letter of 9 June he wrote to his father that he 'can't stick those horrid fellows who write home to say war is adorable'. He goes on to describe a 'Horrible Thing lying in the parados':

> We can afford to laugh at corpses, if we do not know them when alive, because with them it is a case of what the men call 'nappoo fineesh': we can joke with men badly wounded who are going to recover: but when a German bullet – and a reversed one at that – strikes a man on the head and takes the scalp clean away, and still lets him live for two hours, the joke is there no more.[41]

But if Graves was beginning to perceive the darker side of war, this perception was not intruding upon his ideological acceptance of it or of the ideologies perpetuating it, in particular Christianity. On the contrary, his war experience thus far seems to have provided an impetus to his flagging Christian beliefs, and he wrote from behind the lines in July that he had attended communion with 'many of his brother-officers' and that such 'services meant much more to him out in the war zone than they had done at home'.[42]

The war had also done nothing to extinguish Graves's passion for George 'Peter' Johnstone. The only depressed letter Graves despatched during his first few months in France followed upon news sent by his cousin from Charterhouse that 'Peter' was not the pure and chaste individual that Graves took him to be. This alarm was, however, soon assuaged by 'Peter' himself who wrote saying that he had been 'ragging about in a silly way' and promising henceforth to eschew such behaviour for the sake of their friendship.[43] Before the Battle of Loos, Graves wrote a 'farewell' letter to Peter. It is indicative not only of Graves's continuing feelings for 'Dearest Peter', but also of a very conventional acceptance of his situation:

> This is in case I die. If I do, it'll be young and happy and in splendid company, without any fears of Hell or anxious hopes for Heaven: I leave

all that to God: no good building on doubts. I should have liked to write something fine and lasting by which nice people hereafter might remember my name but childlessness loses its sting when I think that you who mean infinitely more to me than myself are going to be a greater poet than I could ever be and that perhaps I have sometimes helped you to understand and love, and so in a sense may live in you when my body is broken up, and have a share in all your doings.[44]

A spirit of self-sacrifice, and self-abasement informs this utterance; the implication is clear that Graves thinks his death less important than 'Peter's' life. Religious doubts are quelled, and 'all that' is left to God. Such unexceptional sentiments which might have been written by any number of young subalterns on the Western Front, are only suprising when viewed in relation to the tough, sardonic tones of *Goodbye to All That*. As we shall see, Graves's re-writing of his experience in his autobiography, elides much of his initial reaction to the war, and is very concerned to be neither 'wet' nor 'unmanly'.

The debacle at Loos did not quell Graves's high mindedness. Although he reported to Eddie Marsh having witnessed 'awful scenes', nevertheless he told his parents that the battle had been 'a great experience'. And despite the company of his fellow officers whose 'sole topics of conversation are wine, women, racing, hunting and musical comedy', he is thoroughly impressed with 'the men', whose behaviour at Loos he describes as 'splendid', and with whom he says he 'gets on very well'.[45] They are a source of comfort to him, and perhaps more than his brother-officers, enabled Graves to idealise his regiment. On first joining the Royal Welch Fusiliers, Graves had been impressed with their tradition, and now, being part of that tradition gained particular significance to him. Writing to Edward Marsh again in December 1915 he says, 'I have to live up to my part here as I have learned to worship my Regiment: in sheer self-defence I had to find something to idealize in the Service and the amazing sequence of R W Fus. suicides in defence of their "never-lost-a-trench" boast is really quite irresistible. Result: I am getting horribly Praetorian and drill-bookish . . . '[46] It is significant that this romantic idealisation of the regiment is dependent upon the self-sacrifice of men, willing to die to preserve its good name. Suffering is at the heart of the ideal.

Graves's other sources of comfort in the trenches remained

'Peter' and poetry, and these two were not entirely unconnected. 'Peter', as I mentioned earlier, is described to Edward Marsh in a letter of October 1915 as 'wholesome-minded and clean-living'.[47] Even in the 1957 edition of *Goodbye to All That* 'Peter's' letters to Graves whilst at the front are described as 'something solid and clean to set off against the impermanence of trench life and the sordidness of life in billets'.[48] In 1915 as in 1957, Graves is anxious to assure his respective audiences that his relations with 'Peter' are 'clean'. Implicitly it is the sexual which is 'dirty'. 'Peter' was not only credited with virtue, but also with the name of 'poet'. He is, Graves declared to Marsh, 'a poet long before I'll ever be'.[49] In Graves's view it was impossible to be a 'good' artist without being a 'good' person.[50] Peter fulfilled both criteria, or so Graves believed.

For himself, Graves felt after Loos that 'an inspiration' had come to him 'of what the New Poetry [was] to be'.[51] He was anxious to respond to Marsh's earlier criticisms of his old-fashioned technique, and to become part of the Georgian movement. On 24 February 1916 he wrote Marsh a long letter in which he commented upon the recently published *Georgian Poetry* anthology, described his admiration for Charles Sorley, and went on to speak of his own work. He cannot praise the anthology enough; it is his most 'treasured possession' in France, it is 'splendid' and he 'love [s] nearly every piece in it'. But 'most of all' he loves Rupert's contributions, '"Heaven" and "The Great Lover" and "The Soldier" and all the rest'.[52] That Graves could still admire 'The Soldier' after Loos, is a fair indication that he had not as yet begun to question any of the ideological underpinnings of the war; there was no radical questioning of the idea of 'noble sacrifice'.

His avowed admiration for Brooke's war sonnets, also indicates that Graves had not quite perceived the slightly oppositional tenor of Sorley's work, or if he had, could not or did not relate it to Brooke's position. Sorley was the first to offer the trenchant critique that Brooke had 'taken the sentimental attitude'.[53] This was an attitude that Sorley's own poems sought to avoid. Graves speaks of reading the recently and posthumously published *Marlborough and Other Poems* (Sorley was killed in action near Loos on 15 October 1915):

It seems ridiculous to fall in love with a dead man as I have found myself doing but he seems to have been one so entirely after my own heart in his loves and hates, besides having been just my own age and having spent just the same years at Marlboro' as I spent at Ch'house.[54]

Two months later, in a letter to Sassoon, Graves returns to his admiration for Sorley which he says is shared by 'Peter'. Evidently Sassoon was also interested, and had been making enquiries about Sorley and specifically about his sexual orientation. Graves writes: 'What did your Marlburian say about Sorley, and was he "so"? As his book contains no conventional love-lyrics and as he'd reached the age of 20, I conclude he was.'[55] In May 1916 then, Graves implicitly identifies himself with Sorley (as well as with Peter and Sassoon) as being 'so', by which I think it is fair to understand, homosexual. His self-image does not seem to have undergone any radical change thus far due to his war experience.

But if we return to his earlier letter to Marsh, we find Graves remarking that he has 'altered a bit' and '*C'est la Guerre*'. The latter phrase is mooted as a possible title for his forthcoming book because,

It has a laugh and an apology in it and expresses just what I want, an explanation – an excuse almost – for the tremendous change in tone and method and standpoint which you must have noticed between the first and last parts of the verse-cycle, a hardening and coarsening and loss of music. It gives a clue, then, to the contents of the book and yet has nothing highfalutin' about it which would make me ridiculous in the eyes of the Regiment and of Ch'house: which is most important.[56]

It can hardly be suprising that Graves felt that both he and his poems had been hardened and coarsened by the war. Part of this process apparently involved a regression into an affirmation of the values embodied by Charterhouse and the regiment. We will recall that in his last term, Graves had been involved in a critique of his school and of its involvement with militarism. But soon after volunteering he returned to Charterhouse and found the school 'a grand place',[57] and in the quotation above, there is a clear wish to accommodate both school and military ethos and to be accepted within the bastions of conservatism. Along with this went the beginnings of a more profound change in his identity, from homosexual to heterosexual, but in order to demonstrate this we must turn to the poems themselves.

The war poems in *Over the Brazier*, most of which were written whilst in France, provide an intriguing record of Graves's psychological development and his ambivalent reactions to his soldiering and to the war. Several of them are concerned with the issues raised in the letter to Marsh discussed above. The relationship between, war, art, and sexuality is explored. The first four poems in the 'La Basée' section of the book, 'On Finding Myself a Soldier', 'The Shadow of Death', 'A Renascence' and 'The Morning Before the Battle' are most interesting in this connection.

'On Finding Myself a Soldier'[58] reminds us that 'hard' and 'coarse' are relative terms. The poem hardly justifies either epithet, but it does attempt to articulate something of the changes Graves felt he had undergone. The poem takes as its central idea the 'flowering' of self-hood; it is a poem about maturation, the movement between bud and bloom. The poet begins by asserting that his 'bud was backward to unclose,/A pretty baby-queen' and goes on to suggest that he never doubted 'when her heart should show', it would be coloured 'Like the flush of dawn on snow'. But now 'aghast' he finds the bud has metamorphosed into 'Twelve flamy petals ringed around/A heart more red than blood'. Discounting as I think we must, the tempting pun on 'queen', nevertheless we are obliged to recognise that Graves figures his 'budding' as specifically female. And clearly we may read the bud/flower metaphor as pertaining to both his sexuality and his poetry. But the implications of the final image are less transparent. The change from 'the flush of dawn on snow' to full-blooded red, implies a loss of delicacy, and perhaps a violent loss of innocence. What is not overthrown as yet, however, is the gender of the flower. Graves is, I think, influenced in the poem by the idea to be found in Carpenter's writings and elsewhere, that a homosexual constitutes a 'female' soul in a 'male' body. He further equates this 'femininity' (as does Carpenter) with his art. Graves seems to be saying in this poem, much the same as he said in his letter to Marsh: that on becoming a soldier his work has developed in a harder, coarser way than he anticipated. What is of more interest in the poem than the letter, however, is the ambivalence of the 'flamy petals' around the 'heart of blood'. Intrinsically this is by no means an unattractive image; we are reminded of the multifoliate rose of love, ardent and passionate.

The three poems that follow give different weight to the opposed positions within Graves's ambivalence. Both 'The Shadow of Death' and 'The Morning Before the Battle', dwell on the negative aspects of his war experience, whilst 'A Renascence' is unremittingly positive. The first of these poems argues that the war will kill both himself and his art. He will die, 'With battle murder at [his] heart/Sad death for a poet!' Again his 'pretty little soul' is equated with his 'art' and both are imaged as 'a baby' who has now become a 'changeling accursed'. The poem ends like this:

> To fight and kill is wrong –
>   To stay at home wronger:
> Oh soul, little play and song,
>   I may father no longer![59]

'Battle murder', Graves asserts, is morally justified, but has the negative consequence of killing, or at least changing, his art. Although the 'baby' soul is not gendered in the poem, Graves's persona is most definitely male, and this maleness is, of course, associated with fighting and killing, which in the final analysis constitutes the 'right'. Graves laments the death of his former art and soul, but the implication is that this sacrifice is for a good cause.

'The Morning Before the Battle' again describes a premonition of death, but this foreboding is now rendered through contrasting images of a garden. The poet walks amidst flowers carelessly singing, pinning roses on his breast, and reaching for a bunch of cherries. But then a cold wind blows, and blights 'every beauty with chill breath':

> I looked, and ah! my wraith before me stood,
>   His head all battered in by violent blows:
> The fruit between my lips to clotted blood
>   Was transubstantiate, and the pale rose
> Smelt sickly, till it seemed through a swift tear-flood
>   That dead men blossomed in the garden-close.[60]

Although the ostensible movement of the poem is negative, it is possible to detect in the sumptuous and sensual imagery here an echo of 'The Dying Knight and the Fauns' with its late Victorian tendency to endow death with aesthetic and erotic appeal. The argument of the poem suggests that beauty is blighted, but the ambivalent language of this stanza expresses a sado-masochistic fantasy in which fruit and blood are equated, and 'dead men' are said to 'blossom'. These blooms are clearly related to the red heart and flaming petals at the close of 'On Becoming a Soldier', and they contain the same uncertainty.

There is a suggestion in the three war poems we have discussed so far, that whilst the loss of previous aspiration and potential is lamented, there are moral and aesthetic compensations to be gained through the experience of war and suffering. This positive aspect of war becomes the overt subject of 'A Renascence', a poem in which suffering is openly embraced as a creative force, and the victory of the 'masculine' over the 'feminine' manifestly celebrated:

> White flabbiness goes brown and lean,
>   Dumpling arms are now brass bars,
> They've learnt to suffer and live clean,
>   And to think below the stars.
>
> They've steeled a tender, girlish heart,
>   Tempered it with a man's pride,
> Learning to play the butcher's part
>   Though the woman screams inside –[61]

The poem goes on to conclude that 'they' have learnt to 'stab with the stark bayonet/Side by side with fighting men' and that despite death, from 'their travailings and groans/Poetry is born again'.

This chilling utterance, like Rupert Brooke's 'The Soldier', but more violently so, equates 'cleanliness' with suffering, and with a brutal machismo. Dreaming of the stars is forsaken for the remorseless 'rationality' of 'masculine' thought. Tenderness is abandoned, whilst physical and emotional 'toughness' are celebrated. So much is clear. But two questions remain. To whom does Graves's third person plural pronoun refer, and what is the role of the 'woman' within? Of course Graves's 'They' could be taken to embrace all his fellow soldiers, but it is possible to argue that the title and the last line imply that he has 'poets' specifically in mind. A letter written some months later adds weight to this argument. In February 1917 he remarks to Robert Nichols:

My idea of a poet is a woman suffering all the hardships of a man; hardening her weak softnesses; healthy and clean, loving the elements, loving friends more than life itself, proud, whimsical, wise, simple. But appreciating the refinements of Life as much as the harshnesses . . .[62]

This is very adjacent to the ideas expressed in 'A Renascence'. In the poem the 'woman' within is not so much defeated as made into part of a process of transmutation. It is surely not fanciful to suggest that 'her' screaming is related to 'their travailings and groans' which 'give birth' to poetry. We uncover a metaphor in which the poet is both 'mother' and 'father' to the poem; the latter is the product not only of the suffering caused by the war, but also the suffering entailed in the relationship between the internalised male and female. Sado-masochistic sexuality is central to both the experience of war, and the writing of poetry. The 'woman' within is tortured, whilst the 'man' learns 'the butcher's part.

Both the poem and the letter under discussion are ample testament to the struggle Graves felt was underway with respect to his identity. They also demonstrate little in the way of anti-war sentiment, rather the reverse. A minority of the other poems in *Over the Brazier* hint at the less palatable aspects of trench warfare in a way that most popular poetry of 1915–16 did not, (I think particularly of 'Limbo' and 'The Trenches') and the war is referred to in one poem as 'silly' and 'mad'. But elsewhere consolation is very much in evidence. 'The Dead Fox Hunter',[63] for instance, deals with an incident at Loos, in which a severely wounded officer lying in no man's land had jammed his fist into his mouth to stop himself crying out, thereby halting dangerous attempts to save him. Graves found the corpse, hit in seventeen places, still with the knuckles forced into the mouth.[64] From this grisly story Graves managed to shape a poem which not only celebrates the dead man's heroism, but also in a rather jolly way anticipates his arrival in heaven where 'Justice must provide/For one who rode straight and at hunting died.' The poet gleefully imagines the inauguration of a heavenly hunt in which 'the whole host of Seraphim complete/Must jog in scarlet to his opening Meet'. For evidence that this recourse to improbable, metaphysical consolation was neither wholly ironical nor entirely unserious, we may turn to another poem 'Big Words' which also hints at that renewal of Christian faith mentioned earlier with respect to Graves's time in France.

'Big Words'[65] neatly expresses the tension between positive and negative experiences of war. The poem begins with the poet indicting himself for 'whining' of approaching death. This, he asserts is 'weak' and 'ungracious'. Much of the rest of the poem is devoted to a hymn of praise to explain why he is 'satisfied' with his past and present. This begins with the mention of 'winning confidence' prior to the war on rock climbing expeditions; a confidence that the war has consolidated. Graves goes on to talk of 'winning faith in the wisdom of God's ways' and finding 'it justified' even in the 'chaos' of war. He has also, he says, won 'love that stays/And warms the heart like Wine at Easter-tide' – an image that inevitably resonates with the idea of loving sacrifice through its associations with the Eucharist. The poet's 'cup of praise/Brims over', and he asserts that he is ready to die. The poem concludes, however, with a less cheerful couplet: 'But on the firestep, waiting to attack,/He cursed, prayed, sweated, wished the proud words back.'

On leave in England, however, the proud, 'Big Words' were in the ascendant. Writing to Sassoon in May he speaks of being 'desolated' at having 'deserted' both Sassoon and the battalion, and goes on to say that although he can't 'pretend to like Fricourt more than this heavenly place' (i.e. Harlech), he 'honestly would go back tonight' if he could. He asks Sassoon to send him as 'much battalion news' as possible.[66] This mood only intensified the longer he stayed in England, and was no doubt encouraged by another hiccup in his relationship with 'Peter'. This time it was 'Peter's' mother who caused the problem. She had precipitated 'a great, a hardly bearable disaster' on finding and reading all Graves's letters to her son. Graves himself takes up the story in another letter to Sassoon:

So terribly has she been shocked at finding quotations from Samuel Butler and Carpenter and people in them and at such signatures as 'ever yours affectionately, Robert' and 'best love, R' that she has extracted a promise from the poor lad that he will have nothing to do with me till he leaves Ch'house. Complications too long to enumerate leave no loopholes of evasion for either of us, so I am now widowed, laid waste and desolate.[67]

Towards the end of the same letter, Graves wrote, quoting the popular soldiers song '"I want to go home" – to France.' A month later on 23 June, Graves is champing at the bit. He is 'restless and enthusiastic and want-to-get-back-to-the-boys-ish'. He has 'no Peter to illumine the gloom in an atmosphere clogged with moral and actual smut.' He goes on:

Ohe! Roll on the trenches! I hear you've been risking your precious life again among them craters: I am pleased, damned please, you're doing so well; wish to hell I was with you – go on risking, and good luck. It's a man's game![68]

Little could illustrate so trenchantly as this, the paradoxes of both Graves's and Sassoon's sexuality. Despite being 'widowed', Graves admires and wishes to play the 'man's game'. Sassoon, as we have seen, was in a similar position.

Graves got his wish soon enough, for by July he was back in France, where he went up the front line on the 15th to play his part in the Somme offensive. This did not last long. For on 20 July Graves was so severely wounded that he was left on a stretcher to die at the Casualty Clearing Station. But he somehow refused to fulfil medical predictions, and survived a tortured journey first to a field hospital, and then on to the base hospital at Rouen. He arrived back in England on 3 August and remained in hospital until the 26th of that month. He then spent until November convalescing. It was during this period that he consolidated his relationship with Sassoon, who was also in England recovering from trench fever. The two men spent a considerable amount of time together, reading and amending each others' poems, and discussing their attitude towards the war. There was some talk of trying to get posted to Egypt, but it seems that Graves was won over to Sassoon's more heroic proposition that they had to go back to France to lead their men, and to uphold the 'good reputation' of poets.[69]

On being passed fit for active service then, Graves returned to the 2nd Battalion in France, but once there it was quickly perceived that he was not fit enough for trench duties, so he was attached to the Headquarter Company. But Graves's health was precarious and in the very cold winter of 1917 he contracted bronchitis and was sent back to England. This was the end of his service abroad. He spent the next several months in and out of hospitals, suffering from both his weak lungs and 'nerves'. The symptoms of the latter condition included an inability to use a telephone properly, a phobia about train travel following his horrendous journey from the front whilst wounded, and an obsessive fear of gas such that any unusual smell was enough to trigger a trembling response. He was also subject to 'not wholly rational swings of mood'. Despite all this, he was not sent to a hospital specialising in nervous disorders, but instead found himself at a convalescent home situated in Osbourne House on the Isle of Wight.

It was from here that Graves began a tentative correspondence with 'Marjorie' who was a nurse he'd met whilst in hospital at Oxford. It is of this relationship that Graves writes in his autobiography that he found it difficult to adjust to woman love.[70] And this seems to be an accurate remark since the relationship ended before it had really begun. Graves found out that Marjorie was engaged to a subaltern in France, and decided therefore to end the correspondence. Honour and loyalty towards his comrades in arms are the ostensible motivation for this moral rigour, but it is also likely that Graves was not wholly unrelieved to find an excuse for terminating this liaison. For contrary to the account in *Goodbye to All That* Graves was still in touch with 'Peter Johnston' at this stage. When Graves had returned home from France wounded the previous year, intercessions with Johnstone's mother were made, and before leaving for France again in January 1917, Graves had met Johnstone and had 'a long talk with him', finding him 'extraordinarily intelligent'.[71] Presumably whilst in hospital in Oxford, and then on the Isle of Wight Graves had little chance of meeting with his protégé, but that his emotions were still considerably engaged with 'Peter' is evidenced by the reaction when Graves heard in July that 'Peter' had been arrested for soliciting a corporal near Charterhouse. This news coincided with Sassoon's protest against the war. Graves's two closest friends were both in trouble, and Graves was mortified by their respective actions.

On 12 July Graves wrote to Eddie Marsh in great distress firstly about Sassoon's protest: 'It's an awful thing – completely mad – that he's done. Such rotten luck on you and me and his friends, especially in the Regiment.' Graves goes on to say that he thinks Sassoon to be 'quite right in his views but absolutely wrong in his action' and says that for himself he is 'a sound militarist in action however much of a pacifist in thought'.[72] Graves did not waver from this ambivalent position; he even volunteered to fight in the Second World War, but was refused on the grounds of his age and health.[73] We will have more to say about his attitudes to army service as the story of his relationship with Sassoon unfolds. But for now we return to his letter to Marsh, which also contained news of 'Peter'. Graves writes that he has had 'the worst possible news about . . . Peter who appears to have taken a very wrong turning and to have had a mental breakdown'. Apparently Graves could not bring himself to tell Marsh that his erstwhile favourite had been accused of a (homo) sexual misdemeanour.

Graves's reaction to his two friends' troubles was contrasting. He completely abandoned his relationship with 'Peter', such 'low' sexual expression being regarded as 'dirty' and beyond the pale. But Sassoon was to be 'saved' from his own actions, and Graves wangled himself away from Osbourne House and back to the mainland in order to pull strings and intercede on Sassoon's behalf. The break with Johnstone is taken by Graves's biographers to indicate the end of Graves's 'pseudo-homosexuality'. Paul O'Prey goes so far as to talk of Graves being 'cured' by the experience.[74] But matters are not quite so simple as this, and in my view Sassoon's protest also played a part in Graves's wilful pursuit of a heterosexual relationship in the ensuing months. For Graves now found that both his closest friends had committed illegal, dissident actions which were too much for his own deeply and conventionally Puritanical morality. Rather than the fine idealisation of blood-brotherhood to be found in Edward Carpenter's writing, it seems likely that Graves now perceived homosexuality as leading to legal and social aberrations which he was anxious to avoid. Hence, I think, Graves's seeking out of Nancy Nicholson in August 1917.

The Nicholsons periodically rented a house near the Graves's, in Harlech, and Robert had become friendly with Ben Nicholson when home on leave in March 1915. At the same time Graves had also met Ben's sixteen-year-old sister, Nancy, but at first took little notice of her. It was not until he had seen Sassoon safely despatched to Craiglockhart Hospital, and had some leave in Wales that his relationship with her began to develop. When he called on the Nicholsons on a Friday evening at the end of August 1917, he found Nancy 'boyishly dressed as a bandit',[75] in preparation for a fancy-dress dance at another neighbour's house. Graves accompanied her to this function and their friendship developed from there in the course of the next few months. They were engaged by December, and married in January 1918, only six months after the 'worst possible news about "Peter"'.

Nancy was not only 'boyish' in fancy dress. She wore her hair short, preferred trousers to skirts, and was described by Graves in a letter to Sassoon as 'a capable farmer's boy'.[76] Certainly she relished her work in the Women's Land Army, and was aggressively feminist in her attitudes, all of which seems to have made it easier for Graves to make the adjustment to 'woman love'. His change of emotional direction is indicative, I believe, of a turning away (which must have been, at least in part, self-conscious) from his homosexual feelings, frightened of their implications. As we have seen, his early war poems articulate an internal division between what he took to be the 'masculine' and 'feminine' sides of himself. If the 'feminine' or homosexual side led to actions like those of 'Peter' and Sassoon, Graves would promote the 'masculine' side of himself, so that by 1920 he could write categorically that, 'in a poet the dominant spirit is male'.[77] But this is to jump ahead. In 1917–18 his adoption of a heterosexual role caused considerable awkwardness with various friends to whom he felt he had to explain himself.

In a letter to Robert Nichols of November 1917, for instance, Graves begins by saying how glad he is that they are both 'taking the same line about the war'. Later, he feels obliged to offer this strange apologia:

It's only fair to tell you that since the cataclysm of my friend Peter, my affections are running in the more normal channels and I correspond regularly and warmly with Nancy Nicholson, who is great fun. I only tell you this so that you should get out of your head any misconceptions about my temperament. I should hate you to think I was a confirmed homosexual even if it were only in my thought and went no farther.[78]

This is very defensive indeed, and it is noticeable that Graves now wishes to disavow even chaste homosexuality. He is in full retreat from his previous feelings and commitments.

But some of these were not as easily dealt with as the letter to Nichols implies. The homosexual circle in London centred upon Robbie Ross, for instance, with whom Graves and Sassoon socialised in London, needed to be dealt with circumspectly. In the same month as his letter to Nichols quoted above, Graves also wrote to Sassoon and mentioned that he had seen Nancy who was 'working on a small farm at St.Ives Huntingdonshire.' Graves goes on to instruct Sassoon like this:

Robbie doesn't like the idea of her. So you can quiet him down, *if he mentions her*. She's doing a children's book with me. Otherwise leave her out of the conversation. I don't want to have unfriendliness and I'll

not even allow dear Robbie to bully Nancy. I'll parade her one day for
your approval.[79]

Graves anticipates difficulties with Ross, and even though he has
enough confidence in the friendship with Sassoon to broach the
subject of Nancy, there is still the need to flatter Sassoon by
speaking of 'parading' Nancy for approval. This should not be
suprising. Apart from 'Peter', Sassoon had been Graves's closest
friend. And now this 'friendship' was to be complicated by the
presence of a woman. From this point on relations with Sassoon
became progressively more strained and distant. It could be argued
that the source of tension between the two men was their different
attitudes to the war. But it seems to me that the issue of the war
became inextricably entangled with Graves's decision to pursue
Nancy. They appear to be distinct issues, but I submit that they
were intimately related. Graves considered Sassoon's behaviour to
be 'mad', just as he construed 'Peter's' behaviour as a 'mental
breakdown', and it is likely that Graves considered both of their
actions to be 'unmanly'. He meanwhile, was anxious to assert both
his sanity and his manliness.

The first hint of difficulties in the relationship between Graves
and Sassoon comes shortly after the latter's incarceration at Craiglockhart, and the start of Graves's relationship with Nancy. In
August 1917, Sassoon wrote to Graves from Craiglockhart about
contributing to an anthology to be edited by one Bertram Lloyd.
Graves replied that he would not contribute to this book because
'one' didn't want to 'make oneself cheap' and because he was
worried that Lloyd 'might (as Bobbie would say) be a Conscious
Object and bring discredit on the dear old Regiment and get me
court-martialled and sent to Craiglockhart for contributing to his
book'.[80] Graves goes on to pass this off as a joke, but it must have
seemed a desperately cruel jest to Sassoon. Graves is clearly letting
Sassoon know what he thinks of Conscientious Objectors, and
rubbing in the message of loyalty to the regiment and to friends.
Further evidence that Graves wished to distance himself from
Sassoon's protest, is offered by Graves's decision to change the
dedication on his forthcoming book, *Fairies and Fusiliers*. This
was published in November 1917, and was originally to have been
dedicated to Sassoon, but in September Graves changed his mind,
dedicating the book to the Royal Welch Fusiliers instead. Sassoon

took this graciously, and Graves replied:

Dearest Sassons,
  If you'd been anyone else you'd have thought me a first-class four-let-
ter man for changing the dedication like that, but you know it wasn't
meant for anything, except that I was afraid at the last moment of a
dedication to an individual for fear of jealousy from Gosse, Ross,
Marsh, Masefield or anyone like that of my 'friends and lovers' not to
mention the family. Also, I thought that to point my devotion to the
regiment would strengthen my expression of hatred for the war.[81]

Graves may indeed have feared 'jealousy' amongst his 'friends and
lovers', presumably including Nancy. But that he was also frightened of being too closely identified with Sassoon's protest is
certain, and the dedication to the regiment is suitably martial. He
was not going to offend the mores of either Charterhouse or the
army through such a dedication. How Graves thought this would
contribute to expressing his 'hatred of the war' is obscure to us
now, and depends on the kind of paradox within all of Wilfred
Owen's work, i.e. those hate the war most intensely who have
fought the hardest and lost their comrades; in order to be a 'good'
pacifist one has to have fought well.

  When we consider the war poems in *Fairies and Fusiliers* written between 1916 and 1917, the force of this paradox is abundantly clear. On the one hand there are poems which unabashedly
celebrate the regiment and its achievements, on the other there are
intimations of sadness and loss. What is demonstrably absent is
any kind of protest against the war. As we see in poems like 'The
Legion', 'To Lucasta On Going to the Wars – For the Fourth
Time', and 'The Next War' Graves accepts his situation, and that
of his comrades, with a proud fatalism. In the first two of these
poems, Graves returns to his classical education to furnish him
with metaphors figuring his own situation and opinions. 'The
Legion' constitutes a conversation between Strabo and Gracchus
who sit at their wine whilst the Legion passes by under their
window. In reply to Gracchus' question 'Is that the Three and
Twentieth'?, Strabo vehemently denies that it is, asserting that the
Legion died 'in the first year of this damned campaign/. . . and
won't rise again'. He further suggests that whilst Rome mourns
for her dead sons, both he and Gracchus also deserve pity for
surviving the war to see the 'Legion come to this'. A very unflat-

tering description of the new conscripts is then given, which one could easily imagine a surviving regular of the First or Second Battalion of the Royal Welch Fusiliers applying to the replacements of 1917 and 1918. But Gracchus clearly articulates Graves's own position in the closing lines of the poem. He chastises Strabo with a celebration of the Legion:

> They all try, Strabo; trust their hearts and hands.
> The Legion is the Legion while Rome stands,
> And these same men before the autumn's fall
> Shall bang old Vercingetorix out of Gaul.[82]

It is not difficult given the dedication of the book to the Royal Welch Fusiliers, to see the obvious application of these sentiments to their situation. We should also notice the imperialist patriotism implicit in the poem; Graves's political conservatism is plainly expressed.

But it is a conservatism of a radical kind, in which politicians are despised and only the virtues of the regiment extolled; the implications of this position are militaristic, and quite opposite to Graves's assertion that in dedicating his book to the regiment it would strengthen his expression of hatred for the war. In 'To Lucasta On Going to the Wars', Graves's problematic position is easy to discern. The poem begins with an evasion of political responsibility:

> It doesn't matter what's the cause,
>   What wrong they say we're righting,
> A curse for treaties, bonds and laws,
>   When we're to do the fighting!
> And since we lads are proud and true,
>   What else remains to do?[83]

One can readily appreciate how Graves's situation led to this bellicose expression, but one should not, I think, condone it. The implications of these lines seem to me both frightening and dangerous. For it is surely *crucial* to any moral consideration of war to discuss whether the end justifies the means, and like Thomas Hardy's character Burdett, one is doubtful whether *any* 'end 'is worth the reaching by so red a road'.[84] Separating soldierly virtues 'pride', 'truth' (by which, I take it, Graves means true to each other) 'fighting', from their political meanings is to celebrate militarism, and all the suffering it entails, for its own sake.

That Graves is struggling with such implications is evident elsewhere in the poem. The Fusilier in question, going to the wars for the fourth time 'hating war', is neither going because he is courageous, nor because of love, hate, anger or fear; it is because 'he's a Fusilier/And his pride keeps him there'. There is an overt tension here between hating war and loving the fighting, or at least the esprit de corps, the 'pride' that it engenders. Paradoxically this is politically potent writing. Precisely the same kind of mental attitudes are encouraged in officers and officer cadets today. They are taught that their role is not political, and that their first duty is to their comrades, their unit, their service. It is a way of abnegating political responsibility for the exercise of a brutality which is always implicitly or explicitly considered to be necessary.

'The Next War'[85] demonstrates the depths of Graves's conservatism at this period of his life. The poem begins with a description of children 'With bows and arrows and wooden spears,/Playing at Royal Welch Fusiliers'. Graves poses the question as to whether they have been 'warned' how their games will end. He goes on to tell them, arguing that from the first moment of such play they are bound by 'fate' to act 'As champions of this stony ground,/Loyal and true in everything,/To serve your army and your King'. They will have to be prepared to suffer to 'keep safe those joys /That belong to British boys', protecting Wales from 'Prussians' and 'Slavs'. There will always be another war 'dirtier' but 'more glorious', and 'the cruellest team will win'. Graves goes on to draw a portrait of awful politicians engendering terrible suffering, whilst children play at being soldiers. The poem is circular in its form, and is composed in rhymed quadrameters all of which helps to create the dominant tone of acceptance and inevitability. Despite the recognition that 'new foul tricks unguessed before/Will win and justify this war', protest is implicitly useless. The boys have to learn to 'hold your nose against the stink/And never stop too long to think'. They have to 'play the game' of being Royal Welch Fusiliers as best they can.

All three of the poems from *Fairies and Fusiliers* that we have considered so far touch lightly upon the 'horror' and 'pity' of war; these aspects remain undescribed and appear in the poems, as in this sentence, merely abstractions. In only one or two poems (I think particularly of 'The Last Post' and 'A Dead Boche') does Graves actually describe some graphic detail from his trench experience. The majority of poems act rather as a way of mediating his experience, of seeking ways to accommodate it positively. 'The Assault Heroic' and 'Two Fusiliers' find consolations which are less concerned with regimental pride, than they are with love and art. The former poem internalises the war, seeing it as a battle within the self. Its starting point is 'Five sleepless days and nights' which leaves the poet threatened by the 'dungeon of despair'. The poet's 'foes' are the inhabitants of that doleful place who tempt him to join them with their taunts:

> To-day we've killed your pride;
> To-day your ardour ends.
> We've murdered all your friends;
> We've undermined by stealth
> Your happiness and your health.
> We've taken away your hope.[86]

But this 'assault' upon the poet is countered by his 'spear of faith', his 'shield of laughter' and his 'sharp, tongue-like sword/That speaks a bitter word'. With these attributes he defies despair and 'alchemises' the aggression of his enemies until they are defeated. Implicitly the poem is about Graves's ability to overcome despair through art. Faith and humour are allied with the tongue-like sword to transform the negativity of his experience into artistic 'lumps of gold', or 'instant fruit'. Like Brooke, Sassoon and Owen, Graves also recognises inspiration for his art in war.

'Two Fusiliers' is also intimately related to Sassoon and Owen, and echoes sentiments to be found in Brooke's war sonnets. The poem was written with Sassoon in mind, and Owen's 'Apologia Pro Poemate Meo' is thought to have been inspired by it.[87] Certainly 'Two Fusiliers' shares the theme of love between comrades that is also the basis of Owen's poem. Graves begins by celebrating the fact that he and the 'other' fusiliers have survived and that they do not need either 'pledge or oath' to 'bind' their lovely friendship fast'. It is already secured by the experience of shared suffering; they are 'bound' by 'wire and wood and stake', by Fricourt and Festubert, by 'whipping rain', and by 'all the misery and loud sound'. Nothing can bring people closer together than this shared suffering:

> Show me the two so closely bound
> As we, by the wet bond of blood,

By friendship, blossoming from mud,
By Death: we faced him, and we found
Beauty in Death,
In dead men breath.[88]

Implicitly, heterosexual, erotic love is nothing compared with
'blood brotherhood'. Despite his adoption of a heterosexual persona during 1917, this poem still displays the influence of Edward
Carpenter. And the sado-masochism involved in the homoerotic
relationship is overt. It is blood that 'binds', along with the
'whipping' rain and misery; and there is beauty in death. The last
line implies that the dead remain an inspiration to life and song.
Love and art are the product of slaughter.

Given that Graves felt like this for Sassoon[89] even after meeting
and becoming engaged to Nancy Nicholson, it is no wonder that
tensions developed in their relationships. But before speaking
briefly of these, a few words are necessary about 'Fairies' rather
than 'Fusiliers'. In view of my preceding argument, and because of
the adoption of the word 'fairy' to denote, in an aggressively
dismissive way, a male homosexual, it is tempting to read into the
title of Graves's book an expression of sexual ambivalence. But in
1917 the word 'fairy' was not widely used in its popular, collo-
quial application to homosexuals.[90] Nevertheless, it is not difficult
to perceive how the word has been homophobically displaced to
denote someone who is 'unnatural' and less than a 'real man'.
Although it is not applied in such a muscular way by Graves, still
his usage makes an interesting binary opposition to 'Fusiliers', and
one that bears upon Graves's conception of 'manhood' and his
self-image as 'manly'.

'Fairies' are, of course, part of the trappings of late Victorian
culture, and in Ireland of the 'Celtic twilight'. Doubtless Alfred
Graves had introduced his son to the land of faery at a relatively
early age. And certainly it is with childhood and children that
Robert Graves associates 'fairies'. Graves, like Brooke and Owen,
was particularly fond of children and mentions in letters from
France seeking out children to play with when at rest behind the
lines.[91] He also speaks in a letter of 1917 about the 'real fairies'
being children.[92] And the 'fairy' poems in his book are child-like
in form, comprising nursery rhymes, songs and ballads couched in
plain language with simple and definite rhythms and rhyme. Many
of them express a yearning for childhood, and none more so than

'Babylon', which begins:

> The child alone a poet is:
> Spring and Fairyland are his.
> Truth and Reason show but dim,
> And all's poetry with him.[93]

It has been opined by more than one commentator, that such poems were wilful evasions of his war experience, and certainly this cannot be denied. I would only wish to add that the poems seem to me to evince a Romantic nostalgia, wherein childhood is viewed as a time of sexual 'innocence', and it is this which is appealing to Graves. He was anxious to assert his heterosexual manliness, but also expresses his ambivalence about this, and the poems about fairies constitute part of that ambivalence; they express a Puritanical longing to retreat from the adult world of sexuality altogether. Both of Graves's biographers agree that there was something childish in his relationship with Nancy,[94] and certainly from late 1917 until quite some time after the war, Graves's poetry had much more of the 'fairy' about it than the 'Fusilier'.

Accordingly, in his correspondence with both Wilfred Owen and Sassoon in 1917–18, Graves is forever telling them to 'cheer-up'. This did not go down particularly well with either of them as they were both writing their darkest poems at this time. It could be argued that Graves was never particularly close to Owen. Like Sassoon, Graves offered Owen some rather patronising advice, and treated him as a 'discovery'. Owen was both flattered and amused by this,[95] but there was little intensity in the relationship. Graves's friendship with Sassoon was far more involved. But relations between these two were strained by their different reactions to the war, by Graves's relationship with Nancy, and by their different artistic directions. At the heart of their problem was an inability to confront or discuss openly the place that sexuality had in their relationship and in relation to all the other issues. It might be objected that nobody could have done this in 1918. But this is to forget that both writers had read Edward Carpenter; they had both corresponded about Sorley being 'so'. Nevertheless, Sassoon was too fastidious to raise the topic with Graves, and Graves wanted to deny any homosexuality on his part altogether. Their often acrimonious correspondence continued until a major row over *Goodbye to All That* which eventually caused a lengthy breach in their relationship which was not healed until 1957.[96] In some of the letters written between 1918 and 1933 the problematic relations in the Graves–Nancy–Sassoon triangle are touched upon, and Graves articulates the fact that upsets between himself and Sassoon affect Graves's relationship with Nancy adversely.[97] Love between the men is made mention of, but the sexual aspect of this is denied by both parties, and instead there is a tendency to indulge in the giving and receiving of pain. Rather than dignified silence, the correspondence becomes on several occasions a study in the exchange of insult and aggression.

Graves spent the rest of the war on home duties. If he had been fit there is little doubt that he would have gone back to France. In November 1917 he wrote, 'I am still able to fight again and I feel I must'.[98] The doctors, however, did not agree, and by February 1918, having been posted to a cadet battalion in Rhyl, he is expressing shame at the contrast between his own situation and Sassoon's. Graves's position was particularly difficult because he had so vehemently insisted in the face of Sassoon's 'pacifism' that the war had to be fought: 'I believe in giving everything', he had written to Sassoon in an attempt to out do his friend in the rush for martyrdom.[99] But Graves's 'giving' at least in terms of active service remained in the realms of theory, since the army would not let him resume such duties. Meanwhile, Sassoon went out to be wounded again, whilst Graves attempted to consolidate his relationship with Nancy, and continued to write poems of 'country sentiment' rather than impassioned outcries about the war.

When the war came to an end, the cessation of international hostilities could not banish the 'neurasthenia' from which Graves continued to suffer sporadically, and with varying degrees of intensity, for the next seven years. This time was spent living quietly and impecuniously with Nancy and their growing family, firstly at Boar's Hill just outside Oxford and then at Islip. Graves studied for a B.Litt. at Oxford, and otherwise attempted to earn enough from his writing to meet his obligations. This proved impossible, and the young couple were obliged to rely on their respective families and friends for financial assistance. Like Sassoon, Graves and Nancy flirted with socialism in the immediately post-war years, but their 'revolutionary' idealism did not prevent them embarking on a disastrous capitalist enterprise when they opened a grocery shop at Boar's Hill. Attraction to left-wing ideas was a passing phase, and one gets the impression that Graves did not think very profoundly about politics, preferring to devote his intellectual energies to psychology and, of course, to poetry.

His studies in psychology were prompted and encouraged by his friendship with W.H.R. Rivers, and by his continued problems with shell shock. There is some debate as to the nature and extent of treatment Graves received for his nervous illness. Martin Seymour-Smith reiterates Graves's later claim that he was not treated at all.[100] But the letters make explicit reference to visiting a 'nerve man' in London in 1921, who advised Graves to rest and do no work at all for several months[101] (advice that Graves seems to have ignored). Whether this was an isolated occasion or whether such consultation was repeated remains obscure. What may be said with certainty is that Graves's contact with Rivers, though it does not seem to have taken the form of strict psychoanalysis, was highly influential in Graves's thinking about poetry. His two prose books of this period, *On English Poetry* (1922) and *Poetic Unreason* (1925) are both based on the idea that lyric poetry embodies psychological conflict in a manner similar to dreams, and that 'true' poetry is composed in a trance-like state akin to hypnosis. Rivers was heavily consulted about the first book, and the influence of his thought is apparent in the second, despite his death in 1922. Poetry was conceived of as a species of therapy for both writer and reader. Technique is the aspect of the art which enables the writer to communicate, and rescues him from narcissism.

To discuss either Graves's post-war poetic theories or his poetry in any detail must remain beyond the scope of this study. But before going on to discuss *Goodbye to All That* it is I think worth making some broad remarks about his work between 1918 and 1929. The most crucial point to be made is that it represents a continuation of the preoccupations we have observed in his war poetry, and particularly those concerned with gender and identity, love and violence. As we have seen, in the middle of the war he considered the poet to be a 'woman suffering all the hardships of a man'. And we observed in some of the early poems, a concern with the gender identity of the poet, and how the war is bringing about change in his self-image. Graves's immediately post-war speculations developed these ideas. In *On English Poetry*, Graves conceives the poet as someone who, because of 'unusual complications of early environment', has developed a number of 'rival sub-personalities' which create conflict between themselves, and with the dominant controlling personality. Poetry is the articulation of these conflicts and sometimes of their resolution.[102]

The place of gender in relation to poetry is broached in a most interesting, and I think, significant way. Firstly, in a section dealing with people who write some poetry and then stop, or are moved to write by extraordinary stress of emotion, Graves argues like this:

The temporary writing of poetry by normal single-track minds is most common in youth when the sudden realization of sex, its powers and its limited opportunities for satisfactory expression, turns the world upside down for any sensitive boy or girl. Wartime has the same sort of effect. I have definite evidence for saying that much of the trench-poetry written during the late war was the work of men not otherwise poetically inclined, and that it was very frequently due to an insupportable conflict between suppressed instincts of love and fear; the officer's actual love which he could never openly show, for the boys he commanded, and the fear, also hidden under a forced gaiety, of the horrible death that threatened them all.[103]

I suspect that Graves's 'definite evidence' is culled from his own experience endorsed and reinforced by the testimony of Rivers. But Graves attempts to divert the reader from the temptation to think of Graves as 'loving' his 'boys' during the war, by immediately raising the question of gender in the next section of the book:

The poet's quarrelsome lesser personalities to which I have referred are divided into camps by the distinction of sex. But in a poet the dominant spirit is male and though usually a feminist in sympathy, cannot afford to favour the women at the expense of his own sex. This amplifies my distrust of poets with floppy hats, long hair, extravagant clothes and inverted tendencies.[104]

The relation of this passage to Graves's biography hardly requires commentary. Having turned away from a homosexual identity, he now protests the necessity for a dominant masculinity in poets, and expresses homophobic 'distrust'.

But this new direction in his love was not without cost, and although as I have stated the bulk of his poetic output following *Fairies and Fusiliers* attempted to avoid the war, still he could not quell its hold upon him. In *Country Sentiment* (1920) where

210

poems celebrating his new family life in the country predominate, there is nevertheless a small section of war poems. These are divided between expressions of self-punishing guilt – survivor-guilt, and guilt for killing – and expressions which attempt to refine the attitude to war he had taken in opposition to Sassoon; despite all its horror, Graves argues, it still had to be fought. In a poem entitled 'Retrospect: the Jests of the Clock' he even concludes that 'he'll be ready again: if urgent orders come,/To quit his rye and cabbages, kiss his wife and part/At the first sullen rapping of the awakened drum . . . '[105] And in 'Hate Not, Fear Not'[106] Graves enjoins his reader to 'Kill if you must, but never hate' and to 'Fight cleanly' without the intrusion of hate and fear. Quite how this 'cleanliness' relates to the Western Front is not articulated, and it is difficult for us now to imagine any such appalling violence as 'clean'.

If Graves was torn between guilt and his more aggressive feelings in the war poems, there are further troubling psychological problems hinted at in other poems in *Country Sentiment*. 'Outlaws' and 'Ghost Raddled' in particular, strike one as pointing forward to the less cosy collection, *The Pier Glass* (1921), and doing so because they are emanating from his war experience, even though war is not the ostensible subject. In 'Outlaws'[107] Graves figures the 'aged gods of fright and lust' clinging to life, lying in wait 'Greedy of human stuff to snare/In webs of murk.' These 'old gods' are said to be 'almost dead' and starved of their 'ancient dues' amongst which are numbered 'an unclean muse'. The poem is about Graves's fear of lust and 'dirtiness'. It seems to me that it expresses his lingering fear of the homosexual feelings that he does not wish to be trapped by. Similarly, 'Ghost Raddled' has a cast of ghosts and demons which bring with them all manner of horrors. In response to a request for a song, the persona tells his interlocutor to choose from a catalogue of 'clouded tales of wrong/And terror.' Amongst these we have visions of 'blood choking gutters' and,

Of lust frightful, past belief,
  Lurking unforgotten,
Unrestrainable endless grief
  In breasts long rotten[108]

The poem concludes with two rhetorical questions which ask how a song can be made in a house which belongs 'To a blind December'. This is chilling in more ways than one. And we might fairly infer from this that all was not absolutely happy between Graves and Nancy already. Again Graves seems troubled by a lust that is buried, and that he wishes to avoid, but it, as well as other violent ghosts, come back to torment him. The poem is about punishment and self-punishment.

In Graves's next volumes, *The Pier Glass, Whipperginny,* and *The Feather Bed* there is no shortage of sado-masochistic imagery. Graves himself described the mood of the first of these books as 'aggressive and disciplinary'.[109] Love is seen over and over again to involve a terrible violence as Graves explores the conflicts between his Puritanism, his sexual identity and his war guilt. In several of these poems men and women are imaged involved in a conflict to the death. Both 'The Coronation Murder' and 'The Pier Glass' focus their attention on women who have murdered their lovers or husbands, and are unrepentant in their revenge. Other poems deal with the vicissitudes of love with less obvious vehemence, but the reciprocal exchange of pain is not hard to detect. The most concentrated expression of Graves's sexual difficulties, and his philosophical treatment of them during the early 1920s, is to be found in the long narrative poem, *The Feather Bed.* Here, amongst other matters, Graves begins the reinterpretation of Biblical Christianity which was eventually to lead him to the development of his own mythological system in *The White Goddess.*

The story is described in the prologue as 'a study of a fatigued mind in a fatigued body and under the stress of an abnormal conflict'.[110] The poem describes a male lover whose beloved jilts him in favour of a convent. In Graves's own words, 'this staggering rebuff to the young man's typically bullying attitude in love leads him to invent the monstrous libel in compensation; which libel is merely flattery to his own wounded pride'.[111] The 'libel' concerns two nuns at the convent, one of whom harbours a lesbian desire for the young man's beloved, and the mother superior who is envisaged trying to seduce the young man. All this takes place within a framework wherein Graves in a rather Blakean way is anxious to explore the fall into division, and the 'conflicting powers of doubleness' that arise from this fall. He envisages Lucifer as the most advanced 'aspect of God' who represents the 'spirit of reconciliation' and 'peace', and is, significantly enough for my argument 'single-natured, without gender'.[112]

The images of female threat and violence in this, and other poems of the period, together with the self-condemnation implicit in much of the writing seems to me to figure Graves's fear of the 'feminine' within himself as much as any external figure. Having said that, it is inconceivable that Graves's relationship to both his mother and Nancy are unimportant here as well, and we cannot say for sure what neuroses of their own interacted with those of Graves. But what we can suggest is that Graves sees the 'masculine' part of himself as guilty; guilty of killing in the war, guilty of clumsiness in his relations with women, guilty of disloyalty to male friends like Sassoon, guilty of rebuffing the 'feminine' part of himself. This draws upon his head the desire for punishment which is delivered by the avenging 'feminine'. This masochism inevitably has as its corollary the sadism implicit in various of the female characters' words and actions.

In later years as Graves pursued his studies in mythology further, and his relationship with Laura Riding displaced after much turbulence his relationship with Nancy, Graves elevated the experience of male masochism into a poetic and theological doctrine. This is the end of a process which began with those first poems of the war wherein the conflict between 'male' and 'female' in the poet was figured. Graves progressively externalised the 'female' into the position of his Goddess and Muse. In a displacement of the Puritanical and patriarchal trinity, Graves conceived the threefold White Goddess. She is the 'triple muse' in her roles of mother, lover and layer out. She presides over the endless dialectic between destruction and creation. The poet serves the muse and bears her cruelty in order to create. The White Goddess is said to preside over the destruction and eventual resurrection of the poet and his powers. In the poems dealing with the Goddess, however, there is much more emphasis on her cruelty, and the annihilation of the poet, rather than any redemptive powers.

Although Graves's mythological scheme is ostensibly anti-patriarchal, it tends in fact to repeat the ambivalence towards the female which is a dominant characteristic of patriarchal society. Graves both fears and reveres the female. She is made into a Goddess of cruelty and vengeance who, like the Christian God, punishes in order to save. She is externalised as fixedly 'other', again re-inscribing the essentialist categories upon which the dominant in our (and Graves's) society depends. And, although the emphasis in Graves's scheme is upon male masochism, the inevitable corollary of this was a reciprocal sadism. This may be detected at work not only in Graves's poetry, but also, to some extent at least in his life. The choosing of successive 'Muse' figures to inspire his poetry, whilst accepted by his second wife, cannot have been the source of much pleasure to her. Rather the reverse. And the 'failure' of various 'Muses' to live up to Graves's rather high expectations, was also the source of pain.[113]

Despite this, I think we are obliged to acknowledge that, unlike Sassoon, Graves fought to develop his own anarchistic rebellion to post-war, bourgeois English society. He fought a long battle against his inherited values, and certainly succeeded in overturning some of them. His voluntary exile in Majorca following the publication of *Goodbye to All That* is emblematic of this strife to escape his past, and re-make himself. That in the final analysis his work embodies much that can be traced back to dominant ideologies; that his rebellion was contained by them, should not blind us to the potential his writings have for making us question our own assumptions about gender and sexuality, and aiding our own self-discovery. But this is to anticipate a conclusion, before we have discussed *Goodbye to All That,* arguably Graves's most lasting contribution to war literature.

The book was written very quickly in 1929 when Graves's affairs were in a very traumatic state. In 1926 he had gone to Cairo to work at the university there, and the American poet Laura Riding had accompanied the Graves entourage, beginning a ménage à trois which was to last for some little while before the inevitable bust-up. This came in 1928–9 and by this time involved another man. The violent close of these interrelationships has been described by both Martin Seymour-Smith and Richard Graves, and need not detain us further here, but to observe again that sado-masochism was not merely restricted to literature, but was very much operative in life. And some of the pain of recent events is certainly responsible for the aggression and bitterness which informs parts of *Goodbye to All That.*

Paul Fussell has pointed to much that is of importance about the book. He notes that it is 'no more a "direct and factual autobiography" than Sassoon's memoirs. It is rather a satire, built out of anecdotes heavily influenced by the techniques of stage comedy'.[114] The book, according to Fussell is full of black comedy, which exposes the absurdity of war, and in which almost all the characters are either fools or knaves.[115] Thus Graves articulates a 'goodbye' to an England and its institutions which he has come to despise.Whilst agreeing with most of this, what I wish to contest is Fussell's implication that Graves's book is thoroughly and coherently anti-war. In my view it suffers from the same kinds of ambivalence that we have noticed in the poetry. Whilst demonstrating that war is absurd, Graves at the same time articulates his pride in the Royal Welch Fusiliers, a pride that has got everything to do with their fighting prowess. A whole chapter of the book is devoted to the regimental history and tradition, all of which is reported entirely without irony.[116] And, although Graves exposes the ridiculous snobbery of the officers mess at Laventie, on the next page he is telling us with evident satisfaction that the Royal Welch Fusiliers had made it 'a point of honour to dominate no man's land from dusk to dawn'.[117] We should also note that Graves himself is specifically implicated in this honour and bravery. For he describes how he is tested by being sent out on a patrol immediately upon joining the regiment. This is a 'test' he passes, and continues to pass.[118]

As we have already noticed, Graves's attitude to Sassoon's protest against the war was founded on his belief that one had to remain loyal to one's comrades. And, much to Sassoon's disgust, Graves felt that to take a pacifist stance was to invite from one's comrades not only an accusation of disloyalty amounting to cowardice, but also the charge of 'bad form'[119] or not 'behaving like a gentleman'.[120] All this is faithfully recorded in *Goodbye to All That*. Graves contends quite rightly that Sassoon oscillated between 'happy warrior' and 'bitter pacifist', describing his (Graves's) own attitudes as less heroic but more consistent. So Sassoon's protest against the war is reduced in Graves's account to an aberration. The implication is that to be anti-war is a justifiable stance up to a point. But one is not to articulate this in action which prejudices one's loyalty to the military virtues embodied in regimental traditions.

Further evidence for Graves's ambivalence may be found elsewhere in the book. Despite the black comedy informing much of the description of his battle experience, we also have some of his more light-hearted letters from the front reproduced,[121] and we have passages which speak of his alienation from the home front and his wish to be back in France when he is home on leave.[122] But more telling than this is the theme of Graves's sexual identity which, whilst it is not particularly foregrounded, nevertheless remains an important, if not central, concern. As Samuel Hynes has recently observed, the book has a tri-partite structure dealing with both pre- and post-war England, two distinct places separated by the cataclysm of the war. It is a record, Hynes argues, of personal and social change, moving us from the conventional pieties of Edwardian England through the war, and into a post-war England characterised by disenchantment and disintegration.[123] One cannot but agree. But Hynes does not develop his thesis much further in the direction of the specific personal changes that Graves undergoes and describes. And it is these that I am particularly interested in.

What I wish to contend is that the chronology of events in *Goodbye to All That* is manipulated in order to articulate as a sub-plot the idea that the war made a 'man' out of Graves. I have already quoted passages from the account of his schooldays wherein Graves speaks of the 'pseudo-homosexuality' resulting from a 'prep' and public school education. Many, he says, never recover from this 'perversion'. But *Goodbye to All That* is very concerned to record Graves's 'recovery'. In the 1929 edition, Graves says that he 'recovered' from 'pseudo-homosexuality' by a 'shock at the age of twenty one'.[124] In the 1957 edition this sentence is removed. In the earlier edition, the inference that the incident when he is told that his beloved 'Dick' had 'made a certain proposal to a corporal in a Canadian regiment' is responsible for his 'recovery' is then, clearer than in the later version. But in both the news of 'Dick's' transgression is said to, nearly 'finish' Graves, and in both the paragraph in question concludes, that with so much slaughter about 'it would be easy to think of him [Dick] as dead'.[125] This crucial event in the autobiography is said to take place in October 1915, whereas in fact it happened in July 1917. It seems to me that the point of this shift is to demonstrate a coherent progression from 'pseudo homosexuality' to heterosexuality. Instead of the awkward fact that Graves was corresponding with Marjory whilst still in contact with 'Dick/Peter', which implies the suddenness of the change in Graves's orientation, we have a time interval of two years introduced, in which this implicit transition takes place.

It is during this time that the 'old' Graves is indeed nearly finished. And, as Samuel Hynes points out, the incident of his severe wounding and subsequent recovery is figured in more than one poem as a death and resurrection to a new life.[126] What emerges in the autobiography after his wounding is a 'new' Graves who falls in love with 'Marjorie'. And this falling in love occurs precisely at the end of Graves's soldiering in France. He has experienced and survived Loos and the Somme; he has experienced and survived the chatter of both his men and fellow officers about the qualities of French women. And, although his Puritanical reaction to this chatter is recorded, we also feel the force of Graves's fascination with it. He returns to England ready to fall in love with a woman.

The fact that he found the transition to 'woman love' difficult, however, is recorded, and the reasons for giving up his pursuit of Marjorie:

My heart had remained whole, if numbed, since Dick's disappearance from it, yet I felt difficulty in adjusting myself to the experience of woman love. I used to meet Marjorie, who was a professional pianist, when I visited a friend in another ward; but we had little talk together . . . I wrote to her after I had left hospital, but finding that she was engaged to a subaltern in France, I stopped writing. I had seen what it must feel like to be in France and have a rival at home. Yet her reproofs of my silence suggested that she was at least as fond of me as of him. I did not press the point, but let the affair end almost before it started.[127]

This is a fascinating passage. Graves is anxious to create the idea that in the (fictional) time between 'Dick's' fall from grace and the meeting with 'Marjorie' his affections were not intensely engaged. Yet, as we have mentioned before, the reasons offered for not pursuing Marjorie suggest that loyalty to men overrides his affection for the woman. Ostensibly we are being told about Graves's honourable relinquishment of a 'conquest' but the significance of the passage is, unintentionally, rather greater than this. Despite changing the chronology Graves is using this relationship as a stepping stone to his relationship with Nancy. The reader is being told implicitly that Graves is now capable of pursuing a relationship with a woman, but that her attractions are not strong enough to induce him to act in dishonourable ways. The sub-text implies that Graves's feelings were still heavily involved with his fellow soldiers, and so much so as to prevent him pursuing a relationship even when encouraged.

Between the abandoned relationship with Marjorie and the pursuit of Nancy the incident involving Sassoon's protest is interposed. We are then told that, 'In the summer of 1917, shortly after the episode with Marjorie' he had taken Nancy to a 'musical revue'. Following this, he says, he begins to correspond with her, and he meets her again on leave in October. The transition to loving Nancy is made via Marjorie and after Sassoon's implicitly 'unmanly' behaviour. The narrative is organised in such a way as to demonstrate the progressive stages of Graves's rites of passage to manhood. The book offers no psychological investigations or rationalisations for his adoption of woman love, and so the audience is left to infer that the war has revealed his 'true nature'. At the close of the war, Graves describes how his loyalty to the regiment is now overshadowed by his loyalty to Nancy and his new-born baby daughter, Jenny. Graves realises that he has ceased to be a 'British Grenadier'.[128] Despite the hardships endured, the horrors perceived, the legacy of 'neurasthenia', and despite the absurdity and black humour informing the book, nevertheless we are left with this positive outcome for Graves; 'pseudo-homosexuality' has given way to the roles of father and husband. Graves has, through the war, proved himself a 'man'.

Some may object that I am giving undue attention to this theme, and foisting an interpretation upon the book without sufficient evidence. But Graves's publication of *But It Still Goes On* the year after *Goodbye to All That,* indicates that part of what Graves was attempting to say goodbye to, was sexual confusion. The play involves a homosexual, David, and a lesbian, Charlotte, who both pursue heterosexual relationships out of desperation and a desire to be 'normal members of society'.[129] David has served in the war, and in discussion with Charlotte explains 'how a platoon of men will absolutely worship a good-looking gallant young officer'. He goes on:

Of course, they don't realise exactly what's happening, neither does he; but it's a very strong romantic link. That's why I had the best platoon and then the best company in the battalion. My men adored me and were showing off all the time before the other companies. They didn't bring me flowers. They killed Germans for me instead and drilled like angels. It was an intoxication for them; and for me.[130]

There is much in 'David's' situation that might be applied to Sassoon or to Graves himself. This is a succinct expression of the sado-masochistic, sacrificial love which informs so much writing of the First War. But this is not primarily Graves's theme in the play. What he appears to be criticising is the way in which homosexuals attempt to form heterosexual relationships, and the way that this repression gives rise to violence. A fantastically tangled web of relationships is developed in the course of the play which ends in murderous bloodshed. Graves's attack is ostensibly about Edwardian sexual hypocrisy, but the extraordinarily bitter and aggressive tone of the play, gives the impression that Graves's anger is about sexuality itself. The character, Dick, who voices acerbic denunciations of society in the play, has this to say about sex: 'Sex is fear. Loneliness sometimes; that's a fear. Or dullness; that's another. Or fear of personal extinction. Say, generally, fear of death. Copopulation!'[131]

What is said to go on and on and on, at the end of the play is suffering; a vicious cycle of sexual confusion, frustration and violence. We might draw the conclusion that Graves in 1930 felt that he had experienced enough of this, and in escaping to Majorca with Laura Riding said 'goodbye' to it. But all his subsequent writing is bound to the problem of sexuality and creativity, and his White Goddess, as I have already argued is a means of coming to terms with his own ambivalence. The Puritanism of his childhood is then displaced but not finally conquered.

After 1929, Graves deleted the war poems from his collected oeuvre. It was as if he wished to forget 'all that'. Sassoon spent twenty years remembering the war, Graves wanted only to put it behind him. And perhaps one of the reasons for this difference is that Sassoon still found the 'love' between men in the trenches inspiring, whilst for Graves it was threatening; it seems likely that it gave rise to homosexual feelings that he wished to, and finally did, deny. Nevertheless, Graves's war poems at the beginning of the war have much in common with the other poets I have dealt with here. Consolations are found in sado-masochistic love, in pride and loyalty. In *Goodbye to All That*, Graves re-writes his experience so that consolation inheres in the gaining of manhood through the suffering of war. The motif of love between the men is played down in order to secure a projected self-image of 'man-liness'. What is demonstrably not present is any articulation of pacifism, or rigorous political analysis which might raise a critique of the war's causes or conduct. But Graves's suffering goes on after the war in England, and it is in order to escape that he leaves for Majorca. He spent the rest of his life devising a philosophical and psychological rationalisation of the sado-masochism consequent upon his inherited Puritanism, and the suppression of what he took to be the 'feminine' within himself. If this led to something of reconciliation in his art and life, tragically in old age Graves could still articulate the ambivalence about the war that we have charted here. He expressed pride in having served with the Royal Welch Fusiliers, and sorrow at having killed Germans.[132] Some things did indeed go on and on. They still do.

There is an undated poem belonging to the war years, which was not published until 1988. It is a sonnet entitled 'Trench Life', and it makes an appropriate end to this chapter in so far as it takes us back to the beginning of this book, and to the idea that each of the poets we have considered suffered greatly before the war, and then found in the conflict not only more suffering but suffering that could be celebrated. The sonnet's concluding sestet is as follows:

> Yet we who once, before we came to fight,
>   Drowned our prosperity in a waste of grief,
> Contrary now find such perverse delight
>   In utter fear and misery, that Belief
> Blossoms from mud, and under the rain's whips,
>   Flagellant-like we writhe with laughing lips.[133]

Notes

1   B. Bergonzi, *Heroes' Twilight: a Study of the Literature of the Great War,* London, (1965), 1980, p. 154.

2   R. Graves, *Poems about War,* London, 1988.

3   R.P. Graves: *Robert Graves: the Assault Heroic, 1895–1926,* London, 1986, pp. 3–12.

4   Ibid., p. 47.

5   R. Graves, *Goodbye to All That,* London, (1957), Harmonds-worth, 1960, pp. 20–1. Hereafter referred to as *GTAT57.*

6   Ibid., p. 19.

7   Graves, *Robert Graves: the Assault Heroic*, pp. 44–5.
8   Graves, *GTAT57* pp. 21–5.
9   Ibid., p. 23.
10 Ibid., p. 40.
11 Ibid., p. 41.
12 R. Graves, *Goodbye to All That*, London, 1929, p. 75. Hereafter referred to as *GTAT29*. See also *GTAT57*, p. 44, where the phrase 'sex feeling' has been replaced by the word 'love'.
13 *GTAT57*, pp. 44–5.
14 Ibid., p. 45.
15 R. Graves, *In Broken Images: Selected Correspondence*, P. O'Prey, (ed.), New York (1982), 1988, p. 35.
16 *GTAT57*, p. 39.
17 Quoted in Martin Seymour Smith, *Robert Graves: his Life and Work*, London, (1982), 1987, p. 63.
18 Graves, *The Assault Heroic*, p. 178.
19 *GTAT57*, p. 204.
20 Seymour-Smith, *Robert Graves*, p. 21
21 Ibid., p. 74.
22 Ibid., p. 73.
23 Letter of R. Graves to E. Carpenter, 30 May 1914. MSS 386–234, Sheffield Public Library.
24 Ibid.
25 *GTAT57*, p. 46.
26 Ibid., p. 53.
27 R.P. Graves, *The Assault Heroic*, p. 110; Seymour-Smith, *Robert Graves* p. 31.
28 See, E. Carpenter, *The Intermediate Sex*, London, (1908), 1909, pp. 40–1.
29 Graves, *Over the Brazier*, London, (1916), 1975, p. 7.
30 Seymour-Smith, *Robert Graves*, p. 73.
31 Graves, *In Broken Images*, p. 30.
32 Graves, *Over the Brazier*, p. 16.
33 See R.P. Graves, *The Assault Heroic*, p. 116.
34 Graves, *Over the Brazier*, p. 12.
35 Ibid., p. 15.
36 J. Vickery, *Robert Graves and the White Goddess*, Lincoln, Nebraska, 1972, p. 7.
37 R.P. Graves, *The Assault Heroic*, p. 115.
38 A.P. Graves, *To Return To All That*, London, 1930, p. 323.
39 Graves, *In Broken Images*, pp. 31–2.
40 A.P. Graves, *To Return To All That*, p. 325.
41 Ibid., pp. 326–7.

42   R.P. Graves, *The Assault Heroic*, p. 129.
43   *GTAT57*, p. 104.
44   R.P. Graves, *The Assault Heroic*, p. 130.
45   Graves, *In Broken Images*, pp. 34–5.
46   Ibid., p. 39.
47   Ibid., p. 35.
48   *GTAT57*, p. 103.
49   Graves, *In Broken Images*, p. 35.
50   Seymour-Smith, *Robert Graves*, p. 76.
51   Graves, *In Broken Images*, p. 35.
52   Ibid., p. 39.
53   Letter of C.H. Sorley to Mrs. Sorley, 28 April 1915, quoted in *The Penguin Book of First World War Prose*, J. Glover and J. Silkin, (eds.), London, (1989) 1990, pp. 28–9.
54   Graves, *In Broken Images*, p. 40.
55   Ibid., pp. 47–8.
56   Ibid., p. 41.
57   R.P. Graves, *The Assault Heroic*, p. 117.
58   Graves, *Over the Brazier*, p. 18.
59   Ibid., p. 19.
60   Ibid., p. 21.
61   Ibid., p. 20.
62   Graves, *In Broken Images*, p. 65.
63   Graves, *Over the Brazier*, p. 28.
64   *GTAT57*, p. 133.
65   Graves, *Over the Brazier*, p. 27.
66   Graves, *In Broken Images*, pp. 45–6.
67   Ibid., pp. 50–1.
68   Ibid., pp. 51–2.
69   *GTAT57*, p. 192.
70   Ibid., p. 204.
71   Graves, *In Broken Images*, pp. 57 and 63.
72   Ibid., pp. 77–8.
73   *GTAT57*, p. 280, *In Broken Images*, p. 286.
74   Graves, *In Broken Images*, p. 78.
75   R.P. Graves, *The Assault Heroic*, p. 182.
76   Graves, *In Broken Images*, p. 88.
77   R. Graves, *On English Poetry*, (London, 1922), New York, 1972, p. 38.
78   Graves, *In Broken Images*, p. 89.
79   Ibid., p. 88.
80   Ibid., p. 81.
81   Ibid., p. 82.

82   R. Graves, *Fairies and Fusiliers*, London, 1917, pp. 3–4.
83   Ibid., p. 5.
84   T. Hardy, *The Dynasts*, III, 5,v, London, 1978, p.601.
85   Graves, *Fairies and Fusiliers*, pp. 51–2.
86   Ibid., pp. 72–4.
87   D. Hibberd, *Owen the Poet*, London, 1986, p. 121.
88   Graves, *Fairies and Fusiliers*, p. 7.
89   See Graves, *In Broken Images*, p. 95. He writes to Sassoon, 'So glad you're still fond of me: and I of you, dear poet, like hell, even as per previously published statement in "Two Fusiliers".'
90   The OED cites a club in New York of the 1890s as the source of this usage, but it is unlikely that this was well known in England until later. Whether Graves was aware of its secondary meaning is uncertain. *In Broken Images*, p. 86, contrasts 'fairies with rouged lips and peroxide hair' with the 'real fairies: the colonel's kids'.
91   A.P. Graves, *To Return to All That*, p. 326.
92   Graves, *In Broken Images*, p. 86.
93   Graves, *Fairies and Fusiliers*, p. 14.
94   R.P. Graves, *The Assault Heroic*, p. 184, and Seymour-Smith, *Robert Graves*, p. 60.
95   See W. Owen, *Collected Letters*, London, 1967, pp. 499, 500, 595–6.
96   See Graves, *In Broken Images*, p. 347.
97   Ibid., p. 158.
98   Ibid., p. 89.
99   Ibid., p. 85.
100 Seymour-Smith, *Robert Graves*, pp. 90 and 97.
101 Graves, *In Broken Images*, p. 125.
102 Graves, *On English Poetry*, pp. 123–4.
103 Ibid., pp. 37–8.
104 Ibid., p. 38.
105 R. Graves, *Poems About War*, London, 1988, p. 55.
106 Ibid., p. 62.
107 R. Graves, *Country Sentiment*, New York, 1920, pp. 50–1.
108 Ibid., pp. 64–5.
109 R. Graves, 'Author's Note', *Whipperginny*, London, 1923, p. v.
110 R. Graves, *The Feather Bed*, London, 1923, p. 2.
111 Ibid., p. 4.
112 Ibid., p. 26.
113 Seymour-Smith, *Robert Graves*, pp. 440–7, 513–19, 533–43.
114 P. Fussell, *The Great War and Modern Memory*, London, (1975), 1977, p. 207.

115 Ibid., pp. 196–220.
116 *GTAT57*, Chapter 11, pp. 72–8.
117 *GTAT57*, pp. 110–11.
118 Ibid.
119 *GTAT57*, pp. 215–16.
120 See Graves, *In Broken Images*, p. 85.
121 *GTAT57*, pp. 91–101. Graves has edited these letters, neverthe-less the relatively light-hearted tone is retained. A.P. Graves also reproduced some of his sons letters from France in *To Return to All That*, pp. 322–31. Implicitly his (A.P.G.'s) purpose was to demonstrate that his son's bitterness about the war was retro-spective.
122 *GTAT57*, pp. 120 and 188–192.
123 S. Hynes, *A War Imagined: the First World War and English Culture*, New York, 1990, pp. 427–31.
124 *GTAT29*, p. 40.
125 *GTAT29*, p. 220, and *GTAT57*, p. 143.
126 Hynes, *A War Imagined*, pp. 428–9.
127 *GTAT57*, p. 204.
128 Ibid., pp. 229–230.
129 R. Graves, *But It Still Goes On*, London, 1930, p. 248.
130 Ibid., p. 245.
131 Ibid., p. 294
132 Seymour Smith, *Robert Graves*, p. 567, R.P. Graves, *The Assault Heroic*, pp. 117–18.
133 Graves, *Poems About War*, p. 53.

6

Conclusion

In the foregoing chapters I have tried to plot the sufferings and the attitudes to suffering of the four most famous and revered English writers of World War I. The point of this procedure has been to demonstrate the way that their inherited ideologies, Christianity, imperialism, Romanticism, at once advocated the idea of suffering as a good, whilst simultaneously creating and sustaining that suffering. We have seen, in other words, that Brooke, Sassoon, Owen and Graves, not only imbibed these ideologies as abstract ideas purveyed to them by parents and teachers, but also *lived* them in the sense that the values, the world view implicit in the ideologies informed their sense of self, and their struggles for self-definition. At the heart of these ideologies lies the idea of self-sacrifice. Christianity defines love by the idea of crucifixion; its adherents are instructed to 'take up' a cross and follow Jesus, that the greatest love is to 'give' one's life 'for a friend', and that 'those who are Christ's have crucified the flesh with the affections and the lusts thereof'. Imperialism uses these ideas for its own political ends. In the nineteenth century, the role of Christian soldier becomes confused with missionary, as armies are despatched to conquer the heathen, and save souls, whilst appropriating their lands and abrogating power to the Christian state. The Empire thus established is then defended in the name of Christ and Christianity. All this depends on a notion of 'manhood' which rigorously denies to 'masculinity' the full range of emotional life, rendering aggression and stoicism as paramount virtues whilst gentleness and the ability to nurture are regarded as 'weaknesses'. Romanticism begins as a critique of such values but soon re-inscribes them by displacing religion with art. In order to create, and in order to authenticate the 'self' one has to suffer. Thus for Oscar Wilde Christ is seen as the type of the artist,[1] and D.H. Lawrence can speak of the artist's necessary 'crucifixion into isolate individuality'.[2] In relation to love and to sexual politics, Romanticism through its aspiration to transcend binary oppositions in higher syntheses, tends to encourage an essentialist view of 'masculinity' and 'femininity' as fixed opposites, and to promote an idea of 'love' which suggests that metaphsyical fulfilment resides in the synthesis of those opposites. Sexuality thus tends to become idealised, removed from the body, inscribed in the mind. And it meets Christianity in a willingness to 'die for love'. As we have seen, it is true that some late nineteenth century 'Decadent' writers in the Romantic tradition equated art and the artist with homosexuality. But this was clearly a reaction to imperialism's definition of 'masculinity'. In other words, essentialism was adhered to through the suggestion that art was 'feminine' and that artists necessarily were effeminate. And in so far as to be 'womanly' was viewed as being willing to suffer self-abnegation then the artist was again bound to suffering; hence the proliferation of sado-masochistic images in late-nineteenth-century poetry.

These then were the ideologies, religious, political, aesthetic that Brooke, Sassoon, Owen and Graves inherited and struggled with in the early years of this century. In the case of all but Owen, the powerful influence of 'prep' and public schools was added to strict Puritanical, Edwardian family life, to provide an 'education' in which the ideologies I have outlined above, with all their attendant confusions and distortions were writ large. At Rugby, Marlborough and Charterhouse these poets suffered and were taught that suffering was good. Segregated from women, they were taught about the love between David and Jonathan, surpassing the love of women. Such love was greater than erotic, heterosexual love because it was supposed to be chaste, cerebral, 'higher' than the loins. So all sexuality was regarded as 'beastly', and that between men as most 'beastly' of all. They and their schoolmates were being invited to love and not to love simultaneously. Suffering the torments of frustrated desire, they were taught to regard such experience as positive, morally uplifting. At the same time, Brooke, Sassoon and Graves harboured their aesthetic ambitions, which also took them in the direction of homosexuality and of suffering. Feeling opposed to the prevalent 'hearty' atmosphere, they developed self-images in which they saw themselves as to one extent or another 'feminine'; and this femininity was in conflict with the muscular 'masculinity' to which they also bore allegiance. They fell in love chastely with boys, and on leaving school took their sexual confusions and sufferings with them.

Wilfred Owen only differed by belonging to a lower class and thus not experiencing a public school. But the intensity of his home life was a more than adequate replacement, and in the conflict between his mother and father he identified a battle in which he sided wholeheartedly with his mother; he learnt to think of himself as 'not a normal manly fellow'.[3] Both religion and art were implicated in this self-image, and suffering was de rigueur to both. His sexuality was rigorously repressed, and so, as in the case of his more wealthy peers, neurotic conflict ensued.

It was not only Brooke then, who found in the outbreak of war a relief from pressing perplexities and sufferings. He could image the war as an opportunity to experience 'cleanness', because during and after his nervous breakdown which was consequent upon his unresolved bisexuality, he viewed all sexuality as 'dirty'. His self-hatred spilt over into a virulent dismissal of homosexuals and women, leaving only a concept of 'manliness' which was predicated upon the ability to inflict and endure suffering. Painful self-sacrifice was lauded above pleasurable self-expression. Love was redefined in terms of slaughter; in order for sacrifice to ensue, killing was a necessity. Owen too had had his pre-war nervous collapse, and was eventually seduced by the war and its promises of suffering, love and poetry. His attitude to sexuality was never quite so extreme as Brooke's, but we can observe in his work a similar mysogyny, a similar suspicion of heterosexual erotic love, and an elevation of a sado-masochistic homosexuality into an ideal 'greater love'.

Neither Sassoon nor Graves had nervous breakdowns before the war, but there is ample evidence of their unhappiness. Sassoon, self-divided, between 'hunting-field' and 'gentleman writer' actively disliked women, and recognised himself as homosexual, but prided himself on his chastity. He was unfulfilled in both love and work. The war offered him an opportunity to unite the man of action with the contemplative, to experience a 'redemptive cleanliness' in the act of sacrifice, to write a poetry in which the extremes of love and hatred could be figured. It offered him suffering in all its forms. For Graves this was also true. Although he was younger than the other writers I have dealt with here, his experience of Charterhouse had not imbued him with an optimistic estimation of his immediate future. Rather the reverse; he felt that the miseries of Charterhouse, which were a product of his non-conformity, would only be continued at Oxford. The army, I suggest, offered the promise of a temporary resolution of the conflict in sexual identity between the 'man's man' who boxed and mountaineered and the aesthete who wrote poems and read Edward Carpenter. The war offered a way of proving his 'manhood' through courageous sacrifice, of experiencing Romantic 'blood brotherhood' as idealised by Carpenter, and again proved by sacrifice. And from all of this suffering he could fashion poetry.

Brooke died en route to Gallipoli. There is no reason to suppose that he would have reacted much differently to the others had he lived to witness combat. Some of his jingoistic imperialism may have been modified, but I think it highly likely that he would have clung to the idea of 'noble' suffering and sacrifice as ultimately consolatory. It also seems likely that had he lived long enough, his pre-war neuroses would have been adversely affected. Certainly in the case of the other three writers dealt with here, the war exacerbated their neurotic conflicts rather then providing resolutions to them. Martin Seymour-Smith's observation that Graves's neurosis 'was not caused by war experience but relentlessly uncovered by it'[4] may be applied to Owen and Sassoon as well. This is important because there has been a tendency even in fairly recent discussions to suggest that 'shell shock' or 'neurasthenia' was caused solely by the war and arose out of the repression of fear. What I have tried to demonstrate is that the subjects of this study brought to the war complex problems of self-identity which were rendered even more problematic in the maelstrom of the trenches. Fear certainly played a part in the development of their war neuroses, but this was not simply, (or even primarily) fear of death or injury, but rather, I believe, fear of the intensity of love they felt for other men, and fear of the ferocity of the sado-masochistic impulses they experienced, exaggerated to an intolerable degree by their war experience.

The trenches provided a venue for the heightening of emotional conflict which had its origins prior to the outbreak of the war. This is a crucial point in my argument, since it counters the possible objection that the attitude to suffering expressed in the war writing I have dealt with, is simply contingent upon the inevitable sufferings entailed by the war; that the degree of suffering endured in itself *necessitated* a consolatory attitude. By closely examining the pre-war experiences and attitudes of the writers involved, I have demonstrated that on the contrary, it was not the war that initiated particular ideological responses to suffering; these were in place well before the outbreak of hostilities.

As a result, the attitude to war expressed in the writings of Owen, Sassoon and Graves is rarely unequivocal. If crass patriotism, imperialism, and chivalric notions of heroism are sometimes exposed in their writing, the 'realities' which enable this critique paradoxically become the means by which other positive values may be located in war. Thus the suffering and horror endured by the troops ennoble them, redefining heroism as passive and masochistic rather than active and sadistic. The fact that those who were killed, often died whilst attempting to kill others is often elided from these writings so that 'sacrifice' can be seen as an act of love, rather than an act of appalling violence. This together with the fact that the non-combatant home front en masse is habitually figured as totally callous, ignorant, unfeeling and jingoistic, vitiates the moral and political impact of the writing. Whatever radicalism exists in their work is contained by values integral to dominant ideologies, and in particular Christianity and Romanticism. Sassoon, Owen and Graves all had difficult relationships with the established Church, but none of them escaped the early imprint of Puritanical values.

The same may be said of the three psychologists who treated the subjects of my study. Dr. Maurice Craig who was responsible for the pre-war 'stuffing' of Rupert Brooke was the least enlightened of these, and his is the most obvious case of extremely conservative 'moral' and political interventions being made in the name of medicine. As has been noticed elsewhere, the war brought about some advances in the treatment of neuroses, and there was a wider dissemination of Freudian ideas than prior to the conflict. Both W.H.R. Rivers and Arthur Brock belonged to the enlightened vanguard – Sassoon and Owen were lucky in this respect to be treated by them. Nevertheless, despite the progressive orientation of their respective 'therapies', these, like the poems of their recipients, were also vitiated with conservative ideologies. Both Sassoon and Owen were subject to moral and political exhortation which exacerbated rather than 'cured' their neurotic conflicts. Perhaps Graves was fortunate to escape such treatment during the war. But like his older friends, England was a place of suffering for him, before, during and after his experience of the battlefields in France.

It might be argued by some that the implication of this, and of my study as a whole is to suggest that Brooke, Sassoon, Owen and Graves were atypical in their respective reactions to war because of their preceding psychological dispositions. On the contrary, as I intimated in the introduction, it is my contention that the problems of sexual identity, and the sado-masochsim experienced by these writers were (and still are to some extent) endemic to English society. The writers I have dealt with only differed from others of their class and educational background in their power to express such conflicts in memorable ways. Other writers associated with World War I who differ in class and gender from my subjects, and were omitted from my study for this reason, nevertheless share various conflicts and attitudes which have been discussed here. In the life and work of Ivor Gurney, for instance, one finds a pre-war history of nervous illness which at least in part seems to have derived from sexual difficulties inspired by an extremely Puritanical attitude to bodily functions.[5] In joining up he sought, and for a time found, relief from his mental difficulties, but after he was gassed and invalided back to England in 1917, there began a process of mental deterioration which eventually led to his permanent incarceration in a mental institution to the time of his death in 1937. In his published literary work, his poems and letters, we find an attitude to pain which suggests that suffering should not only lead to artistic achievement, but should also have a just reward in fame. We also find some of the most moving of First War 'love' poems addressed to his comrades.[6] In Vera Brittain's autobiographical war writings too, we have a thorough depiction of war-time masochism. Through the account of her brother's, her fiance's, and her male friends' experiences we are given insight into sexual repression and confusion, and the will to suffer. We are shown that she shared this sexual repression and wished to emulate their suffering.[7] And, in her need for consolation, despite the overt pacifism espoused in the book, Brittain nevertheless sanctifies her losses through the idea of noble suffering. As my quotation from Brittain in the introduction indicates, she was more self-conscious about her masochism than her male counterparts, but what tends to be elided from her account is the balancing sadism. Of course, she was not privy to any aggressive actions of her male friends and relations, and if she shared these vicariously by letters this is not indicated. So we have the portrait of these volunteers as victims, passive sufferers, rather than active agents who were killing as well as being killed. As for her own aggression this is levelled at her parents in a manner not entirely unlike Sassoon's anger towards civilians, but in Brittain's case there was the added frustration of being treated like a second-class citizen by her father, and the expectation that she should nurse her mother rather than wounded soldiers. There is, in other words, a greater rationale for her anger, yet she admits at various points that she behaves badly in this regard.

More obviously pertinent to my theme of sado-masochism is the career of T.E. Lawrence, omitted from this study because he was not a war poet or a 'war writer' in the sense that the others are. But Lawrence was a great friend of Graves after the war, and they corresponded about their sexual difficulties. Lawrence shared something of Graves's Anglo-Irish inheritance, as well as his fierce Puritanism. This gave rise to severe psycho-sexual problems. Lawrence was chastely paedophilic but gained sexual satisfaction by being flogged to the point of emission.[8] His is an extreme example of the problems I have been dealing with in this book.

I have mentioned only three of the more famous war writers not included in my study, but other books, studies and anthologies reveal the widespread occurrence of experiences and emotions akin to those of Brooke, Sassoon, Owen and Graves. E.M. Forster correctly identified Frederic Manning's *Her Privates We* as a 'love story',[9] and Richard Aldington raises the issue of male friendship and 'sodomy' in the prologue to *Death of a Hero*.[10] Martin Taylor's anthology *Lads*[11] testifies to the range and depth of male poems of love and friendship to arise out of the First World War. Not all of these relationships were necessarily characterised by sado-masochistic impulses, but the idea of sacrifice as an agent of 'greater love' is very common; heterosexual love is often compared and found wanting. Similarly, in Fred Crawford's comprehensive survey of World War I poetry, we receive a sense of just how many minor poets gave expression to ideas concerning the nobility of suffering and sacrifice, the redemptive quality of the love between soldiers.[12]

Having said this leads to the further question of whether there were different points of view expressed wherein political protest was not muted, masked or compromised by consolatory expressions of love. Although, of course, it is impossible that anyone could escape the bondage of inherited ideologies completely, the answer to the question is yes, and it is interesting that these expressions have not gained the same kind of publicity as that afforded the writers I have dealt with. We have already had occasion to mention Charles Sorley. His great poem 'When you see millions of the mouthless dead' explicitly repudiates the kind of consolatory attitudes expressed by so many other war poets, and his 'All the Hills and Vales Among' mocks the public school enthusiasm and heroics which attended so much that was written early in the war. In his letters we find an extraordinary intelligence deployed in an acute political analysis of his situation as a volunteer soldier. Some of this is worth quoting. Here is Sorley writing in November, 1914:

England – I am sick of the sound of the word. In training to fight for England, I am training to fight for that deliberate hypocrisy, that terrible middle-class sloth of outlook and appalling 'imaginative indolence' that has marked us out from generation to generation. Goliath and Caiaphas – the Philistine and the Pharisee – pound these together and there you have Suburbia and Westminster and Fleet Street . . . But all these convictions are useless for me to state since I have not had the courage of them. What a worm one is under the cart-wheels – big clumsy careless lumbering cart-wheels – of public opinion. I might have been giving my mind to fight against Sloth and Stupidity: instead, I am giving my body (by a refinement of cowardice) to fight against the most enterprising nation in the world.[13]

Sorley went on in another letter written a few months later to make his critique of Rupert Brooke's war sonnets. Brooke, he says, is 'far too obsessed with his own sacrifice, regarding the going to war of himself (and others) as a highly intense, remarkable and sacrificial exploit, whereas it is merely conduct demanded of him (and others) by the turn of circumstances . . . He has clothed his attitude in fine words: but he has taken the sentimental attitude'.[14] Quite so.

Arthur Graeme West was also capable of writing poems which

embodied a critique of the 'sentimental attitude'. Having been to the war as a private soldier, he returned to England where he met and read the work of conscientious objectors. This, in his own words, resulted in a 'violent revulsion from . . . old imagined glories and delights of the army . . . its companionship, suffering courageously and of noble necessity undergone – to intense hatred of the war spirit and the country generally'.[15] Evidently West had perceived the way in which comradeship and suffering could become the means to an ideological justification of war. He refused to perpetuate such ideas further, but like Sorley did not have the courage of his conviction. He went back to France where he was killed in 1917.

West's story raises the issue of conscientious objection, and the fact that there were those in England who had opposed the war from the first. Samuel Hynes has chronicled this, and makes the important point that such opposition is contrary to the widespread myth that opposition to the war in England was consequent upon the battle of the Somme and was dependent upon people who had actually experienced the war. On the contrary, Hynes notes, members of the Independent Labour Party voiced antagonism towards the war in August 1914, and 'journals like the *Nation, War and Peace,* and the *Labour Leader* published anti-war editorials; anti-war poems began to appear almost as soon as war poems did . . . There was strong opposition in Cambridge . . . and in Bloomsbury.'[16]

But it is not this resistance that has been remembered and celebrated. And I would suggest that the reasons for this are ideological. The poems of Brooke, Sassoon, Owen, and Graves have come to 'represent' the First War through partial readings which have sought to find therein a compassionate denunciation of war. Protest *and* consolation excite audiences to a comfortable and comforting vision of World War I wherein 'human' values are said to be asserted by the poems which mediate the unspeakable. This liberal–humanist reception of the texts works finally to accommodate the grotesque and enables societies to wage further wars in the name of England, Christ and freedom. The sentimental attitude prevails.

To advocate, as my study implicitly does, pleasure as a proper goal of endeavour, and to argue that the struggle for liberation from oppressive ideologies is one of the prerequisites of that aim, might seem to some equally sentimental. Perhaps there is no answer to this impasse but to reiterate in plain fashion the burden of my argument about sado-masochism. Pain and suffering are, of course, inevitable experiences in life, but our attitude to these experiences seem to me vital. And what I object to is the notion that suffering is a good, whatever the suffering is for. That is to say that the abstraction of suffering from its political meanings is pernicious and allows the propagation of the oppression and warfare that has constituted so much of the sad history of this century. Not the least part of this history concerns the coalescence of sexuality and suffering. It has been suggested recently that the poetry of World War I, because so much of it is love poetry addressed from males to males, has a subversive tendency in terms of gender politics. Although I have some sympathy for the direction of this argument, it seems to me finally to be simplistic and unsatisfactory. The problem my study has sought to illuminate is that this homosexual or homoerotic love was predicated upon violence; that in order to express gentleness, tenderness, loving kindness, and love for each other men had to go to war. Furthermore, in order to assert the power and importance of male loving, the subjects of my study felt constrained to denigrate heterosexual eroticism. Thus in reacting in some respects against dominant ideologies, they succumbed in others which led them finally to endorse violence. And it is this circumstance that I wish to deplore.

The poets of the First War struggled with their cultural inheritance as we struggle with ours. We do them no favours by mythologising them or their writings. We should not tell our children old lies. If Owen amply communicated the untruths embedded in chivalric notions of militarism and imperialism, it is our task, I think, to take up his cause in order to further expose the ideological structures which enabled him still to celebrate aspects of warfare. This cannot and should not be done from a position of complacent superiority; self-interrogation is the beginning and end of studies such as this. The agents of coercion are not easily countered by idealism, and to speak of 'love' is to risk a descent into Romantic escapism. Nevertheless, in a way, this study has been about love, its difficulties and its lack. And in a sense the debates that rage about gender politics today are about the definitions and applications of love in the political sphere. I hope I have made some tentative contribution to that debate here. I can think of no more appropriate way to conclude than by quoting some lines from a poem by Herbert Read in which he figures his men as 'modern Christs' suffering their 'bloody agony'. In such expression he aligns himself with the other subjects of my study, and articulates something that triggered the voyeuristic thrill I experienced as a sixteen-year old when I first encountered First War poetry. This book is the result of my endeavours to understand my own voyeurism; to understand what it was that was attractive about war and war poems. Sado-masochistic love, I suggest is the key to such understanding. And in two lines from the poem, Read encapsulates his sense of loving loss; a sense we all must feel as we read of the grievous lives and circumstances of the killers and the killed in World War I:

'O beautiful men, O men I loved,
O Whither are you gone, my company?[17]

We are left to wonder that such passionate love, should have such violence and destruction as its context and legitimisation.

Notes

1 O. Wilde, *De Profundis, the Works of Oscar Wilde,* G.F. Maine, (ed.), London, 1948, pp. 853–88.

2 Quoted by F. Kermode, *Romantic Image,* London, (1957), 1971, p. 18.

3 W. Owen, *Collected Letters,* H. Owen and J. Bell, (eds.), London, 1967, p. 150.

4 M. Seymour-Smith, *Robert Graves: His Life and Work,* London, (1982), 1987, p. 76.

5 M. Hurd, *The Ordeal of Ivor Gurney,* Oxford, 1984, pp. 195–8.

6 See for example, 'Song of Pain and Beauty', 'Servitude', and 'To His Love', *Collected Poems of Ivor Gurney,* P.J. Kavanagh, (ed.), Oxford, (1982), 1985, pp. 35–41.

7 V. Brittain, *Testament of Youth,* London, (1933), 1979, pp. 114–23, 240–89 and *passim.*

8 Seymour-Smith, *Robert Graves,* pp. 108–9. See also J. Meyers, (ed.), *T.E. Lawrence: Soldier, Writer, Legend,* New York, 1989.

9 J. Marwil, *Frederic Manning: an Unfinished Life,* Sydney, 1988, p. 272.

10 R. Aldington, *Death of a Hero,* London, 1929, p. 26.

11 M. Taylor, (ed.), *Lads: Love Poetry of the Trenches,* London, 1989.

12 F. Crawford, *British Poets of the Great War,* Selinsgrove, 1988, pp. 21–65.
13 J. Glover and J. Silkin, (eds.), *The Penguin Book of First World War Prose,* London, 1989, p. 25.
14 Ibid., pp. 28–9.
15 Quoted by S. Hynes, *A War Imagined: the First World War and English Culture,* New York, 1991, pp.147–8.
16 Ibid., pp. 81–7.
17 H. Read, 'My Company (i)', in *Lads,* pp. 81–2.

Index